Anonymous

Past Days in India

Sporting Reminiscences of the Valley of the Soane and the Basin of Singrowlee

Anonymous

Past Days in India
Sporting Reminiscences of the Valley of the Soane and the Basin of Singrowlee

ISBN/EAN: 9783744743594

Printed in Europe, USA, Canada, Australia, Japan

Cover: Foto ©ninafisch / pixelio.de

More available books at **www.hansebooks.com**

PAST DAYS IN INDIA.

PAST DAYS IN INDIA,

OR

SPORTING REMINISCENCES OF

THE VALLEY OF THE SOANE

AND

THE BASIN OF SINGROWLEE.

By A LATE CUSTOMS' OFFICER,
N. W. PROVINCES, INDIA.

LONDON:
CHAPMAN AND HALL, 193, PICCADILLY.
1874.
[*All rights reserved.*]

LONDON:
PRINTED BY VIRTUE AND CO.,
CITY ROAD.

CONTENTS.

CHAPTER		PAGE
I.	Sport in the District of Mirzapore	1
II.	Game on the Kymore Plateau	7
III.	Wild Pigs—their Numbers	13
IV.	Trade crossing the Valley of the Soane	19
V.	A Singrowlee Story	25
VI.	Description of a Hankwa continued	31
VII.	The Camp visited by a Leopard	37
VIII.	Jones and Smith each get a Lesson	44
IX.	Jones shoots a large Snake	51
X.	Mementoes of Tigers	57
XI.	The Sambhur Hankwa	64
XII.	An Elephant Outwitted by a Jackal	70
XIII.	An Adventure with Hornets	77
XIV.	Crossing the Soane	84
XV.	Specimens in the Sands of the Soane	91
XVI.	The young Lion meets an Elephant	97
XVII.	Utilising the Carcase of the Wild Cat	103
XVIII.	A Dog carried off by a Leopard in broad Day	109
XIX.	Strong Remedies in time	116
XX.	Defence of the Camp	122
XXI.	Brown's Page of Natural History	128
XXII.	The Water-hole at Muggurdah	134
XXIII.	The One-eyed Tiger shot	141
XXIV.	Visit to the Jheel at Ghurwar	147
XXV.	Sitting up for a Tiger	153
XXVI.	Discovery of the Coal Mine	160
XXVII.	Robin Hood Armament	166
XXVIII.	Casualties by Wild Beasts	172
XXIX.	The Tiger's Declaration of War	178

CONTENTS.

CHAPTER		PAGE
XXX.	The Herdboy's Folly	185
XXXI.	The lean Khansamah's Story	192
XXXII.	The Planter visited by Tigers	198
XXXIII.	A Flock of Parrots	205
XXXIV.	The Under-keeper's Statement	212
XXXV.	The old Woman's sad Lot	219
XXXVI.	A Must Elephant	226
XXXVII.	Narrow Escape of one of the Party	232
XXXVIII.	Jones has a weakness for Brahminee Ducks	239
XXXIX.	Pretended Humility of the useless Bushes	245
XL.	The Parliament of all Created Things	252
XLI.	The Mastiff's Speech	259
XLII.	Following up the Trail	265
XLIII.	The Monkeys each take a Header	271
XLIV.	A Parody	277
XLV.	After the Sambhur at Putwut	283
XLVI.	The Lazy River	289
XLVII.	The Storekeeper's Account at Fault	295
XLVIII.	The largest Tigers shot for some years	301
XLIX.	Tigers at the Ghagur	307
L.	Ringing the Antelopes	313
LI.	Difference in Venison	320
LII.	How to Prepare Venison	326
LIII.	Antelopes Migrate	331

REMINISCENCES OF
PAST DAYS IN INDIA.

CHAPTER I.

SPORT IN THE DISTRICT OF MIRZAPORE.

ALTHOUGH there are doubtless many districts in India where a tour of a month or two may be very agreeably spent, yet, from all that I have seen or heard of, I would unhesitatingly give the palm, for sport in general, to Central India, and *par excellence* to the district of Mirzapore.

Previous to the great Indian Mutiny my lot in life was to be stationed at a central point on the Kymore range of hills in the Mirzapore district, whence duty called me to make journeys of various lengths in different directions. Bachelor as I was, and somewhat fond of the gun, I contrived to combine pleasure with duty in my various tours. Isolated from all society, confined strictly by my official duties within certain limits of country, it frequently happened that months passed without my having intercourse with any fellow-Christian. Living wholly among the native population then, being sometimes the sole European within a radius of sixty miles, and much more than that in some directions, I necessarily came into contact with a large amount of Indian rural life and scenery.

Poor human nature (as Mr. Pecksniff hath said) is too apt to flatter paper-stainers in general, that what they may have to say must needs be interesting to the public at large; and, as I cannot plead exemption from human frailties any more than other poor mortals, I now propose taking an imaginary party on a rather discursive sporting tour from Chunar right away to Singrowlee, and the borders of Rewah, merely premising that the several sporting incidents are the experience of either myself, my brother, or related by some of our acquaintances.

In those days it was not only usual, but absolutely necessary, for intending travellers in the district to obtain an introduction to, and a perwannah (vernacular for general order) from, the district magistrate located at Mirzapore. This perwannah would be addressed to all native superintendents and deputies of rural police-stations in the line of route intended to be taken by the exalted travellers therein referred to, ordering the said police officials to render every assistance to the travellers in the way of seeing that the villagers gave no unnecessary annoyance in supplying, or rather in *not* supplying, such russud (or forage) as might be required, or that they could supply, both to man and beast. This perwannah also implied that the said travellers were under sublime protection, and that their safety and well-being would be required at the hands of the local police. In those days and in most districts strangers travelling in the interior without such a document were liable to much annoyance, extortion, and petty insults from the villagers, and frequently from the subordinate police themselves.

Presuming that such an order has been obtained, and a party of six gentlemen (no ladies) made up for a holiday tour of one or two months, the requisite tents for themselves, and a sepoy's paul for the servants, with horses for each of the gentlemen and an elephant or two if procurable, together with the requisite number of camels for the transport of all the baggage being provided, time and place for starting from agreed upon, we think of making a start.

I must here, however, ask a question. Did any of my readers

ever go to a picnic where everything went off satisfactorily—where the knives and forks, or the ham or fowls, mustard or salt, or something considered essential, was *not* forgotten? If so, all that I can say is, that you may consider yourself very fortunate.

A holiday tour in the interior of any wild district of India is only a locomotive picnic on a large scale, in so far as almost everything comestible and potable (except water and milk) has to be provided beforehand and carried with the party, and anything forgotten on starting must perforce be dispensed with, after the first day's march. The police perwannah enables the traveller to get fodder and grain for the horses, &c., and coarse rice, pulse, firewood, common earthen cooking pots for the servants, and such like small articles, together with a few fowls, a lamb or a kid wherever procurable.

In travelling in the interior of any district of India, it is not prudent for Europeans to trust to the chapter of accidents to supply themselves with whatever they may require independent of their guns. Hence it becomes necessary to lay in a good stock of condiments—preserved meats, a few tins of biscuits, liquors of sorts that may be required, together with everything requisite for sporting purposes on an abundant scale, these sorts of articles not being procurable in the heart of most districts.

As it would be far from either fair or wise to throw upon one person all the trouble of looking after everything before and after starting, when the party is made up a mutual arrangement is entered into whereby one looks after the horses, camels, &c., seeing that everything connected with them is provided, and the animals are well looked after on the journey by syces (or native grooms), camel-men, &c. Another undertakes the baggage department, looking also to the setting up and taking down the tents, and so on; another looks after the liquors, cheroots, &c., taking daily account of what is expended; another undertakes the office of paymaster-general, having custody of the general cash-box, and keeping a strict daily account of expenditure therefrom; to another is confided the duties of caterer, and so on.

By thus dividing the responsibility and trouble, things go on much more agreeably than when left to one person, or to the very questionable forethought and care of the native servants, as is generally done. These Indian servants are many of them very clever managers (too much so at times), as Europeans, whether stationary or travelling, find out in the long run to their cost; for when parties travelling have been unwise enough to leave nearly everything to the wisdom and care of their excellent khansamah (head native house servant or butler), they find too late that several indispensable articles have been entirely forgotten, or of others an insufficient stock laid in; while of liquors, although an ample stock might have been laid in, suddenly, long before the journey is over, the report is, "The beer or brandy is all expended, sir."

Under the careful superintendence, then, of Messrs. Jones, Brown, Robinson, and Co., all arrangements are at length supposed to be satisfactorily completed, not by any means omitting a large supply of pice (Indian copper currency); hazy doubts, nevertheless, flying about the minds of the heads of departments as to something important having been omitted or mislaid, a start is at last made.

The first day's journey on such expeditions ought always to be a short one (six to ten miles), otherwise, by overtasking men and animals at the first going off, worse progress is made subsequently; besides, the first day's march being a short one, should anything have been forgotten, the distance is not much to send a man back for whatever may be required. Baker's bread in quantities being cumbersome, is most usually dispensed with, a good supply of atta (flour with the pollard in it) and fine flour answering the purpose of making chuppatties, or hand-bread, cakes, and puddings.

Having now brought my reader to the first encampment, before proceeding further I would make a little digression. I have often thought what a vast fund of interesting as well as useful information, once stored up in the memories of intelligent Mofussilites (all residents in the interior of India are so called), but daily vanishing thence, is lost to the public in general, through the disinclination of actors in the various scenes to sit down now and then for an hour, and record the most striking events of the past week.

Many, in excuse, will say, "Oh, I can't write well enough for the public to read."

Your neighbours, Tom, Jack, or Harry So-and-So, at the next indigo factory or station, form each one of the public as much as I do, hundreds of miles it may be from you, and yet when you go to visit them you are glib enough with your tongue, and when you get the steam up, who but you keeps the table in one continuous roar? No, you don't hit the bull's-eye when you say you can't write; the truth is, you are too lazy or too indifferent to take the little trouble required.

About tigers, many a useful story of their different humours, &c., which would act as warnings, or guides, as it may be, to neophites, might be set down in simple language, adhering, of course, closely to fact. Your story, after going through half-a-dozen hands or more, will have embellishments enough to make you doubt the paternity of your own bantling, should you meet with it subsequently in print, forwarded by other hands than your own.

I have alluded markedly to tigers only, but there are many incidents of Indian rural life which would doubtless prove highly interesting and useful were they recorded and published.

In nine cases out of ten, the man who can tell a story well will be able to write it well, if he only tries. Of course, there are exceptions. There are men to whom it would make no difference whether they had the finest Gillott or the stump of a mainmast, they could not write down the simplest incident in an intelligible manner, not for the life of them.

The beginning of December is about the best time for making

an excursion into the interior of most districts, as by that time the country generally will be pretty well dried up after the annual rains, and the various roads will have been put in order.

Leaving Chunar, a fortress on the bank of the Ganges, now an invalid depôt, and ascending to the table-land of the Kymore range of hills, the scenery is not very attractive until we approach the Ghâts, or passes, descending to the lovely Valley of the Soane.

The chief point of interest is the Fort of Bidjeyghur, seen in the distance to the left. Those versed in Indian history will recollect this fort having been reduced by Major Popham, at the time of Cheyt Singh's somewhat justifiable rebellion in the days of Warren Hastings.

CHAPTER II.

GAME ON THE KYMORE PLATEAU.

THE sport to be obtained close to the high road to Singrowlee, before approaching the Ghâts, is not much. Game of different kinds may be had, if a party will camp for two or three days at every ten miles' march, and make short spurts out in search of it. On the table lands of the Kymore, chiefly between the Karamnassa River and Shahgunge, vast droves of antelopes used to be met with, small herds being common. Two distinct species are met with, feeding promiscuously. The full-grown fawn-coloured bucks are larger than the black ones, but the latter yield the better venison. Many persons, however, assert that the black is nothing but an old fawn-coloured buck, but it is hard to believe that certain animals grow smaller as they grow older.

As plenty of wild pigs may be driven out of the sugar-cane fields, and a tiger or two from some patch of jungle, I shall suppose my party to have been satisfied with a few days' sport on the tableland of the Kymore, and then to have proceeded towards the celebrated Valley.

Leaving Chupka, a small village directly on the Singrowlee road, about one mile behind, we come to the top of the Kowie Ghât, which is a monument to the engineering skill of one of the present worthy judges of the Súddur Adawlut, or High Court, at Agra, who was then magistrate of the district of Mirzapore. From this point the delightful Valley of the Soane opens to view, and presents as pretty a *coup d'œil* as one may wish to see.

A little to the left, fronting us, stands out prominently the Peak of Mongeysur, the extreme western point of a bold spur of the Kymore, and about six miles distant; between Mongeysur and the Ghât, the hill recedes to the eastward, forming a fine amphitheatre clothed with thick jungle; in the distance fronting us, we see the beautiful Soane, like a silver ribbon, meandering to the east till hidden by Mongeysur, and to the west till lost in the bosom of the hills. In the extreme distance fronting us, the scenery is further set off by undulating hills, and the banks of the river thickly clothed with picturesque jungle; we also catch a glimpse of the Rehund, a tributary of the Soane, almost on the horizon, towards the west.

At our right, distant about nine miles, is the Fort of Agoree, in ruins now, but formerly a place of no little note in these parts. Agoree used to be the residence of the ancestors of the Rajah of Burhur, but had then been deserted for many years in favour of the present raj-barree, or native palace. A trip to the ruins used to be a favourite excursion for picnic parties.

At one time some pretty mosaic was to be seen in the old fort, but successive visits of Vandals, who have dug out and carried off mementoes of their visit, have destroyed the completeness of the design. It is a great blot on the Anglo-Saxon character that few of them can go anywhere without leaving unsightly traces of their visit, either in disfigurement of various kinds, or inscribing their insignificant names for future visitors to see, and, it is to be hoped, condemn as ultra-snobbish. In its palmy days, this fort and its defenders are said to have successfully repulsed sundry assaults made on it, with the view of chastising freebooters issuing thence.

The foreground of our picture is filled up with the village of Murkoondee to our left, with the Ghagur winding past it, about three hundred and fifty feet below us, Owie fronting us, with Sulkhun still further on, and their adjacent lands, and two respectable hillocks immediately under Mongeysur, called Mor Bhya, or My Brothers, where the noble sambhur deer love to congregate; our right is chiefly filled up with more or less thick jungle.

In descending the fine Ghât, as also on the tableland above and below it, we may possibly enough see, even in the middle of the road, one or more funnel-shaped holes scratched out by some bear, whose instinct or acute sense of smelling out the whereabouts of his tit-bit—the white ant's nest—is astonishing.

The writer has seen numbers of holes made by bears, some of which had been dug out in the driest weather, right in the middle of a hard road or bye-path. These animals, in that part of the country, are very independent gentlemen in a general way, caring little whether it be the Queen's highway or any one else's, so long as their wants are supplied.

Bruin will seldom do a man any harm at night, unless by accident he comes upon him at the turn of a bush, or disturbs or molests him in any way; he is, on the whole, well disposed and liberal, inclined to live and let live. Should he, however, meet a human being in the daytime, it is a very different thing, for if he sees any one at even twenty or thirty yards' distance, unless it is too much out of the direct course he may at the time be taking, he will generally charge, and then it all depends upon the party's fleetness of foot for escape, if a native, or upon his presence of mind, and the goodness of his gun, if a European, as to who shall come off second best. Earl St. Maur, a few years ago, got dreadfully mauled through not being quick enough in getting out of the way of a bear that he had wounded.

If a party, travelling in the interior of any wild district of India, and who is conversant with the dialect, has any desire to hear incidents of jungle life, a promise of buksheesh to the first village shikari (sportsman), or aheer (herdsman), will draw out an abundance of anecdotes illustrative of life in the jungles.

In the course of his journeys on duty the writer once heard the following story, related as an actual occurrence, and confirmed by a party resident on the borders of Rewah.

Three or four aheers (herdsmen) were one day tending their buffaloes in the jungle near Murkoondee, when one of them suddenly came upon a bear at the foot of a tree, half buried in the hole he was digging to get at a white ants' nest.

Signalling to his companions they soon joined him, and all stood for some time, silently watching the bear, who was too intent upon trying for a meal to notice them, when suddenly the idea of punishing Bruin entered the mind of one of them, who quickly communicated his plan to the others. It was then arranged that the two boldest and most powerful of them should silently approach and jump upon the back of the bear, while his head was buried deep in the hole, and by main force keep it there until the others had tied a small buffalo-bell round his neck.

Having succeeded in securely fastening on the bell, they let the bear go, nimbly enough getting out of his way, and then the antics he played, and the awful row he made in trying to get rid of the sonorous bell, sent the aheers into fits of laughter.

The poor animal is said to have been seen or heard of for four days in different parts of the country, and it is supposed to have traversed between one hundred and two hundred miles, being at last found dead of fright and starvation on the borders of Rewah, fifty miles from where he had the ornament put on.

We have most of us heard of the parliament of rats, meeting in solemn conclave, to contrive some scheme for circumventing their common enemy, the cat, and of the proposal to bell the cat. But when one more thoughtful than the rest put the question, Who was to bell the cat? they one and all prudently declined the perilous feat, and dissolved the meeting, leaving their descendants to the present day, it is supposed, mourning over the degeneracy of their race, in not being able to produce a champion capable of carrying out the above notable scheme. We may have often heard of the proposal to bell the cat, but the writer never before or since heard of belling the bear being actually carried into practice.

The writer also heard the following story on another occasion. The incident is said to have occurred at the top of the Ekpowa Ghât, (or "one foot-pass," so named from its extreme narrowness), in some of the jungles near the precipice, not far from the village of Romph, which is about one and a half miles from Chupka.

A solitary aheer one night led his buffaloes into a bit of jungle, with which he was not well acquainted, and being apprehensive of a chance visit from tigers or bears, he collected his herd under a large tree, when they had done feeding. While his animals were chewing the cud of meditation, the aheer thought proper to consult his personal safety by climbing up the tree, and the night being cold, wrapping around him his thick black blanket, he seated himself on one of the stoutest branches.

Not long after making himself comfortable, a bachelor scion of the bear family, happening to pass that way, had his attention drawn to the black object up in the tree. Thinking it to be one of the fair sex of his species, and being on amorous thoughts intent, he very soon climbed up, and, seating himself conveniently alongside of the supposed fair one, began, bear fashion, to try and ingratiate himself into her favour.

Meanwhile the aheer, finding himself in somewhat of a fix, and perceiving the mistake of the young bear, thought it would be best to humour the animal until he gathered his wits about him, and contrived some scheme for extricating himself from his unpleasant predicament. So, when young Master Bruin said "Boo" to him (which he understood to mean, "Good evening, miss"), he very politely answered, "Boo-hoo," meaning, "Good evening, sir."

This kind of confab, together with sundry nudges on the part of Bruin, went on for some time until the aheer had released his arms from the folds of the blanket, when steadying himself with his left arm, he gave the bear a sudden push with his right hand, sending him clean off the branch.

Not knowing exactly what to think of such a repulse from the supposed fair one, being rather verdant withal, the bear, after shaking himself a bit, and rubbing his nose, came to the sage conclusion that his company was not wanted, and so made tracks for another part of the jungle. As the writer does not vouch for the truth of any merely hearsay stories, they must be taken *cum grano salis*.

CHAPTER III.

WILD PIGS—THEIR NUMBERS.

WHILE on the road, if the party have started sufficiently early, they may possibly see one or more droves, or sounders, of wild pigs, scampering off to their different lairs. Pig-shooting in the valley, from the nature of the country, is not always safe. This sport may be had to any amount on the table-land within five miles of the ghâts, and where scrubby jungle or sugar-cane fields abound.

Pig-*sticking*, however, in the open, uncultivated country of the table-land, is always dangerous, owing to the soil being friable, and full of holes made by rats, foxes, etc., giving an ugly purl to hard-riding man and beast, very probably dislocating a shoulder, or it may be breaking a neck, or ruining a good horse.

It always was astonishing to the writer how the cultivators managed to reap any crop at all from fields on the table-lands of the Kymore, and within two or three miles from the ghâts and jungles. The swarms of wild pigs in those days were something wonderful. Frequently, on moonlight nights, when out on official duty, the writer has, according to season, seen rice, gram, wheat, or other fields, thickly studded with wild pigs gorging themselves. While out for a walk, morning or afternoon, his dogs have often turned a pig out of a small bush that he should never have thought capable of concealing the gentleman. Were it not that the tigers and leopards thin the swarms of pigs considerably, the fields might as well lie fallow; as it is, the marvel is how the cultivators manage to live, after paying their rent and other charges.

We will suppose the party to have descended the Kowie Ghât,

or pass, and arrived at Sulkhun. Here a halt of ten or twelve days is made, to enable the party to enjoy their fill of the abundant sport that used to be had in the neighbourhood, this being a favourite rendezvous for tiger and sambhur shooting, and sport in general.

Here Messrs. Jones, Brown, and Co. have a glorious opportunity of being initiated into all the science and mystery of venery, or rather wood-craft. Venery is applied to all connected with deer alone; *wood-craft* teaches everything connected with forest sport—biped and quadruped.

An experienced Indian shikari will tell by the droppings of a deer whether it is feeding peaceably in the neighbourhood, or has been alarmed and fled. He will readily distinguish the footprints of a leopard from those of a wolf, or a large dog; and by careful inspection will be able to tell whether a tiger has recently passed, and whether he is roaming for prey, or has had a good meal.

The writer, knowing the country and its ways, having been unanimously elected president of the mess as well as caterer, has the charge and management of things in general, and consequently his voice is all-powerful. The president, therefore, has prudently sent on a tent and a considerable part of the baggage the night previous from Adulgunge, with certain *sub rosâ* instructions.

The consequence of the president's forethought was that, when the party arrived at Sulkhun they found a tent ready pitched, several ghurras (water-pots) of Soane water, and breakfast waiting to be put on the table. The order for breakfast was not needlessly delayed, and having refreshed themselves with one or more tumblers full of the delicious Soane water, and then with a bath, the party sat down to a hearty meal, their appetites sharpened by the bracing morning air.

Jones, dry soul, with a taste for Bass, incontinently shouts out for a bottle of beer, but the president, with his deep bass voice, sternly says, "No," and quietly explains that at certain places he intends interdicting alcohol in every shape until the day's work is over. He has found by experience that more fatigue can be undergone, and better results obtained, on coffee and tea than on claret or beer, not to mention brandy.

All acquiesce except Jones, who, after breakfast, bribes the khansamah (butler), and thus surreptitiously obtaining a bottle of beer, succeeds in nearly finishing it before being discovered. Thereupon a council of war being immediately held, the delinquent pleading guilty, is amerced in a light fine of three dozens of beer of like brand.

After breakfast, while enjoying their pipes or cheroots, the president enlightens the rest as to some of his hitherto mysterious movements, and separate conversations with sundry scantily-clad natives. Having sent off an express the day previous from Adulgunge, with certain instructions for a native shikari, whose dwelling was either at Murkoondee or Sulkhun, said shikari, whom we will call Sewgolam, presented himself that morning. The result of that interview was, that there was every chance of some excellent tiger-shooting the next day, as Sewgolam reported that there was a family party of tigers at the Jherria, and two at the Ghagur—both mountain streams, tributaries of the Soane.

In order to benefit fully by the capital khubber (information, or news) received, it was proposed and agreed upon, that not a shot was to be fired in that neighbourhood for some days, lest the tigers should be scared away. It was further agreed to, that under a good guide, provided by Sewgolam, the day's shooting should be had in the jungle towards Putwut. Sewgolam was then directed to purchase the requisite "victim," and make the necessary preparations for a grand "hankwa" (or drive of wild animals) on the following morning, and report progress in the evening.

In accordance with the above arrangements, some with rifles, others with double barrels, one loaded with No. 6 or 7, the other with ball, attended by three servants and the guide, the party starts on foot in search of what they can get, the caterer hinting that, as the larder was empty, those who did not succeed in bagging anything should have no dinner.

They had not proceeded far when a spotted deer dashed past, but was speedily arrested by a quick, well-aimed shot from Brown, while a magnificent peacock, roused by the report, flew up with a whirr, and was making off, until a charge of shot by Robinson dropped him. Almost at the same time, a hog-deer, darting past, was fired at by Jones without success, who attributed the fault to the deer; the president, however, growled out that it was the *beer*.

Jones, soon after that, had another fine chance at a ravine deer, but missed again, and on reloading his double barrel made the discovery that he had forgotten his caps, and as it was too far to send a man back to the camp, or for him to return without the guide, he was no little nuisance to the rest, troubling first one and then another for a few caps.

Brown having bagged another spotted deer, Wilcox a hog-deer, Smith a pig, Robinson a couple of young peacocks, and the president several brace of black and grey partridges, and one of hares, with a few green and wood pigeons, being all rather tired with their scrambling walk, the party returned to camp about four o'clock well loaded.

Jones not having contributed anything to the larder, besides having been troublesome, the president was unanimously called upon to read him a lecture on the impropriety of his conduct, which was thereupon done, and the delinquent being penitent and promising amendment, he was pardoned.

After a good wash, and a glass of beer, with a little biscuit and cheese, the party proceeds to examine the day's work. The president at once condemns the old peacock, but orders his splendid tail-feathers to be carefully preserved. The deer being skinned, the saddles and haunches were ordered to be hung up, well out of the reach of prowling leopards and tigers, the rest being given to the servants. One saddle was ordered to be roasted, and a haunch made into savoury steaks, while the best parts of the hares and feathered game were to be made into a hunters' stew, no mean dish to set before a king even. One hare was, however, withdrawn, to be made into a splendid curry by Ramjaun, *artiste*.

While engaged in giving these and other orders, Sewgolam, shikari, is announced. He reported that, after leaving the gentlemen in the morning, he went immediately with two trusty men to a certain place on the banks of the Jherria, and, after a careful inspection of the neighbourhood, he found perfectly fresh traces of three tigers, the old ones and a young one, nearly full-grown. Moreover, he said that, to make as sure as possible, he had cautiously tracked them, as far as he durst go, to the bed of a dry nullah (channel or watercourse), thickly overgrown with jungle, and which evidently had been their den for a considerable time past.

He further reported that, directly on his return, he sent off the two men to the adjacent villages, warning all hands that their services would be required for a grand hankwa early the next morning. He also said that he had procured a "victim," a young buffalo, which, as soon as he should leave "the presence," he would proceed to securely tie up, and get the machauns (or platforms) ready.

Having finished his report, and all that he had done being approved of, Brown, who was a veritable negrophile, sympathizing right off with the oppressed coloured people, noticing Sewgolam pressing and rubbing his abdomen, asked what was the matter with him.

On learning that he (Sewgolam) was subject to an infirmity, a bad stomach-ache, Brown, philanthropist as he was, began condoling with him, giving him a great deal of wholesome advice, *more medico*; and to prove that his sympathy was not in words only, roared out for the brandy, a certain quantity of which was to be taken internally at once, and he was to take away a certain quantity to be used as an embrocation.

On the brandy being brought and poured out, the president, who understood Sewgolam's *ruse*, but was quietly enjoying the fun, suggested to Brown that the dose prescribed internally was not a quarter strong enough, and that no embrocation was necessary. Whereupon the bottle and glass being handed over, Brown, seeing a good second mate's nip poured out, protested that such a dose as that would kill a poor man unaccustomed to strong liquors, or at least would send him into a sleep from which he would not awake until the middle of next week, and so they would lose all their fine tiger-shooting.

The president simply answered, "Wait and see," and, handing the glass to Sewgolam, Brown was not a little astonished to see the marvellous facility with which the brandy disappeared, without causing any wry face, but, on the contrary, with every mark of satisfaction. Thereupon Brown gained a wrinkle in Indian experience. Sewgolam then, having received his rookhsut (or permission to retire), departed to tie up the "victim," and make the requisite and final arrangements.

CHAPTER IV.

TRADE CROSSING THE VALLEY OF THE SOANE.

AS dinner would not be ready for some time, and an hour's daylight still remaining, the party amused themselves with a stroll in the environs of the camp, the president taking the opportunity of enlightening the others respecting the commerce traversing the Singrowlee road.

Sulkhun and the adjacent villages carry on a great trade at the commencement of the cold weather, in buggye, a species of grass very plentiful over the hilly parts of the district. It is valuable from being so plentiful, as it is made into string and rope, which is used for most ordinary purposes. It is a cheap substitute for sunn (or hemp), the latter being little cultivated in those parts, and when absolutely required, it has to be brought from a great distance, and is consequently too expensive for common use.

The villagers towards Kone, and other directions, cut and bring this buggye by bullock-loads for sale to Sulkhun, &c., where it is again sold to parties who come from Allahabad, Mirzapore, Benares, &c., for it. These middlemen themselves also take it, sometimes only to Ahrorah, a large mart near Chunar, whence it ultimately reaches the above places, where it is made into string, and is used and highly prized for lacing charpoys, or native bedsteads, tying the rafters and framework of native huts, &c.; it is also made into rope, and is used for drawing water, and for the heel and head-ropes of horses, &c.

There is also a considerable trade carried on in the dried flower of the mowah-tree, a very elegant and useful tree. This flower is about the size of a full-grown white-heart cherry, although some may be met with as large as a walnut; it is fragrant and full of saccharine matter, for which reason bears, wild pigs, porcupines, &c., are very fond of it. The mowah flower is gathered, dried, and eaten by the poorer natives, but by far the greater part is sold to those pests of every village, the kulwars, or keepers of hedge pothouses, who, by rude distillation, extract from it a spirit, not of much body, but apparently very intoxicating. When new, it has a fine aroma, but is very insipid, and when stale it appears to acquire strength and a very vile smell.

The beauty of the mowah-tree calls forth the admiration of every one, and their great numbers in the valley, but especially near rocky ground, where there is a sufficiency of soil (in which favourite spots they seem to delight, growing luxuriantly), impart a charm to the landscape which would be materially diminished without them. The mowah is one of the most valuable trees in the Kymore range, the wood being of excellent quality, suitable for a variety of purposes, but the tree is seldom cut down on account of the value of the blossom and seeds.

The flower would yield a good per-centage of sugar, but whether a sufficient quantity could be procured to make it a profitable commercial speculation is very doubtful, owing to the universal demand there is for it by the native distillers. A sharp, pleasant vinegar, but of little body, may also be obtained from the blossoms. From the valley of the Soane and neighbourhood, and even from Singrowlee and Sirgoojah, great numbers of bullocks are annually loaded with the dry blossom, and sent to Ahrorah and other large marts for the kulwars.

The seed or nut of the mowah is also of great commercial value, as it yields fotty-seven per cent. of a very excellent oil. A French gentleman succeeded in making good soap and candles from the mowah oil, the candles resembling those made from stearine.

Residents at the large stations, such as Allahabad, Benares, &c.,

doubtless flatter themselves that they get the purest ghee, or clarified butter, used in all Indian cookery, and yet the bunniahs (traders) are very apt to adulterate their ghee with mowah oil, nor is the sophistication easy of detection.

The way it is done is this: the mowah oil is allowed to settle in large vessels, and in course of time it throws up a white granular substance, scarcely distinguishable from good ghee. This, which may be called the essence of the oil, is then carefully collected and well mixed with the ghee. This substance of the mowah oil being perfectly innocuous, no harm results from the sophistication, except to the pocket of the consumer.

The high road to Kone, Singrowlee, Sirgoojah, &c., running directly across the valley, the whole of the commercial traffic either way necessarily passes Sulkhun; hence at times, generally morning and evening, droves of bullocks laden with salt, sugar, spices, cloths, &c., may be seen plodding their weary way.

"In the merrie month of May," the jungle on either hand between Kowie Ghât and Putwut puts on its holiday dress, and has a very gay appearance, the prass (*Butea frondosa*) and other flowers being then in full bloom, some of them perfuming the air to a considerable distance with their delightful fragrance.

The prass is a very useful plant, its broad leaves making capital extempore drinking-cups, while its dried flowers yield an orange dye, very pleasing to unsophisticated village maidens. The fibres of the roots also are made into very serviceable and strong string, which, while moist, is very pliable, and will bear a great strain, but, if allowed to dry, soon breaks.

The prass, nevertheless, is a great eyesore to zemindars (landlords) from its abundance, tenacity of life, and the great difficulty there is in eradicating it. Burning the stump, or cutting it into small pieces, seems to have little effect, unless perseveringly repeated.

The jhar, or wild plum, is also extremely abundant on the Kymore generally, and in the season the fruit may be gathered free to any extent, thousands of cartloads if required. This wild plum, when gathered fully ripe, and stewed with plenty of sugar, is very pleasant eating. Numbers of wild animals, biped and quadruped, are glad when the plum ripens.

This is another plant that is exceedingly troublesome to dislodge, owing to the singular vitality of its roots, as a little bit, an inch or two long, if left in the ground, will very soon begin to sprout. This plum has been known to throw out suckers more than twenty feet from the parent stem, so that, effectually to eradicate it, it is absolutely necessary to trace the ramifications of its roots, and carefully burn the rootlets. The labour of unearthing the tap-root is not a trifle, a huge cavity or well being required to be dug out, if the bush is of any considerable size.

The valley of the Soane in those days, but especially the neighbourhood of Sulkhun, was a favourite rendezvous for tiger-shooting and sport in general, and the report of a "kill" from the shikari was looked for with not a little eagerness, and seldom without fail if parties went at the proper season. Certain places on the banks of the Ghagur and Jherria seldom failed of yielding fine sport. No less than six tigers, in fact a whole family, have been the result of one hankwa at the Jherria, only two of which, however, were bagged at that time. The writer will vouch for a tigress and two nearly full-grown cubs being bagged at one time at the same place, the male tiger and one cub escaping.

The Mor Bhya, or "My Brothers' Hill," under Mongeysur, used to be a famous place for sambhur deer, which were either stalked or driven by the usual hankwa. The head and shins of this deer (after being properly shaven), stewed under the superintendence of a connoisseur, are a dish for a king. Its recuperative properties are not generally known, and sometimes when known are not duly appreciated.

The usual game to be met with in the vicinity of Sulkhun consisted of tigers, leopards, bears, sambhur, spotted deer, wild pigs, porcupines, peafowl, curlew, jungle-cocks, black and grey partridges, wood and green pigeons, quails, ortolans, and doves. Further on, in the woods between Sulkhun and Putwut, nylghau (or blue ox), the largest Indian deer, being more like a horse than a deer, and about the size of a Suffolk pony, hog-deer, and occasionally the pretty little ravine-deer, may be had.

The shades of evening drawing on rapidly, it was time to return to camp, as it is not safe for any one living or being camped close to any heavy jungle to be out after dusk, that being the time when all wild beasts issue from their respective lairs in search after prey.

On arrival at Sulkhun in the morning, the president had quietly sent off a man to the mullah (ferryman and fisherman combined) at Putwut with orders to try and get some fish, and on the return of the party from their stroll, they found a man waiting with a fine mahseer, or Indian salmon, for which a liberal price was given, and a hint to bring fish every day to the camp.

The khansamah having been summoned, the fish was made over to him, with directions to boil it immediately, as an agreeable addition to the fare for dinner. Then, while refreshing themselves with beer and pipes or cheroots, the president took the opportunity of giving certain advice and directions to be strictly observed next day, if they wished the hankwa to be successful.

In the first place, on going out shooting in the jungles, it is best to wear a sombre dress, brown or olive green, so as to be assimilated as much as possible in colour to surrounding objects; also white collars and gay neckties should be discarded, as well as the regulation belltopper (chimney-pot hat), the ugliest and most uncomfortable head-dress ever invented, and utterly out of place in the jungles. A brown or an olive-green felt wide-awake will be found by far the most handy and comfortable.

The reason for wearing sombre apparel while out shooting in the jungles is this—glaring white or gay colours in large masses *moving about*, not being common in the jungles, instantly attract the attention of wild animals, and make them wary of approach, or by rousing their suspicion, cause them to start off at a tangent beyond shot.

Another thing to be observed is, that when two or more persons go together into the jungles, stalking after deer or other game, they must proceed very cautiously and as silently as possible, making signs in place of speaking, as any talking above a whisper will infallibly alarm animals which may, unknown to you, be behind the next bush, and so scare them away.

If these precautions are absolutely necessary for successful shooting on foot, they become doubly so when seated on a machaun, or platform, at a hankwa. When once seated in a tree on a machaun, the most perfect silence and immobility must be maintained. However much annoyed persons may be by flies, mosquitoes, or wood-ants, a finger or muscle must not be moved suddenly to drive them away; they must just allow the pests to peg away at them.

CHAPTER V.

A SINGROWLEE STORY.

TO give an instance of the necessity for silence, &c., when up in a machaun, the president related the following laughable story of a tiger-hunt:—

A certain rajah, or native prince, down Singrowlee-way, had once received some attentions from native friends in Benares, when on pilgrimage to the holy shrines there, and in return for their civilities invited them on a certain occasion to visit him for a change of air. Gladly accepting the invitation, they took with them a few of their friends, and, as a matter of course, a posse of attendants.

On their way down, having seen plenty of evidences of tigers, and heard many stories about them, they were not long with the rajah before they politely intimated their wish to shoot a tiger or two, to take back the skins and skulls as trophies of their prowess and mementoes of their visit.

The rajah, not being deficient in politeness, acceding to their request, agreed to give them at least the opportunity of doing so, and accordingly arrangements were made for a hankwa. The rajah, understanding their character pretty well, advised his new friends much in the same way as the above party has been advised, but these conceited and pot-valiant citizens, being determined on showing their valour, little heeded the advice given them. Moreover, on reaching the trees, and seeing the machauns so near the ground, as they thought, their courage beginning to ooze out, like Bob Acres', made them insist on the charpoys (native bedsteads) being placed higher up in the branches.

As the hankwa had then begun, there was no time to make the charpoys properly fast, so they had to be content with what alterations could rapidly be made. Then, in their anxiety to get off the ground quickly, instead of one or two getting up into each tree, three or four got up into one machaun, taking with them one or two attendants, and a whole armoury of rifles, double-barrels, matchlocks, spears, swords, shields, &c. When settled at last, instead of being still and keeping silence, they would laugh and chatter like a parcel of monkeys, ignorant of their danger.

The consequence was that, when the tiger, annoyed by the great hullaballoo in his rear, advanced close to one of these monkey-loaded machauns, his attention was immediately attracted by the unusual row up in the tree directly in front of him. Having been disturbed in his siesta, Master Tiger, as may be supposed, was not in a very amiable mood just then; and so, making a gallant spring, he alighted on the edge of the machaun, with his two fore-legs only, holding on like grim death, grinning a "ghastly smile," with his face all bloody from his recent feast.

As the fastenings of the machaun were never originally intended to bear the great strain put upon them by a live and kicking tiger hanging on at one side, and as these fastenings moreover were further insecure through the hasty alterations made, they of course gave way, and, the machaun toppling over, down went tiger, machaun, men, guns, swords, spears, &c., in glorious confusion, most of the guns making a perfect *feu de joie* on reaching the ground, to express their sense of the fun of the thing.

The tiger, not knowing what to make of it all, exhibited great discretion in getting out of the *mêlée* as soon as possible, leaving the other animals half dead with fright, while the men and boys of the hankwa, as they came up and learned what had happened, split the welkin with their roars of laughter. The citizens, it is said, returned to Benares much chagrined, and would never more listen to any tiger stories.

The royal Bengal tiger, loose and free in his native jungles, is a very different animal from the woe-begone creature exhibited in menageries in Europe. There is that in his black-striped face and glaring eyes which requires all the courage of a bold man steadily to face. South America and South Africa are said to have their tigers, which properly ought to be called jaguars or panthers, and hunters in those countries are thought not a little of for destroying even one of them, but a real Bengal tiger would eat such cats any day.

Instances have been known of parties up in a machaun waiting for a shot at a tiger, but on seeing him approach, with his head, neck, and paws all smeared with blood from a recent gorge, have been so terrified as to lose their wits. The following story, illustrative of the terror caused by the sight of a tiger, and his fearful roar on being wounded, was related to the president by a credible person as having actually occurred in one of the jungles of the basin of Singrowlee.

A respectable native in those parts was once visited by a braggart native friend, who continually boasted of his courage, and of the wonderful exploits he had performed. On his being asked if he had ever seen a tiger in a jungle, or had heard one roar, he said he had not, but that was the only thing he most ardently desired, and he longed for such an opportunity of showing what a man of real courage and skill was made of. He was soon afterwards introduced to an experienced shikari, who promised to show the brave man how he shot tigers, and that most probably he would hear the animal roar, requesting him to be ready when he should call for him.

A day or two after the interview, having found traces of a tiger meanwhile in a suitable locality, the shikari called for the boaster, and took him with a "victim" into the jungle. Having tied up the animal, and securely fastened his machaun in a tree conveniently near, the shikari mounted with the man, whom he placed behind him, having doubts of his presence of mind, notwithstanding all his vapouring, cautioning him to be silent and motionless.

In about a couple of hours the shikari was aware of the approach of the tiger, and again warned his companion. Presently the tiger came into view, stealthily approaching within springing distance of his victim, but before he could effect his object, the shikari cleverly planted a ball in his back, breaking his spine, paralysing his loins, and causing him to roar horribly. As his companion did not fire, the shikari turned half round upbraiding him, and snaching the matchlock out of his hands, quickly gave the tiger his quietus.

The effect on the braggart of the roar the tiger gave on receiving the first shot was such, that the shikari had scarcely time to fire the second before he felt the man behind him fall forward and seize him in a strong grip, at the same time something sharp penetrated his back. With some difficulty he released his arms, and spoke roughly to the man, but receiving no answer, he felt with his hands and found that the man, through extreme fright, had fallen forwards in a strong convulsive fit, and had made his teeth meet in the shikari's back. In this position he was obliged to remain until the shikari's and the boaster's friends, alarmed at their long absence, coming in search of them, forcibly released him from his strange imprisonment. The man, it is said, never recovered from the terrible fright.

When up in a machaun, too great care cannot be taken of your battery, placing each gun convenient to your hand, but in such a way that it cannot slip through the interstices of the charpoy, and fall to the ground. A sad accident (vouched for by the president) once happened to an old sportsman through some little want of care. He and a friend had gone to the Mor Bhya hillocks, close under Mongeysur, to shoot sambhur, but before the beaters could drive the animals up near enough for a shot, the deer were alarmed by the double report of a gun in front, and broke away on one side.

It appears that the gentleman had placed a double-barrel at his side, and safely as he thought, while he held a pea-rifle in his hands. How it occurred the gentleman could not tell, but the double-barrel somehow slipped through the charpoy, and falling perpendicularly, both barrels went off as the stock struck the root of the tree, one ball going through his right foot, while the other grazed his cap. The gentleman suffered for many months, and when he did get well, he had a limp in his gait ever afterwards.

"Khana tuyar hy, huzoor," or "Dinner is ready, your highness," was just then announced with joined hands and a bow to the president, which welcome news was received with great satisfaction by every one. Proceeding to the dinner-tent, they were not long in discussing the fine mahseer, which was declared to be first-rate. The hunter's stew was pronounced excellent by all, but the president demurred, saying, that, "to be perfect, it wanted a few doves, quail, or ortolans."

A good hunter's appetite having caused full justice to be done to the rest of the capital dinner, especially the hare-curry, the party adjourned to the open, round a glorious fire formed of logs and wood. While enjoying the fragrant weed, after some general conversation, the president said that, having to get up very early next morning, every one must turn into bed betimes; but, as several of the party did not know what a hankwa was, or how it was conducted, he thought it best to give them at once a detailed account, and advised their paying attention to him.

The first thing to be done is to send off an experienced shikari to discover the traces and lair of a tiger. This having been done, and a young buffalo-bull provided as a "victim," the shikari takes it before sundown to the spot arranged for the hankwa or drive, and in the track of a tiger, and fastens it securely to a stake driven firmly into the ground, or to the roots of a tree. The shikari has with him two or three villagers, who have brought their tangarees, or wood-axes, and charpoys, according to the number of sportsmen, which they proceed at once to fasten securely in trees, conveniently situated. Poles are then cut and fastened twelve to eighteen inches above the front edge of each charpoy, and to these poles small leafy branches are tied, hanging downwards, which serve as a screen to the sportsmen on the machaun. These poles are also used to rest the barrels of the guns on, that they may be close at hand.

It is, however, generally best to fasten the charpoys in the morning, as then the leafy screen, being fresh, presents a more natural appearance, the shikari doing it directly he finds the "victim" killed. These preparations being completed, the shikari's party make their way out of the neighbourhood as quickly as possible, knowing that the jungle is no longer over safe, because about that time wild animals of all kinds issue from their various coverts in search of their prey or food.

The shikari having then made his report at the camp, proceeds quickly to his own village, and sends other men to different villages, to give notice of a hankwa the next morning, and to summon all the men and boys not absolutely required for any special duties. As a properly conducted hankwa seldom lasts longer than two or three hours at most, generally in the early morning, and as the villagers engaged in it receive a whole day's pay for their trouble, they are always glad of the summons.

CHAPTER VI.

DESCRIPTION OF A HANKWA CONTINUED.

AT daybreak on the following morning, the shikari, taking one or more crafty men with him, proceeds very cautiously to the jungle to see whether the "victim" has been killed or not. If on his return he reports "a kill," the gentlemen, who by that time have got everything ready, proceed quickly to the spot, but with as little noise as possible, all talking on the way being in a decidedly subdued tone of voice. Some eight or ten of the bravest and most intelligent villagers accompany them, and station themselves in trees, a few yards apart, to the right and left of the trees in which the machauns are. As the duties of these men are more onerous and dangerous than those of beaters, they will have double pay each for their trouble.

While describing the fixing of the charpoys, I should have said that they are placed about ten feet from the ground, this height being generally considered the safest, as the machaun then would be just out of the reach of a tiger, were he to stand up on his hind legs and try to get in. Finding himself foiled, should he still be bent upon mischief, and make a spring, most likely he would go clean over, harming no one, even if the sportsmen were foolish enough to allow him so much time to accomplish all this. Whereas, were the machauns placed some feet higher up, unless at once very high, the tiger's spring would land him nicely in the machaun, beside or on the gentlemen, however unwelcome he might be as an unexpected as well as uninvited visitor. No doubt, in such a case, on making his spring he would be saluted with a volley; still, unless hit in an immediately vital spot, he might have strength enough left to inflict some ugly wounds with his teeth and claws. Accidents happen somehow when least expected, and it is best to take every possible precaution when scheming the overthrow of such a powerful active brute as a tiger, especially as it is well known to sportsmen that wounds from any of the feline race are extremely troublesome to heal.

The villagers who have placed themselves in the trees to the right and left, and at about the same height as the machauns, act the part of, and are called, rokhs or stoppers, their duty being resolutely to stop the tiger coming towards their trees with the view of breaking away, and to make him turn back and go in the road leading right in front of the machauns of the sportsmen. The way this is done is as follows:—When a rokh sees a tiger coming his way, he cries out "hish," or some such sound, not too loud, or else taps the tree once with the handle of his axe, just loud enough to attract the attention of the tiger, and make him apprehensive of some danger in that direction. If this sound is not enough, he taps again louder, and if the tiger still persists in advancing, he throws a stone or a bit of stick at him, which usually turns and makes him go in the direction required.

The position of a rokh, and his duties, are, as already said, more dangerous than that of a beater, although at times some one or more of these latter have been known to be mauled by a tiger, suspecting danger ahead, breaking back and charging the line of beaters. Sometimes the tiger *will not* go to be killed, he *will* break past the rokhs, and that is annoying enough. On one occasion, at the Jherria, one unmannerly brute, not liking the many hints given him to retrace his steps, spied out the rokh, who had placed himself too low in the tree, and acted somehow incautiously, attracting the attention of the tiger too markedly to himself, and the consequence was that the tiger clawed him out of the tree, killing and carrying him off before the gentlemen could descend and attempt his rescue.

The gentlemen having started for the machauns, the shikari

takes all the rest of the men and boys (fifty to a hundred or more), and places them a few yards apart, forming a semicircle in rear of the place where the tiger is supposed to be lying down, preparing for a sleep after his heavy repast. Two or three tomtoms (small native drums) are also stationed, one in the centre of the line of beaters, the others at even distances to the right and left. The shikari then having ascertained that all is ready, placing himself in the centre of the half-moon, signals to the men right and left as far as he can see, and these again pass the signal on till it reaches the gentlemen, warning them that the hankwa is beginning. The signal is always made with the hand, never with the voice. When the return signal from both sides reaches the shikari, he orders the beaters to commence shouting and beating the bushes with sticks, or throwing earth or stones into thick clumps, whilst the drummers kick up the greatest shindy that they can possibly get out of their drums. Altogether it is a pretty row, and you may be sure that the hullaballoo raised quickly wakens every animal couching within a long distance on either side of the line of beaters, causing them to start up, and wonder what on earth is going to happen; they never, perhaps, heard such a row in their life.

As I think it best to describe here what has happened at a hankwa, let us now take a flying leap, *à la* Leotard, into one of the machauns, and lend a hand in what is going to happen. Here we are, then, on the tiptoe of expectation, perhaps stung by one or more of a cloud of mosquitoes, or bitten by a villainous red or black tree-ant, or it may be tickled to the height of irritation by one or more wilful, persevering flies, but dare not move hand or foot to drive them away, momentarily expecting the burst or the stealthy tread, as the humour may be, of the tiger or tigers, and scanning with lightning glance the circumscribed space in front and the bushes beyond, not knowing exactly from what point the game may show itself. See! What is that! Oh, a wild boar only, who "lards the lean earth," scared enough; but who has

D

given the unpractised nerves of some a rude shock. There again! No, that is a bear. He too thinks that the sooner he is out of such a neighbourhood the better, and shuffles off double quick. Perhaps a pot-bellied hyena may sneak past, and be nearly mistaken for a tiger. These and everything else must be allowed to pass without a challenge, as, if an unlucky shot were fired at such small game, the tiger or tigers would be alarmed, and break past the rokhs, or double back on the line of beaters, scattering, and, likely enough, grievously wounding, if not killing, one or more of them.

On one occasion, an inexperienced person was holding his gun on full cock, with his finger on the trigger, and through sheer nervous excitement, on seeing a slight motion in some bushes in front, he pulled the trigger; the consequence was, not only losing his chance of a fine tiger (for the animal was making directly towards his machaun), but the tiger, breaking back on the line of beaters, knocked over two or three, scattering the rest, and making them consult their safety in speedy flight. Unfortunately, one of the beaters, as he turned to escape, received a tap on the back of his head from the fore-paw of the animal, which completely smashed in the skull, killing the poor man instantly. Those who were knocked down escaped with their lives, but had received ugly wounds from the claws of the tiger. A hankwa attended with loss of human life is a serious matter to sportsmen, as it at once becomes a police business, and parties think themselves fortunate if they get clear with a douceur of one hundred rupees (£10) to the family of the deceased, not to mention certain other expenses, besides the delay caused, and perhaps necessitating the break-up of the pleasure-trip.

Then comes the grand sight—one, two tigers show themselves! and bang! bang! go the artillery from one or more trees, making one, or perhaps both, of these hitherto monarchs of the jungle bite the dust in sudden death. Hur—hold your row, will you? Here's another rushing past! Bang! bang! Ha! his back is broken! and then follows a roar which must be heard, for it cannot be imagined or described, and the like of which was on one occasion heard by the narrator one mile off. Owing to the contortions and roars, which rather disturb a fresh hand's nerves, it is somewhat difficult to give a maimed tiger his quietus, but this one gets it at last. Old tigers are much more game and dangerous than young ones only two or three years old; the bones of the former, having solidified, become capable of resisting a leaden ounce ball. Many tigers require several balls before they give in, and while some tigers were being skinned, leaden balls that have struck the thigh-bone, or, in some cases, the skull, have been found completely flattened, as if hammered out. For tiger-shooting, it is advisable to use composition-balls, made of one part tin and two of lead.

On the first shot being fired, the beaters redouble their shouts, making the welkin ring again. When the wounded tiger has received its quietus, the men of the hankwa draw up, and the sportsmen descend from their not over easy perches. The examination of the spoil comes next, and the allotting of due honour to the successful shots, the remarks of the gentlemen being interspersed with those of the villagers, complimentary to the sportsmen, but by no means so to the dead game, or their living female relations. During this interval, by the orders of the shikari, some of the beaters have cut down branches and young green bamboos, peeling off and twisting the outer skin of the latter into a sort of rope, with which, tying up and swinging the recently fierce but now quiet enough monsters, they bear them off triumphantly to the sound of the tomtoms to the sportsmen's camp. The beaters are then mustered and paid off by the paymaster personally, boys getting two, three, or four pice ($\frac{3}{4}d.$ to $1\frac{1}{2}d.$) each, men five pice ($1\frac{7}{8}d.$), the rokhs two annas ($3d.$), and the shikari two or three rupees ($4s.$ to $6s.$).

Lastly, the defunct tigers are made over to the shikari, to skin them properly, and take off their heads (cleaning the latter well), preserving the teeth (either separate or in the skull), and also the claws. Many persons do not give the shikari his present until the separate parts of the trophy have been produced; and this is the best plan, as men of that kind are apt to steal the claws and teeth to sell as amulets. Some people go to the trouble and expense of boiling the carcase down for the sake of the grease, tiger-fat being said to be a specific for rheumatism.

It has been gravely asserted that some Europeans have partaken of tiger-meat; it may be so, but, unless they did it themselves, who cooked it? Respectable Hindoo or Mussulman servants would not touch it on any account. It is true that some superstitious villager will at times carry off a small bit to cook for his infant son, thinking that by eating part of a tiger the child will grow up a bold, fearless man; but superstition makes even English persons occasionally do strange things.

Such, concluded the president, is a tolerably faithful account of a hankwa, or drive of wild animals, the manner of conducting it, and the results. The several incidents, of course, are not always the same, nor are the results—failure, and possibly disaster, instead of success, being sometimes the finale.

The president's explanations and description of a hankwa having taken longer time than was expected, it was somewhat late before the party retired, after orders had been given for them to be awaked at daybreak.

CHAPTER VII.

THE CAMP VISITED BY A LEOPARD.

ON being aroused the next morning, the first report they heard was that a leopard, as proved by his footmarks, had purloined two of the joints of venison that were hung up in the large tree under which they were camped. After the president had berated all the servants for not keeping a watch, the party hastily dressed themselves, Sewgolam meanwhile having reported a "kill," and everything being ready, they proceeded to the Jherria.

They had not long been seated in their machauns, when the hankwa commenced, and after waiting in breathless silence for a few minutes, a fine tiger was seen stealthily creeping along with his ears cocked back, and now and then looking back in the direction of the horrible din. When he had got sufficiently near, and clear of bushes, he was saluted with a badly aimed shot, which made him roar and endeavour to leap over some bushes on one side, but, while on the spring, he was stopped by two shots well planted, which dropped him like a sack. Scarcely had the first one been disposed of before another made its appearance, and coming well in front of all was saluted with a general volley, which proved immediately fatal, as she—for it was the tigress— dropped without making the least groan.

After waiting a considerable time without any more tigers showing themselves, the president signalled to the men to close up. When the beaters had come up and the sportsmen had descended, some of the men reported that a three-quarter grown cub had managed somehow to break past the line after the first shots had been fired. When the tigers had been slung, the party made their way back in high glee to camp, leaving the tigers to be escorted with the customary honours. Breakfast having been ordered sharp, after having refreshed themselves with a good wash, they all waited for the arrival of the procession, which just then came in sight. After again examining the tigers and giving the usual orders, the men and boys of the hankwa were at once dismissed. Breakfast being then announced, they proceeded to discuss it with appetites not a little sharpened by the bracing morning air.

While engaged over their breakfast, the butler reported that a man had brought a porcupine for sale, if the gentlemen would like to have it. By all means, was the general response, as most of them much wished to obtain some good quills, which the caterer, however, somewhat marred by saying that he wanted the animal whole for dinner. Such a thought never having entered their minds, and appearing to excite disgust in some, the caterer was obliged to explain that roast, or rather baked, porcupine was a first-rate dish; and if they allowed that one to be appropriated for the purpose, he would undertake that they should have as many quills as they chose before their return home. The others being still somewhat incredulous, and, moreover, curious as to the mode of cooking, the caterer was necessitated to enter into the following details :—

The porcupine, after being cut open, cleaned, and stuffed with proper seasoning, is enveloped, quills and all, in a thick paste of coarse atta (flour with the pollard and bran in it); the cook then digs a hole in the ground, and smoothing it all round with thin mud, puts in a quantity of live coals. When the hole becomes well heated, the ashes are withdrawn, more live coals put in, and the porcupine on them, and all covered up with live coals and wood. After a sufficient time has elapsed to allow for the porcupine to be properly cooked, the black mass is taken out of the hole and cut open; the head is then cut off, and the skin (the quills coming with it) peeled off easily, the rest being sent to the table, looking and tasting very much like a well-fed sucking porker.

After breakfast, while indulging in a weed and arranging with Sewgolam how to circumvent the rascally leopard that had stolen the best of the venison during the night, the butler, making a profound salaam, or bow, reported that the larder was quite empty; there was nothing in camp but preserved meats. This report at once altered the programme for the day; so it was decided to leave the leopard until the next day, and at once set out to get something to keep the pot boiling. As it was useless to go into the Jherria jungle, the game having all been frightened away by the morning's hankwa, it was resolved to start westward, and then, making a detour south through the jungle, return early to camp.

Taking Sewgolam and three coolies, or porters, with them, they had scarcely entered the jungle a quarter of a mile from camp, when Jones was fortunate enough to see a spotted deer, and potted him before he could make off, or the others make out what he was firing at. While the president and most of the rest were busy sending off the deer and ordering the quick return of the men, two of the party had strolled away, and as they were descending the side of a shady hillock, two noble sambhur deer sprang up from the other side of some bushes, and were making off; one, however, only succeeded in doing so. On hearing the double report, the others soon joined them, when Sewgolam proposing to break up the deer, those who were verdant had an opportunity of seeing another phase of woodcraft, in skinning, disembowelling, and quartering the deer, thereby making a much lighter and more convenient load for the coolies.

By that time the men had returned, and were about to start with the second load, when the president, reflecting a moment, imformed the rest that it was absolutely necessary for him to return to the camp to personally superintend the preparation and cooking of the head and shins of the sambhur, and promised them a dish of soup they would remember for some time. As he required Sewgolam to arrange with him about the next day's proceedings, he advised the rest not to go far into the jungle from where they then were, promising to send them a competent guide with the coolies in a short time.

On his return to the camp, after sending off the coolies with a trusty villager well acquainted with those jungles, the president inquired more particularly into the whereabouts of the thieving leopard, and then despatched Sewgolam to track him carefully to his den, and make the necessary arrangements so as to be sure of him the next day.

The butler was then ordered to bring the sambhur meat and receive orders for dinner, directing him also to have plenty of hot water got ready at once. When the sumbhur was brought, the president directed the horns of the head to be knocked off, and the eyes and tongue removed, the latter to be put in pickle; the shins, after removing the hocks, were then cut off from the knee-joint, and the head and shins plunged into hot water to wash and scald them. After soaking until the stronger hairs were removable by hand, the head and shins were taken out, carefully shaved with a razor, and again well washed with hot water. Next, the head and shins were broken, the brain of the head and marrow of the shins extracted, and, after placing the whole in a large dekchee (Indian copper cooking vessel) or saucepan, with some salt, and enough water to cover it all an inch deep, the cook had strict orders to let it boil for one hour, and then merely simmer for five hours, or about six hours altogether (adding now and then boiling water enough to keep the contents just covered), when the president, tasting it, put in a few drops of sundry herb essences, and a pinch or two of celery salt, with pepper and more salt to taste.

In the meantime two of the coolies had returned to camp with another spotted deer, two peacocks, a brace of hares, and three of a species of pheasant. While the president was busy flavouring the sambhur soup, the others returned, bringing two more peacocks and some partridges. The peacocks being too old, were denuded of their tail-feathers and given to the camp-followers, with the usual parts of the rest of the game. Knowing that the party would be very thirsty after their shooting ramble, the caterer, to give them a refreshing surprise, had a quantity of tamarind-and-honey sherbet prepared, which was pronounced delicious by all, and entirely superseded Bass and other drinks.

The caterer had an eye to effect in preparing the sherbet, for when dinner was announced, and the soup partaken of, the surprise and pleasure evinced at its super-excellence, was quite a triumph, and well rewarded him for the trouble taken in its preparation. A noble hunter's pie, formed of a little of everything shot during the day, gave occasion for the expression of further satisfaction, which increased and reached its climax as the feast was crowned with a dish of feeloze dipped in honey.

Rapping his knuckles on the board and requesting silence, Robinson rose, and, in an eloquent speech, thanked the caterer and president in the name of all for the first-rate dinner they had literally enjoyed; stating that for himself, honestly speaking, he had expected to meet with short commons frequently; instead of which, to his own (and he was sure the rest would agree with him) great and agreeable surprise, they had partaken of more than one dinner, and that one especially, which the best hotels would be unable to produce; ending with proposing a toast to the health of the president, and a call for three hearty cheers.

After the toast had had justice done to it, the president rose, and thanking them in a few words for the expression of their satisfaction, said that he hoped the excursion would terminate as pleasantly as things had gone on, and suggested their all retiring early, as they would have to start at daybreak the next day for a long morning's ramble, in which he hoped to show them some other game.

Retiring, then, from the table they adjourned to the fire, where, while enjoying their cheroots or pipes, and brandy-and-water, the time passed swiftly in going over the incidents of the day, which naturally led to the recital of various sporting reminiscences. Leaving the others for a while, the president went to see for himself that the venison was placed well out of reach of the thieving leopard, and ordered the servants to arrange among themselves for a good watch to be kept during the night. Returning to his companions, he advised their retiring at once, as they would need a good night's rest to prepare them for the next day's sport.

Before daybreak the next morning the khansamah, on bringing the coffee, reported that one whole quarter of the sambhur had been carried off by some animal. On inquiring into the matter, it appeared that the man who was to have kept the first watch had been indulging a little too freely in mowah toddy, and had dropped off to sleep without awaking another man, consequently no watch had been kept again all night. The president, inwardly chafing the while, ordered the remainder of the sambhur to be cut into strips and jerked, determining meanwhile to end the career of the leopard before many hours had passed.

When all were ready, as the party were going to the jungles and rocks to the west of Kowie Ghât on horseback, the president warned them to keep a good look-out and proceed silently, as there was a chance of coming across some wild pigs, bear, or that thieving leopard, returning at early dawn to their several lairs. Not meeting with anything, however, on the road, they all dismounted at the edge of the jungle, where Sewgolam was waiting with men to conduct them to the ascertained quarters of the leopard, whose plain footprints far apart showed that he had returned home at a gallop a few minutes previously.

Proceeding cautiously through the jungle, they came suddenly, at the turn of some bushes, close upon a large bear grubbing for white ants, which, seeing them, rose on his hind-legs prepared to show fight, and was on the point of rushing on the nearest of the party, when a well-aimed shot by Wilcox right in his heart, settled his business.

THE LEOPARD ESCAPES FROM ITS DEN.

Being so near to the leopard's den, it was feared that the shot fired in the chance encounter with the bear would alarm and cause him to escape. The shikari then said, that foreseeing the probability of such an occurrence, he had sent on men on each side to watch where the leopard went to, should he escape from his usual quarters on hearing the shot. It was well that the man had taken such precautions, for, when they came up to the reputed leopard's den, one of the men said that on hearing the report of the gun, the leopard sprang out of his cave, and fled with great speed to a dense jungle in a *cul de sac* of the hill.

CHAPTER VIII.

JONES AND SMITH EACH GET A LESSON.

WHILE deliberating how to drive him out, the leopard was suddenly seen by all, trying to escape up the steep side of the hill. After one or two had tried a long shot at him, a general chase commenced, which was found to be very fatiguing, as they had to make their way over loose stones and boulders, and through thick jungle. Persevering a few minutes longer, they came upon a bit of open ground, and looking about, the shikari pointed out the leopard, lying on a rocky platform, a few yards higher up in front. As the beast was lashing his sides with his tail and growling, it was evident that he intended to show fight, and would probably make a charge, thinking to escape in the rush. As the animal, however, was on the point of springing down on them, Brown brought him down cleverly with his rifle, by a shot in the eye, thus securing a perfect skin, which turned out to be that of a fine male one.

During the examination of the leopard, Wilcox saw what he thought was a hedge-hog, making his way into a hole under a large piece of rock. From the description given it was found to be a porcupine, and it was at once resolved to catch the fellow alive if possible. Finding the rock detached, all the party, with some of the villagers, by their united strength managed to lift it up, and discovered two porcupines, which, on their house being thus rudely broken up, tried to escape. Jones and Smith instantly, but incautiously, stooped down to seize one each, when the porcupines, suddenly raising their quills, taught them a lesson not to meddle rashly with prickly things. Seeing that the porcupines were wanted, the villagers easily captured them by throwing their upper garments on them. Satisfied with their morning's work, and feeling hungry as hunters, it was time to return to their horses, and hasten to the camp for breakfast.

Leaving the shikari and villagers to bring in the game, the party soon reached the camp, and did ample justice to an excellent meal. After breakfast—the shikari, meanwhile, having arrived with the game—while amusing themselves in superintending the skinning of the leopard and the bear (taking the fat also off the latter), Sewgolam said that a villager met them on their return, and reported that there was a tiger at the Ghagur, near Murkoondee. All were rejoiced to hear the news, the shikari being there and then ordered to get a "victim," and make the necessary preparations, and to promise the man who gave the information a reward of eight annas (1s.), as an inducement to others to bring similar information.

Presently, two villagers came to the camp, one bringing for sale a spotted deer-fawn, and the other a pair of tame partridges. Some of the party doubting their being tame, the villager at once let them loose, when, after picking about a little time, and straying to some distance, the man called to them, and the birds immediately flew and settled, one on his head and the other on his shoulder. On such a proof of tameness, the man had no reason to regret bringing the birds to the camp for sale, except the necessity of parting with them. The owner of the fawn, also, was apparently abundantly satisfied with the result of his interview.

The president then said that those partridges reminded him of what he once personally saw at Chunar. Having to cross by the ferry to go to Benares, he overheard some natives apparently betting something about a partridge, which one of them had in his hands. The ferry-boat being about to start, the man handed the partridge (a grey one) to one of the rest, and jumped on board. On the passage, being asked what the matter was, the man said his bird was so tame it would never leave him, and that the other men doubting his word, he (the owner) had a wager of two rupees (4*s*.) that he would cross the Ganges, and from the bank on the other side he would call to his partridge, and it would come to him, and he was then crossing for that purpose. On arriving at the other side, nearly all in the ferry-boat who had listened to the statement followed the man to a little rising ground, whence calling aloud, the partridge, being loosed, flew across the river and settled on the shoulder of its master, seeming glad to be there.

In the afternoon the party took a quiet stroll by the Morbhya hillocks, and round through the Putwut jungles, bringing home a sambhur and a spotted deer, and some smaller game. The stroll having extended much farther than was at all contemplated, as it generally does under such circumstances, when they returned to camp, they were all quite ready for dinner, which was ordered forthwith, and justice done to it. Then, while enjoying their cheroots and grog around the fire, in answer to an observation, the president said that the "victim" does sometimes escape, and is respited for months, or altogether, if grown too old. Tigers do not invariably leave, and return to their lairs from the same direction, and it does occasionally happen that a "victim" is found alive in the morning. A remarkable instance once happened at the Jherria, at about the very spot where the last "victim" had been killed.

A party of gentlemen had come to Sulkhun for a few days' "sport," and engaged the same shikari, who took a "victim" to the Jherria. Going the next morning to see if there was "a kill," he was surprised to find it alive, but noticed that all the hair on its body was turned quite white with terror. Suspecting the cause, he began carefully examining the ground all round, and found the footprints, of different sizes, of no less than four tigers. On returning to camp, taking the victim with him, and reporting the circumstance, the gentlemen being still incredulous, themselves went, and, examining the place, found the shikari's statement to be perfectly correct. It was supposed that the four tigers, attracted very likely by the lowing of the "victim," had arrived nearly together, and being jealous of each other, had passed a considerable time in walking round about, or sitting down and watching "the victim," neither of them daring to strike it for fear of the others pitching into him.

The sight of the tigers all round it, and the hearing of the caterwaulings, roars or growlings so close, had the effect of turning all the hairs on its body white through sheer terror. As the young buffalo had received a mortal fright (usual in such cases), refusing food and even water, and would not live long, it was tied up again the next evening, and on the following morning two tigers were bagged. One of the gentlemen, an eye-witness of, and an actor in, the above circumstances, related them to the narrator.

The next morning, the first report again was, one hind quarter of the sambhur carried away, evidently by a leopard. The shikari, arriving just then with a favourable report of "a kill," was ordered to put a clever man on immediately to trace up the leopard, as it was plain that the real thief had not yet been killed. When all were ready, they started for Murkoondee, where, leaving the horses, they proceeded on foot to the banks of the Ghagur, where the machauns were fixed, and the result of the hankwa was a fine large tiger. The beaters having come up close, and no other tiger appearing, the party were just about preparing to descend, when suddenly a bear rushed out, and was saluted with several hastily-fired shots, which wounded and enraged the animal. Not thinking of any danger from the bear, they were all laughing at his queer antics, while reloading their guns, when those in one tree called out to the others in another to look out, as the bear was climbing their tree (having heard and seen them), apparently bent on mischief.

Those warned had scarcely time to look round ere the bear appeared with his head and fore-paws at one side of the machaun. Fortunately, one of the party in the tree (Brown) had a pair of pistols, which somehow he thought of putting into his belt before starting, and, drawing one of them, fired it within one foot of the bear's throat, causing the brute to let go his hold and fall to the ground, where he soon died. While the little scrimmage was going on up one tree, the others were getting out of theirs, and running to give assistance, the foremost arriving at the foot of the tree just as the bear received his *coup de grâce*, barely managed to jump aside when the brute fell; as it was, he got spattered with some of the blood.

By that time the beaters and all had assembled round the tiger and bear; Brown, who had shot the bear in the tree, receiving great praise and the honours of the day for his presence of mind and steadiness. In his turn, Brown said that he had a strange presentiment of some danger before starting that morning, and seeing his pistols, which he always kept carefully loaded, something urged him to put them into his belt; and well it was that he did so, for their guns having been fired off, and there not being time to load again, one or both of them that were in the tree would to a certainty have been seriously mauled by the wounded and savage brute.

The hankwa having ended so happily, it was resolved by the gentlemen, and readily agreed to by the shikari and beaters, that the tiger and bear should be escorted to camp with special honours. Accordingly, two stretchers having been quickly made, the tiger and bear were placed one on each of them, lying on their bellies, with the head between the fore-feet, the corners of the frames being decorated with green branches. The whole body of beaters were then ordered to provide themselves with similar branches, and to accompany the trophies with as much noise as they chose to make, to give more *éclat* to the affair, an extra reward being promised for their trouble. The party then returned to Murkoondee, and, mounting their horses, rode quickly to camp.

By the time they had washed and discussed a capital breakfast, for which they were all sharp-set, and were lighting their cheroots, their ears were assailed with a din, light at a distance, but perfectly horrible by the time that the triumphal procession reached the camp. The sight was a novelty to most of the spectators, and not a little comical to the gentlemen, for when they had left Murkoondee the beaters rested there a little while to smoke, and make such additions as they thought would do honour to the occasion.

With some coloured and white rags they had made small banners, and with these, and one or two more drums, accompanied by all the idlers of that and other hamlets, they came into camp, drumming, blowing horns, dancing and singing at the top of their voices, to the praise and honour of the gentleman (especially) who put his little gun down the bear's throat, and so on, slightly embellishing the matter.

Also, by the time that the procession reached the camp, a respectably-sized mob had assembled, as the villagers of Sulkhun, with the servants, passing travellers, &c., must needs come to see and hear what all the row was about. As it was high time to get rid of the mob, the paymaster was requested to pay off the beaters, giving each one his share of the extra reward promised them.

When the mob had been dispersed, while the shikari and others were busy skinning the tiger and bear, and collecting the grease from the latter, a company of men were seen approaching the camp, some leading tame bears, others monkeys and goats, while the rest had baskets of snakes. It being too early to go out for their usual stroll, the party thought to divert themselves, as some of them had never seen such performances; and so they ordered the men to commence operations, the president, however, suggesting as little of the drum as possible, having had quite enough of that kind of noise for that day at least.

Several of the performances of the animals elicited hearty bursts of laughter from all, especially the ungainly attempts of the bears at dancing. The sham fight of the bears, however, whether from the animals not being well up in their parts, or that one had hurt the other, would evidently have ended in a real fight, had not the keepers thrashed and separated them. Satisfied with the exhibition, the poor fellows were dismissed with a liberal present, which seemed to please them amazingly.

CHAPTER IX.

JONES SHOOTS A LARGE SNAKE.

THE sun beginning to decline, it was time to take their usual stroll; and it was determined to proceed due west, into the open fields, where some quails and partridges were said to be. After they had gone some distance, Jones indistinctly saw something moving through some tufts of grass, which he thought might be a hare, and, firing quickly a little ahead, chanced to blow to ribbons the head of a large snake, nearly eleven feet long. The body, in its contortions, approaching where they stood, made them quickly give it a wide berth, as the blood was being spattered all about. The attendants, however, with their sticks, soon quieted it, and it was sent into camp to be carefully skinned, Jones intending the skin to be made up into slippers and tobacco pouches. Several brace of partridges and quails, and a few curlews and pigeons, having been bagged, the party returned to camp well satisfied with the whole day's work.

The dinner again gave general satisfaction, not a few toasts being drunk in the course of it; one to the president for a dish of stewed venison steaks, prepared by the cook, under his special superintendence, and which was pronounced A 1. The hero of the day (Brown) bore his honours suitably, when a toast with three times three cheers was proposed and drunk. There being no hankwa the next day, the party sat up late, singing songs, recounting their various sporting experiences, &c. A sudden outcry made one or two rush into the tent for their guns, and on inquiring into the cause of the noise, it appeared that a rascally jackal had had the temerity to attempt the seizure of the fawn, and had nearly succeeded in doing so.

On returning to the fire, the conversation naturally turned on jackals, and the president especially mentioned sundry traits about these animals, and the opinion the natives had of them, relating several anecdotes about them which are current among all classes. One of the party doubting the cunning of the jackal, the president said that, if they would listen for a few minutes, he would relate something of his own knowledge.

Having been on a certain occasion ordered to Singrowlee, on duty which would keep him there for some months, he built a lath-and-plaster bungalow, with a verandah all round, having lattice-work sides. While the rest of the outhouses were erecting, the servants had to stow away the fowls in the kitchen at night in a basket covered with a heavy stone. One morning the cook, who slept in the kitchen until his own quarters were ready, reported that he was waked during the night by a great noise among the fowls, and jumping up quickly, he had just time to see some large animal rushing out with something in his mouth. Seeing the basket upset, and some of the fowls out of it, he put them in again after counting them, and finding two of the largest missing. On examining all round, there were plain marks of a leopard having visited the place.

The next night, although the basket of fowls and the door of the cook-room had been better secured, the leopard had managed to get in again, and carry off two of the next finest fowls. As this sort of robbery could not be allowed to go on, he (the president) determined to sit up the following night, and try and shoot the thief. A goat being bought during the day, he had it well fastened to a peg firmly driven into the ground, a few yards from the bungalow. Then, taking up a position in a dark corner of the verandah, and covering himself with a black blanket, he waited patiently with his double-barrel all ready. The leopard, however, either suspecting a trap, or seeing him (for a leopard's eyesight is very sharp), failed to put in an appearance.

Instead of the leopard, at about two o'clock, when the moon

was well up, a jackal came sneaking up to the goat, and tried his utmost, by making the latter's acquaintance, to throw him off his guard and then spring at his throat. The antics and cunning tricks of the jackal were excessively amusing. Pretending to be very innocent, he tried to entice the goat into a game of play, running round and round him, gradually making the circles less all the time, then making a little spring towards the goat as if to kiss him, as you all have seen a young dog do to an older one.

Not succeeding, he would roll over and over, trying to get within springing distance, or else he would run round awhile pretending to bite the fleas in his tail, each time, however, nearing the goat; then he would run off a few feet and back again, or would, with the semblance of innocent play, run round the goat, making little barks and snaps at him. All, however, would not do—the goat was too knowing a hand to be so taken in, and whenever Master Innocence came too close to be agreeable, down went his head ready to give him a dig with his horns. The agility displayed by the jackal in avoiding the sharp horns of the goat was not a little instructive as well as amusing. This fun lasted for more than an hour, until something that the jackal did tickled him so much that he could not help a burst of laughter. The way that the jackal jumped, and looked astounded at having been so near danger and not aware of it, added not a little to his merriment, during which the jackal made off hot foot. Taken altogether, this opportunity of reading such a page of natural history was well worth the loss of a few hours' rest. As it was getting close upon daybreak, he roused one of the servants, and making the goat over to him, went to get an hour or two's sleep.

All having been so much interested in the different stories, no one had noticed the flight of time, and when the president, hearing the distant cry of some jackals, without looking at his watch, said that it was midnight, and time to go to bed, the others, doubting, looked at their watches, and were not a little surprised to find it just twelve o'clock. Requesting an explanation, the president said that by observing the habits and cries of different animals, and the state of certain plants, after living in the jungles for some time, persons did not much require either a watch or a barometer, as by the above means the hour of the day or night, or the approaching change of weather, might be pretty correctly told. He further said that jackals usually cried every two hours during the night, commencing at six o'clock if the night were dark by then; but at eight, twelve, and four, or about daybreak, they may be sure to be heard if in the neighbourhood and all was still. Of course there might be exceptions, but in well-regulated jackal coteries they might generally be heard at the above hours.

The next morning, on getting up rather late, the first report was that the pet fawn had been carried off, evidently by the leopard. As the fawn by its tameness had won upon all the party, and moreover was intended as a present to a lady friend, the news of its abduction determined them not to leave the place without making the thief pay for all his misdemeanours. While the president was giving orders for a man to start immediately to summon the shikari, that individual was seen approaching, and on arrival, being told what had happened, he said he knew it before the gentlemen had waked. He then said that the leopardess (for he was certain it was the mate of the one already shot) had been carefully traced to the same cave, that men had been left to watch it, and everything was ready whenever the gentlemen choose to go after her.

Breakfast being at once ordered and discussed, and the horses all ready, the party lighting their cheroots started for the rocks where the other leopard had been shot. Leaving the horses at the head of the jungle, they proceeded to where the leopardess was said to be. Going right up to the mouth of the cave, they all, with the shikari, strained their eyes in vain, as nothing could be seen. Fancying that they had been humbugged, they were inclined to be angry at coming on a fool's errand, but the shikari, having questioned his own people, assured them that the leopardess had not escaped. The cave being difficult to enter, it was proposed to smoke the animal out. Accordingly, a long bamboo, with some dry grass tied at one end and set on fire, was thrust into the leopard's den. Suddenly, before any one was aware, out sprang the animal, knocking down Robinson in the rush.

Some moments were lost in the confusion, during which the animal was making off by tremendous leaps, but a fortunate long shot by Wilcox hit it right at the back of the skull and floored it. When brought to the gentlemen, and found to be a leopardess, it was immediately surmised that young ones were in the cave, and a brave little native boy, being asked to go in, at once consented. Presently, a good deal of spitting and growling being heard, the boy was seen creeping back, holding as well as he could a leopard cub in each hand. He said that the cave went a good length, and had then a bend to the left, where he found the young ones by their growling at him, but, being quite dark, he had to feel about to secure them, which he did after much trouble. As the noble little fellow had been much scratched in the encounter, for his bravery and trouble he had a present on the spot of one rupee (two shillings), which seemed to please him mightily.

While looking about, some of them saw some large beehives under the projecting eaves of a perpendicular rock, and wanted very much to try and get them. The shikari, however, advised them strongly not to try it, or they would get stung, but promised that the honey and combs should be brought to the camp by the evening.

The leopardess being made over to the shikari to be skinned, and the cubs sent to camp by some of the villagers, the party taking the rest of the men and strolling through the jungles, came upon a couple of curious whitened mounds, and wanting to stop and explore them, the president advised their proceeding on, promising to tell the party all about them after dinner if they reminded him. Going along further, Jones, seeing some animal making off through the grass, fired quickly and killed, as it turned out to be, a fine porcupine. Further on they shot a deer, some hares, and partridges. As the sun was getting warm, they then returned to the horses, and mounting, soon reached the camp.

Being tired with their long stroll, they did not care to go out again that day, amusing themselves with another fawn and a young monkey, which some villagers had brought for sale. A brood of half-fledged pea-fowl having also been brought, the party found it necessary, as they were forming quite a menagerie, having young leopards, porcupines, partridges, pea-fowl, a fawn, and a monkey, to make arrangements for leaving them all with some of the villagers until their return.

An early dinner having been ordered, while discussing the soup, Smith pushed his plate away, saying that it was not worth tasting after sambhur soup, and wished for a plate or two of it then. The president quietly said that he had given orders for a sambhur hankwa for the next day, and it would depend upon each of them whether they had any more such soup; but he strongly advised them to try and shoot the animals in the head or neck, and so get perfect skins, which were very valuable when properly dressed.

CHAPTER X.

MEMENTOES OF TIGERS.

AFTER dinner, which (barring the soup) again gave satisfaction—the bear's paws of the previous day, baked, being pronounced excellent—when the party were settled comfortably round the fire, the president was duly reminded of his promise. He then said that perhaps they were all aware of the natives being very superstitious, those living far away in the district being even more so than those living in towns. Natives living in or on the borders of the jungles, or forests, invariably erect a small mound of earth on the identical spot, if known, where a tiger has killed any one, otherwise on the spot where the remains were found. This mound is of a conical shape as you saw, being about one and a half or two feet in diameter at the base, sometimes broader, tapering to about six inches at the apex, which is flattened. One or more curiously-shaped earthern vessels may always be seen either on the mound or close by it, and the mound itself ornamented with three or four daubs of coloured wash and a flower or two. Before the coloured wash is applied, the mound is carefully smoothed and whitewashed. The curious-shaped pottery placed on the mounds is never seen in towns, and in the country parts it is never used for any other purpose. These curious things, when once placed on the mound, are never touched by any one, it being considered a sacrilege to do so; moreover, any one wilfully removing them is supposed to be certain of meeting some great calamity.

Wherever the death has been a more than ordinarily tragic one in their estimation, that particular mound is selected, and on a certain appointed day in the year nearly all the females in the village, together with a deputation on behalf of the male inhabitants, go and make poojah, or worship, there, and if the old piece of pottery has fallen or been knocked off by animals, a new one, with much religious ceremony, is put on the top. Every mound is periodically visited, kept in order, and poojah performed before it. All this is done to appease the spirit of the departed, which is otherwsie supposed to enter into that or other tigers, and compel it, or them, to kill other people to avenge his own death. Taking the village of Romph, at the top of Ekpowaghât, as a centre, more than fifty of these mounds may be seen within a radius of one mile, one of these mounds being actually *within* a village, and another a few yards outside of another village. It is for the destruction of the ferocious animals that give occasion for such mounds, that the truly paternal government of India has *reduced* the reward for killing them from ten rupees to five rupees, or from twenty to ten shillings.

To exhibit in their proper light the liberality of the said government and the rapacity of its inferior officers, we will merely suppose the following case, but which has happened over and over again, although not in a precisely similar manner in every case, and to the knowledge of the narrator in more than one instance. A simple shikari of a village, distant we will say fifty to sixty miles, or more, from the station, is foolish enough to shoot a tiger, and *boast of his exploit.* The news soon reaches the native police, who, sending for him, pretend to make much of him, saying that he is a very brave man, has done a noble deed, and rendered the government a great service, will have his head exalted above his fellows, and receive a certificate of honour for his bravery, besides a great reward; and, finally, asking if he is not aware of the great reward given by a paternal government for the destruction of any tiger or other wild beast.

When the poor simpleton confesses his utter ignorance of the reward offered, the police treacherously lead him on to admit that he would like to claim the reward, but did not know how to set about it, or to whom to apply. Having admitted his claim to the reward and his desire to have it, he is from that moment in the power of the immaculate subordinate police. As it is necessary to keep the poor fool in the dark for a few days, he is told to make his mind easy, to go to his usual occupations, and that in a few days the order for the reward will come down.

A week or ten days after that interview, he is again summoned to the local police-station, and informed that a report of the circumstance, and his claim to the reward, having been sent to the magistrate and collector, the account of his great bravery has so pleased all the nobility of the station, that he has been requested to go to the magistrate's office, where no doubt great things will be done to him, and that he had better get ready to proceed at once, and so not lose the good fortune that is evidently awaiting him, and a lot more of similar lies. The poor man has perhaps never been ten miles away from his village, is thunderstruck at hearing that he is expected to go such a long distance, and, after reflection, says he cannot leave his means of subsistence, urging, who was to maintain his family during his absence, and that he would rather decline the intended honour and reward.

The police then ply him with fresh arguments, that all the nobility of the station, the officers of government, and the government itself, would be highly offended at his refusal, and would rate him soundly for wanting to show such bad manners to influential people, and that he ought to have more pride in him, and so on. The poor man perhaps then objects that he has no money to defray the expenses of the journey. The police then come to his aid by suggesting that as he was going to receive such honour and reward, surely his friends would lend him sufficient for all his purposes, seeing it would shortly be repaid. By such arguments the poor fellow is persuaded to pack up the tiger's skin and skull, and present himself again at the police-station, when he is further told that they have received orders to treat him with every distinction, and that he is to be escorted all the way from station to station by one of themselves.

Having got him several miles away from his village, the native policeman, who in reality has charge of him to see that he does not escape out of their toils, blandly suggests that he was guilty of great rudeness in not offering the native officer (his superior) a small present for all the trouble that he had taken in the matter, and that if four annas (sixpence) were then given to him it would prove of great service eventually to the brave man. This is squeeze the first, to be followed by others, on various pretexts, till he reaches the station.

On arrival at the station he is told that he must wait a day or two for the propitious moment in which to be presented to his honour. When the fortunate day arrives, as he is going to the court, he is told that it is customary to give a douceur to the native official who will present him to the gentry, and by speaking a good word for him will insure for him a good reception. The poor man, thinking that, as he had come so far, and had already spent so much, it would not do now to hang back, asks how much is required, and is told that eight annas (one shilling) would be sufficient.

On taking stock of his cash, he says that he has only that much left, but the policeman tells him that he would have no difficulty in borrowing any amount, as many persons would feel honoured in lending such a brave man as much as he required. After receiving the money, the policeman tells him to wait in a certain place, while he goes to make the necessary arrangements. When an hour or two has elapsed, the policeman goes up to him with some fresh lies, that, owing to the immense press of work, his honour the magistrate was obliged reluctantly to put off attending to him that day, but had appointed two days afterwards to receive him, or else says that a fearful dacoity had occurred, and that every one had run off to catch the rascals; or that the head native officer had, a few minutes previous, fallen down in a fit in open court, and that the whole court in consequence was in great confusion.

He then takes him to a kind friend of his, who, he says, will lend the brave man what he requires, and, under pretence of official duty, leaves him to arrange matters. The money-lender bewails his misfortune in, at that particular juncture, not having it in his power to accommodate such a gallant man, but (seeing that the man has a good brass cooking-pot with him) offers to procure a loan if he can deposit anything as security. The poor man, being at a nonplus, and feeling the cravings of hunger, hands over the brass pot, which the money-lender takes round the corner, and, after a few minutes, returns with about one-third the value, saying that it was with great difficulty he had managed to raise so much, mentioning nothing then, however, about interest, but, as a matter of form merely, gets an engagement in writing, acknowledging the receipt of the money, and agreeing to pay exorbitant interest, wholly ignoring the brass pot deposited as security.

The poor man then goes to his friend's quarters, and the policeman happening to come in shortly after, on hearing the matter, pretends great anger, and says he will have the man well punished for his scandalous conduct.

He then tells the poor man that, owing to some bad men having obtained rewards wrongfully, through personating those entitled to them, a recent order had been passed for claimants to present a written claim to prevent fraud. He is then taken to a native writer, who makes out his petition on the regulation stamp paper, and demands one rupee (two shillings) costs. The man, astounded, turns to his police friend, who tells him to pay the demand, as it is only a mere matter of form, and it will be returned to him. After paying the rupee, the poor man informs the policeman that he has not a pice left to procure food with, nor anything on which to raise money, but the policeman tells him not to be concerned about that, as he will feed him for a day or two.

In a day or two he is taken before the magistrate, and hears the order given for the payment of the magnificent reward of five rupees (ten shillings). On going to the cashier to receive payment, he is made to give a properly attested receipt. This being done, he is next informed that it is customary to give the head native officer one rupee; the court costs would be one rupee, eight annas; the paying clerk demanding one rupee for his trouble, and the head native police-officer the same sum for the protection afforded the man on the road, so that by the time he reaches his pretended friend's house he has only eight annas (one shilling) left. Moreover, on presenting his claim, the skin and skull of the tiger were delivered in, and he never sees them again.

On the arrival of his police friend, when upbraiding him for his treachery, the mask is thrown off, the policeman demanding one rupee for his trouble, and the shelter and food given for so many days. The poor man says that he has only eight annas left, which he hands over, and the policeman then snatches away the man's upper garment to indemnify him for the balance. Falling at his feet, the poor simpleton begs for mercy, and that some of the money might be returned, to enable him to reach his home. The policeman, after much entreaty, generously returns the supplicant two annas out of the eight, and with this sum the poor man starts on his return journey of, say, sixty miles to his own village.

Arriving there, a considerably wiser man than before he left, and balancing accounts, he finds that he is *minus* three rupees borrowed at heavy interest for his journey, a brass cooking-pot worth three rupees, one month's food supplied to his family, one month's earnings, one upper garment, and one tiger's skull and skin, which he might have sold privately for one or two rupees, if he had not said anything about shooting the tiger. On the other hand, he finds himself *plus* a good deal of wisdom, no end of ridicule for his folly, one rupee borrowed on a brass pot, and the certainty of a lawsuit for the principal and interest of money had and received on deposit of a brass pot, although the latter, when the trial comes on, is ignored altogether.

As far as memory serves, the main incidents of the above story are absolute facts, having happened to a shikari, who, having a tiger's skin for sale, and being advised to apply for the reward, after very significantly declining the suggestion, related his experience to the narrator. One of the party expressing surprise at the credulity of the villager, the president said that when English men and women, with all their advantages of education and hot-pressed civilisation, could believe in spirit-rapping, table-turning, the Cock-lane ghost, and a thousand other absurdities, it was not to be wondered at that a poor ignorant villager should be taken in by the flattering lies of the treacherous native police. By that time it had got late, and after a glass of grog each, they turned into bed.

CHAPTER XI.

THE SAMBHUR HANKWA.

AROUSED early the next morning, the party were soon ready, and proceeding to the Mor Belya hillocks, mounted their machauns. Soon after the signal had been given, two huge wild boars rushed out, presenting a tantalising opportunity; but, as all had been warned not to fire at anything until sambhur appeared, these were allowed to pass unscathed—a liberty they did not misuse. Presently, five sambhurs came dashing up, three of whom were floored in first-rate style, by as many well-directed shots, the rest of the party somehow missing the chance.

The beaters being a good way off, it was expected that there was more game, and so all were on the *qui vive*. Suddenly a bear showed itself for a moment, but escaped behind some bushes, without giving any one a chance for a shot. After that, half-a-dozen wild pigs rushed out, and were saluted with a volley, which knocked over two; then, almost immediately after that, a spotted deer was springing past, over one of the dead sambhurs, but was noisily requested to stop and join company. Also a couple of peacocks, flying past screaming, suddenly fell heavily to the ground.

The beaters having then come up, the gentlemen descended from their machauns, well pleased with their morning's work, wishing only that the bear had given them an opportunity of cultivating closer acquaintance. Three of the party grumbled at losing their chance of a shot at the sambhurs, owing to being at the moment excessively annoyed, some by flies, and the others by mosquitoes or tree-ants.

On their return, having cleared the jungle, they saw a native ahead running to the camp, and on calling out, he came and reported that a tiger had just killed and carried off a man (a wood-cutter, who supplied the camp with wood) in the Putwut jungle. This news, it may be supposed, created a great sensation, the younger of the party proposing to go at once and attack the tiger in a body.

The president, knowing the danger of such an attempt, suggested that instead of acting precipitately, the shikari should be sent off at once, to see for himself what was best to be done. After sending off the shikari, they proceeded to camp, and breakfast being ordered at once, they all sat down to it with true jungle appetites, little being said in course of it, their spirits being too much damped at the fate of the poor man, losing his life in such a way in their service.

Breakfast having been speedily dispatched, the shikari was soon after seen coming to the camp, and he reported that the tiger was a dangerous one, as, by certain marks, it was recognised by some of his people to be the same one that had killed a man close to a village a few miles off. He further said that the body of the woodcutter had been carried into a patch of thick jungle, into which he had ventured near enough to hear the tiger crunching the man's bones.

The jungle, being much intersected by ravines, was not suited for a hankwa, and as it was necessary to destroy the tiger, before he had become a confirmed man-eater, and the terror of the country for miles round, there was only one way of shooting the brute, which, if the gentlemen declined, he was resolved to undertake himself.

The plan he proposed was dangerous, as it involved the possibility of meeting the tiger, but if the gentlemen were inclined to risk it, he would conduct two, or, at the most, three of them, to some trees close to a small pool of water, and close to the spot where the tiger was, and to which the animal would be sure to resort. He further said that if any of the gentlemen determined

F

upon going, they must get ready at once, so as to be up in the trees before the tiger had finished his meal.

After drawing lots, three of them proceeded very cautiously, without talking, to the spot, and each of them mounting a tree, the shikari doing the same with his matchlock, they waited for the brute. Fortune favoured them, as they had hardly got settled, when the shikari made a sign, and in another moment they heard and saw the tiger, his belly swollen out, his joints cracking as he came on, and his head, breast, and fore-paws all bloody, presenting a horrid picture. Allowing him to stoop down and take three or four laps of water, at a given signal three rifles were discharged with a sure aim, and the incipient man-eater fell dead into the pool.

Directly he was dead, the shikari gave a signal-shout to some men he had left behind, and by the time the gentlemen got down from the trees, the men came up. Taking two with him, the shikari, after collecting the head and other fragments of the body of the man not eaten by the tiger, ordered the men to take them, with the tiger, to the exact spot where the woodcutter had been seized and carried off.

The tiger being then cut open, his undigested meal was taken out and placed, with the head and other fragments, in a hole which had been meanwhile dug by the rest of the men. A few simple ceremonies having been performed, with an artless invocation of the Deity, the hole was covered up, stamped down, and protected with stones, and the usual mound raised.

The shikari then asked the gentlemen if they wanted the tiger to be skinned, and a general negative being returned, it was determined to signalize the act of retribution. Ordering a great quantity of dry wood to be collected, the gentlemen asked the shikari if their native prejudices would be offended by the carcase of the tiger being burnt on the man's grave.

The man answered, "On the contrary, the whole community would be highly pleased, the spirit of the departed pacified by such a speedy sacrifice, and all other tigers prevented for a long time from committing such enormities." As soon as the villagers understood what was intended, they showed no little alacrity in collecting the wood necessary for the pile, which being quickly formed, the tiger was placed on it, and speedily consumed.

On their return to camp, the report of their success had preceded them, and given general satisfaction, allaying the anxiety of those left behind. An unusual circumstance also occurred on offering the villagers some compensation for their time and trouble, as these men positively declined to receive anything, saying that they were amply repaid in the satisfaction they had in assisting at the burning of the tiger, and then respectfully took their departure.

During tiffin (luncheon), as the police might at any time be expected to arrive and inquire into the circumstances of the man's death, it was unanimously resolved to make them instrumental, through their European head, in securing the benefit and protection of the widow, and to this effect a letter was prepared. Shortly after, the poor woman herself came, and, after much explanation, apparently uselessly made, with not a little trouble she was at last got rid of, with a small gratuity.

That, however, was not to be the end of the matter, for while the woman was being dismissed, a great noise of drums and horns was heard, and a procession was seen heading for the camp, escorting a present of honey, milk, sweetmeats, and a lamb, preceded by men respectably dressed. On arrival, the chief of the deputation, in a fulsome laudatory speech, begged the acceptance by the gentlemen of the accompanying trifles, as a small token of the gratitude of the inhabitants of several neighbouring villages, for the destruction of the tiger, and signalising its death in the satisfactory manner they had done. As the refusal of the offering would have grievously hurt their feelings, the present was accepted, and the deputation dismissed with thanks.

Satisfied with their day's work, the party sat down to a capital dinner, the president being troubled with a second application for sambhur soup, himself following the example. After dinner, while enjoying themselves round the fire, one of the party (Brown) remarked how singular it was that the widow of the man that was killed by the tiger could not be induced, even by a direct question, to mention her late husband's name, and wondered what could be the reason.

The president said, "that the natives of India, although so degraded in most respects, yet in some points are extremely delicate and refined in their feelings. It is an almost universal, or at least very general custom, certainly in that part of the country, for a native female of nearly every caste, however low in station or poor she may be, if she has any regard for herself, or respect for her husband, never to address or speak of her husband by his name. It is considered a shame to her, and directly she does so make her husband's name common, her glory departs from her, and she is considered no better than she ought to be. In any village quarrel, one of the terms of reproach used against her is sure to be, the woman that calls her husband by his name. A native married woman in those parts, if right-minded, when she has occasion to speak of or call her husband, always does so as the father, brother, or uncle of so-and-so, naming some male child, and never by his own name."

While they were all talking over the events of the day, the elephant managed to get loose, and, owing to its being a very dark night, came close up behind Smith, without being perceived, until the noise made by flapping its ears, caused him to spring up and get out of the way with no little agility, knowing the huge animal to be somewhat mischievous.

Just as some of them were about throwing brands at the elephant to drive him off, the mahout (head-keeper and driver) came up and took charge of it. Being asked how it was that the animal was loose, he said that he had gone to the village to buy some things, leaving the under-keeper in charge, who had not properly secured the elephant before going to sleep.

His explanation not being considered satisfactory, it was thereupon agreed to by general vote that both keepers should be fined for negligence. This little interlude led to general remarks on the cunning, sagacity, and other qualities of these moving mountains, general surprise being expressed at such a huge animal being able to tread so lightly as to come upon them unperceived. The president said that it reminded him of a rather ludicrous occurrence.

A native, crossing a paddock without any right to do so, did not see a large elephant loose in it. Whether excited by a spirit of fun, or mischief, or both, the elephant gave chase, and coming close up behind the trespasser, without his being aware of it, smelt at his hair with his proboscis, and not liking it, the animal blew the nasty smell out again with a snort. The man, terrified out of his reverie, turning round his head quickly, saw the elephant standing over him, with his trunk upraised, and his great mouth wide open as if he were going to gobble him up at one mouthful.

Uttering a loud cry—"Bapree!" equivalent to "Alas, my father, I'm a gone coon this time"—the man set off running as hard as he could pelt. The elephant stood stock-still awhile, twinkling his eyes, enjoying the fun, until pretending to be frightened, he suddenly turned round, cocked up his tail, and galloped back to his shady quarters under a large tree, trumpeting forth his delight all the time.

CHAPTER XII.

AN ELEPHANT OUTWITTED BY A JACKAL.

AFTER they had enjoyed the anecdote, making their several comments on it, the president said that, although the elephant was noted for his sagacity, the natives have a story current among themselves of an elephant having been outwitted by a jackal, and proceeded to give it in an English dress, as an illustration (with others hereafter) of the story-composing ability of the natives, *not* vouching for the truth of any particle of it, or them.

A cunning member of a community of jackals, living in a thinly populated part of the country, where, owing to the healthiness of the climate, dead bodies were rather scarce, one day, to gratify his own ends, struck up an acquaintance with a solitary elephant. During their daily intercourse, after a time and as a proof of friendship, the jackal undertook to conduct the elephant to different fields, where he might enjoy himself, in the midst of abundance of food in which he delighted.

Having by these means succeeded in gaining the confidence of the elephant, the cunning rascal judged that the proper moment had arrived for advancing his scheme a step further. Leaving the elephant enjoying himself one day in a gram field, the schemer proceeded to the royal palace, and demanded admittance to the king of the jackals on an important matter. Being granted admission and duly presented, the rascal pretended to bewail the attenuated condition of his majesty's body, once so corpulent, and the manifest weakness his highness exhibited, owing no doubt to the impoverished state of the royal commissariat department, and suggested that the flesh of an elephant would soon restore his highness to his wonted health and strength.

Thinking that the rascal was only joking, the king of the jackals angrily rebuked his mistimed levity, saying that it was not seemly for any of his subjects at any time to poke fun at him. Disclaiming such an idea, and pretending to be much hurt at the imputation on his love and loyalty, the schemer, intent on carrying out his object as well as give his majesty a rap on the knuckles, reminded him that, by the laws of jackaldom, he was bound to listen to the suggestions of the meanest of his subjects, and if approved of by a general council to act accordingly.

Summoning therefore a parliament, the king of the jackals stated that for the restoration of the royal health elephant-diet had been suggested as a certain specific, and promised the hand of the eldest princess to whoever of his subjects should be brave enough to procure for the royal household some elephant-meat for dinner that day, adding that the royal larder was in a deplorable condition.

Seeing that all the others remained silent, astounded at the temerity of such a suggestion, the wily schemer who meanwhile, through feigned modesty, had kept himself in the background, stood up, intimating that he had something to say. He then, pretending to have been deeply grieved at seeing the condition to which the royal family had been reduced, stated that he had long revolved the subject in his mind, and believing that he had at length hit upon a plan for replenishing the royal larder, and with elephant meat, had ventured to make the suggestion, leaving it, however, as in duty bound, to his superiors in the community, famed for their wisdom and valour, to carry out the suggestion; but as no one showed sufficient spirit to undertake the enterprise, he humbly offered himself to do so, provided that his majesty commanded all his subjects to obey him (the speaker) for a short time, assuring his highness and the council of the success of his plan, and concluded by expressing his reliance on the fulfilment of the promise his majesty had been graciously pleased to make.

The suggestion was then put to the vote of the council, and, after discussion, the feasibility of the plan having been admitted, the king's order was thereupon given, and an oath of obedience to the daring schemer having been imposed upon all, the wily rascal directed them all to proceed singly, and by different routes, with the utmost caution and silence, to a certain spot indicated.

On arrival, the royal family following and keeping themselves in the rear of the general body, and so farthest from danger, all were to conceal themselves, maintaining the strictest silence, and any one disobeying was to be punished with death by the rest instantly falling upon and devouring him.

Meanwhile he would go hunting, and when they heard his voice they were all to join him with the utmost speed, and then do as he might further command. After making a profound bow to his majesty, and a general one to the council, he left the assembly with the confident bearing of a successful jackal.

Directing his steps to the field in which he had left his friend the elephant, he began cajoling him, hoping that he was satisfied with the fare to which he had had the pleasure of conducting him, and trusting that their mutual friendship would be substantially beneficial. As a further proof of devotion to his friend, he said that after leaving him that morning he went foraging for himself, and in his pursuit of game he came upon a splendid field of fine large sugar canes, to which, if agreeable, he would then conduct him.

The elephant's mouth beginning to water at the news, he confessed that if he had a weakness it was for sugar canes, and desired his friend to lead him to it immediately.

Professing again his entire devotion and readiness to oblige his friend at all times, he desired him to follow. Proceeding by a very circuitous route, so as to excite the impatience of the elephant as well as to give his fellows time to assemble at the appointed place, they at length came to the edge of a large jheel, or swamp, on the other side of which the elephant could see the sugar canes tempting him. Not giving the elephant time to raise any objections, and also the better to disarm suspicion as to the firmness of the swamp, the schemer offered to go ahead first, to try the practicability or otherwise of the passage.

Having previously ascertained the treacherous nature of the swamp, and discovered a passage for himself, the wily rascal, having little or no weight to carry, owing to too long continuous short commons, after making several feints to the right and left, here and there and back again, as if finding out the firmest ground, although in reality only to confuse the elephant when he should follow, at last crossed the swamp. Returning to his friend he said, that if he carefully followed the track indicated by his footsteps, he would be able to cross the swamp without any difficulty.

The elephant, having seen the jackal cross and return, being impatient to get at the sugar canes, trusted implicitly to his report, unmindful of the dictates of prudence. For the first few yards he went on very well, but coming to a soft place he was hesitating, when the jackal encouraged him on by saying, that was only a little hole, and that the ground was firm beyond it. Deluding himself, the elephant went on until his instinct told him plainly that the soil was treacherous, and while deliberating about returning, suddenly the under crust of mud on which he was standing, unable longer to bear the weight, gave way, and he felt himself sinking up to his middle in a bog.

The wily schemer then, pretending great surprise and much concern at his friend's predicament, ran up offering his assistance to get him out, pulling now at his ears and then at his tail. All his efforts being insufficient to move the elephant, he asked if he might call his companions to help him to extricate his friend out of his difficulties, and the elephant, thinking that small help was better than none at all, having given his consent, the rascal set up the preconcerted signal—hooah, hooah, hoo-ah! Hearing the signal, the whole community of jackals, big and little, rose up from their hiding places, and rushing upon the elephant, who was unable to fight or flee, soon smothered him with their numbers.

Too late discovering the treachery of his pretended friend, and feeling himself dying an inglorious death, the elephant gave utterance to these sage reflections: "Never form acquaintance, much less cultivate intimacy, with those between whom and yourself there is great inequality, nor lend a ready ear to the advice of those who flatter only to injure."

The next day a parliament of jackals being convened, the king of the jackals honourably fulfilled his promise by giving his eldest daughter in marriage to the wily schemer, at the same time advancing him to the dignity of prime minister, at which there was a prolonged hoo-o-ah! of general satisfaction, evil disposed members nevertheless envying him his good fortune, as baser minds are apt to do. Just as the story was finished, some jackals close at hand set up loud hooahs, as an appropriate finale, warning the party that it was about midnight and time to turn in.

The next morning, when they had just finished breakfast, a man was brought to the camp, said to have been bitten by a snake. On inquiring into the circumstances, the parties who brought the man in, and who were with him at the time, said that they were passing through the jungle, when the man trod upon the tail of a black cobra, without perceiving it, as the reptile was gliding through some grass, and before the man could jump out of the way the animal turned round and bit him in the leg. On examining the man, he was found to be in a comatose, moribund state, too far gone to do anything effectual to; in fact, before remedies could be brought from the medicine-chest he was dead.

When the other men had removed the body, the president said, in answer to some remarks, that the bite of the *cobra di capello* was always fatal, but the poison of the black species of that class of snakes was extremely virulent, as they saw in that instance, inducing coma in about two minutes, and death in from seven to fifteen minutes, ten minutes being about the average. The best thing for any one to do, who has sufficient presence of mind and fortitude, when he is bitten by a venomous snake, is instantly to take his penknife and cut the bitten part well out, allowing the blood to flow freely and so help to eject the virus; then (if bitten in the arm or leg), have a ligature tied tight with a tourniquet above the bitten part, so as to arrest the circulation of the virus, and so gain time for the application of further remedies.

When a live coal or caustic has been procured, the incision should at once be cauterized, and a strong dose of *eau de luce*, or brandy and water with pounded red or black pepper in it, administered internally, the patient meanwhile being *made* to walk or run about by one man on each side supporting him, and thus forcibly prevent drowsiness.

These remedies, *if applied* in time, will save the person's life; but not one in a thousand knows what to do, or would have the courage to cut a good-sized piece out of his arm or leg; and, as the virus is exceedingly active in operation, every second of time being of importance, while he or his friends are considering what to do, doing the wrong thing, or applying useless remedies, the man's vital powers are rapidly over-mastered, and he dies. Snakestone, snake-root, charms, and incantations are alike superstitious bosh.

Whilst so engaged in conversation, the thannadar, or native police inspector in charge of an outpost, was announced. After making a profound obeisance to all, being questioned as to his business, he said that a report having been made at the thannah, or station-house, of one of the servants of the gentlemen having been killed by a tiger, he came personally to request the favour of their giving him a statement of the circumstances, as he had to make a report to the magistrate of all such cases.

The president having informed the inspector of everything

connected with the man's death, as noted in the foregoing pages, handed him a letter to the magistrate on the subject, and desired him to mention in his report as having received the sum of thirty rupees, to be applied to the widow's benefit, as particularized in his letter, and which amount being then handed to the inspector, he took his leave, making many reverences.

CHAPTER XIII.

AN ADVENTURE WITH HORNETS.

THE tragical death of the woodcutter, and the case of snake-bite, having together cast a damper on the spirits of all, made them desirous of quitting Sulkhun for a time. Accordingly, orders were given for two of the tents to be packed up immediately, transported across the Soane, and pitched at Chopun, under a large banyan tree on the river bank. The shikari being then sent for, the collection of pets, increased by the addition of two bear's cubs, was made over to him, with money for their keep, until their return.

A short time after that, one of the camel-drivers came up, saying that he had been stung by a hornet, and that it was very painful, asking for some medicament. On examining the man's shoulder, the sting of the hornet having evidently been left in the wound, caused the pain and inflammation; but the pipe of a large key pressed on the part soon brought the sting out, after which honey was rubbed in, and a rag moistened with honey being kept on it soon completed the cure.

Sundry remarks about hornets being then made by several of the party, the president said, that once while travelling, his servants preceding him, he came up to the large tree under which the camp was formed, and found the cook and others getting things well under weigh for breakfast. He had just filled his pipe, after dismounting from his horse, and had called for some fire, when first one hornet, then another, then a lot of them, and at last a swarm of hornets, began flying about, and attacking every one, man and beast.

On looking up into the tree, the cause of all the commotion was soon discovered. The cook, it appeared, had lighted his fire directly under a large hornet's nest, and, the smoke annoying them, the whole swarm had sallied out to do battle for their squatters' rights. And successfully too, for in a remarkably short space of time, there was a general cry of cut and run, the horses were plunging and kicking, the camels restive, and all hands frantic.

Fortunately for him, the saddle had not been taken off the horse on which he had come, so, jumping into the saddle, and digging in the spurs, he galloped off at a tearing rate, leaving the servants to get out of the mess that they had caused the best way they could. As it was, he got stung by two of the brutes, by one on the nape of his neck, and by another somewhere else, so that he could hardly sit on horseback.

The whole camp was pursued for several miles by the enraged hornets, and they had to march an extra six miles that day, to get to a proper camping ground. When the servants came up they were in a pretty pickle, so badly stung that he was detained three days there, and then had to make only half a day's march. After that day's experience, when out in the jungles, his servants never forgot to look up into the tree, under which the tents might be pitched, *before* lighting their fires.

That the servants might have time to pack up everything for an early start next morning, dinner was ordered early, and justice done to it. After dinner, while assembled round the fire, the president told them the following story of a man-eater:—

The market-town of Kone, about sixteen miles from Sulkhun, was once seriously incommoded by a large tiger. The brute had become a confirmed man-eater, and, from having killed und eaten about forty human beings, had instilled such terror through a large extent of country as to put a complete stop to all trade for some weeks. The dread was so universal that at length the inhabitants were afraid to leave the precincts of their villages, for even necessary purposes, until want drove them, at the risk of their lives, to hurry in search of needful supplies.

This dreadful brute used to kill and eat people in all directions around Kone, and was artful enough to take up his quarters sometimes in the dry bed of a nullah, or watercourse, across which the district road went, and, from his post of observation, which commanded a view of the road in either direction, he could pick out whichever traveller suited his taste best.

Several shikaris had been sent out after him, but the old brute, as if divining their object, forestalled them by eating some of *them* up, until not even an offer of 500 rupees (£50) would tempt any other shikari to try what he could do. The last victim of the brute was the climax of his enormities, causing a general outcry and burst of indignation throughout that part of the country.

The preliminaries of a native marriage had been gone through some time previously, and a fortunate day had been fixed by the Brahmin (or priest), for the young lady to go to her new home. The dreadful deeds of the man-eater were well known, and made the flesh of nearly all creep when any allusion was made to him, still it was thought that a large party of friends, accompanied with plenty of native music, would effectually scare away a dozen man-eaters, so it was determined to proceed on the fortunate day.

Accordingly, an extra band of musicians having been engaged, as well as several matchlock men, the wedding party proceeded, making a horrid din all the way, till they came to the dry bed of the nullah, when, half of the procession having passed safely, suddenly the man-eater, making a frightful roar, bounded into their very midst, and seizing the bride (a lovely young girl), who was on horseback, as is usual in those parts, made off into the jungle with her before the terror-stricken party could recover themselves to try and rescue the poor girl.

This last act of enormity sealed the doom of the man-eater, for it so happened that a certain indigo planter was at a village a few miles off from Kone, making arrangements for the purchase of lac and other items on speculation. On this coming to the knowledge of the traders at Kone, a deputation of the principal mahajuns (or native merchants), and heads of villages, waited upon him, and offered a considerable sum if he would, being a well-known, fearless man, and a good shot, have compassion on the whole country and rid them of the tiger.

Of course he refused their offer of remuneration, but, as it would take him considerably out of his way, and it would be doing them a service, he said that they must bear the expense of the men required for the hankwa. To which they replied that, if necessary, two or three thousand men would gladly give their services for nothing, if by so doing they could secure the destruction of the much-dreaded brute.

The planter being aware of some officers being in the neighbourhood on a shooting excursion, then told the deputation to provide a man on horseback immediately, to take a note to some other gentlemen at a village a few miles off. When the note had been dispatched the planter instructed the deputation what to do, and to have everything in readiness by the second day therefrom.

After the arrival of the military gentlemen, who gladly accepted the invitation, and came over at once, the party rode to the village nearest the dreaded nullah, and having ascertained that the "victim" had been killed, and all other arrangements effected, they silently made for the jungle, and mounted the machauns, determined if possible to destroy the man-eater.

Everything proceeded well, the dreaded tiger, an old male, coming full into view of all the party, who, by an almost simultaneous report, saluted him with a shower of bullets, not one of which, however, proved mortal.

Finding himself hurt, the tiger gave a tremendous roar, and, standing up on his hind legs, began biting at the several wounds, until overbalancing himself he fell backwards rolling in the sand, growling and roaring awfully. As soon as the spare guns were

THE FIGHT WITH THE MAN-EATER.

brought to bear on him, the party saluted him once more, several of the balls, however, missing such an unsteady mark.

Feeling himself again hit, the tiger bounded up with another fearful roar, and went clean over a clump of bushes, into a ravine much covered with jungle. Every effort to drive the brute out of the ravine proving unsuccessful, the party had to descend after reloading their guns, and try and finish him on foot, *always* very dangerous, and in this instance more so, this brute not having the fear of man before his eyes, besides having been pretty hard hit, and so made more savage. Thinking the tiger to be too much hurt to do any harm, the party were talking and laughing over the fun, when suddenly several of the beaters called out to the gentlemen to take care, as the tiger was creeping up the bank, close to one of them.

Sure enough, they had scarcely time to clear out and stand on the defensive, before the tiger broke through the bushes, and made a charge. Fortunately, two or three balls hit him hard enough to make him stop and roll over, thus giving the party time to retreat and seize the spare guns from the attendants. Advancing again to the attack, the tiger, seeing them, got up with an angry roar, and was about to rush upon them, when he was stopped again by a volley, several of the balls hitting him, but still not mortally.

While the party had again retreated, and were engaged in loading all the guns, the tiger managed to get into another small ravine, out of which, when they were all once more ready, he was with much trouble driven, and again had several balls planted in him, this time with better effect, for he fell down and lay motionless.

As many wild animals are apt to "play 'possum" on being wounded, some of the beaters began pelting him with stones, and one happening to strike on his nose, the tiger, growling, managed to sit up on his hind legs, half dazed. The fair mark then presented was too good to be lost, and a ball, well aimed at the chest, caused the brute at last to hang his head, and fall on his side, dying game to the last.

On being examined, it was found that he had received nineteen balls before he was settled, some of the balls being quite flattened, as if fired at an iron target. When it was found that he was really and truly dead, and not shamming, the noise of rejoicing, made by the immense mob of beaters, was something extraordinary.

Men were then immediately sent off to the surrounding villages, and to Kone, to tell the good news of the destroyer having been himself at last destroyed. Poles were then quickly cut, and the no longer dreaded man-eater, slung on them, was carried in triumph by four men, in front of the gentlemen, and preceded by all the tom-toms (native drums), kicking up a dreadful shindy, all the way to the nearest village, where the gentlemen had left their horses.

By the time they arrived, a great crowd had assembled, and the party was received with every honour, men, women, and children uniting in calling down no end of blessings on them, for having rid the country of such a monster. Nor had the wealthier inhabitants been forgetful of hospitality, for they had prepared such refreshments as their caste permitted them to offer, and the gentlemen could accept.

Jones just then hearing the servants speaking angrily, called out to know what was the matter, and one of the grooms coming up said, that a man had come at that hour of the night asking charity, but whom they suspected to be a thieves' spy. Being brought to the fire by their order, Smith said to him that it was not usual for beggars to go round at that time of night asking for charity, and that he should be well horsewhipped as a warning to others.

The president interposing, said to the man, that they would give him a chance of saving his skin, and that was by giving a truthful account of himself.. They would be able to judge, by his tale, whether he were an honest man in distress, or a thieves' companion, and if honest and in need he should be relieved. After listening to his tale, for the truth of which he appealed to the shikari, who, happening to be in the village, was sent for and corroborating the story, being satisfied as to his honesty and truthfulness, they liberally relieved his necessities. Making a profound obeisance, too grateful to speak, the man took his departure, and it being very late, they all turned in.

CHAPTER XIV.

CROSSING THE SOANE.

THE next morning, after starting off the baggage an hour or so before them, the party set off for Chopun, some on the elephant, others on horseback, while two of them preferred to walk, their horses being led by the grooms. As they were going through the Putwut jungle, one of the party on the elephant (Robinson) seeing a bear among some bushes, grubbing for white ants, tried a long shot, but missed, owing to the unsteady motion of the elephant. The ball, however, told sufficiently near to alarm and anger the bear, for the brute, turning round and seeing the party, came rushing towards them, but suddenly stopped about half-way, his prudence apparently getting the better of his courage, and then disappeared down a ravine.

Passing through Putwut, which is a small hamlet built on rising ground, just beyond high-water mark, and over half a mile of the sandy bed of the river, they at last arrived at the far-famed Soane, and took a hearty draught each of its delicious water, which is slightly impregnated with a mineral taste, making it the more pleasant. Running over a sandy bed, perfectly pellucid, with a gentle murmuring sound, seemingly inviting them, the whole party, man and beast (for the gentlemen had overtaken the camp equipage on the sands) slaked their thirst.

One of the camels so much approved of it, that wanting to enjoy itself thoroughly, it lay down in the water, thereby wetting some of the rice and spoiling some of the sugar and flour of its load, causing no little uproar among the servants; but being admonished as to the impropriety of its behaviour, by a sound cudgelling, it made up its mind at length to get up, and go on its way as a sober and well-behaved camel should do.

The beautiful Soane at this time of the year is at about its lowest ebb, being not more than about two hundred and fifty yards broad, and, at the crossing, scarcely knee-deep. In the height of the rains, it is about a mile wide, and its character totally changed, being then a furious torrent of filthy waters, much the colour and consistency of thin pea soup, whereas then it was a beautiful stream, clear as crystal, flowing gently on, as if the above character were a gross libel on it.

The bed of this river, and of its tributary, the Rehund, is very treacherous in most places, and a stranger, in crossing the Soane especially, should take a guide to show the ford, keeping close to him, otherwise, by following his own headstrong will, he might chance to get fixed in a quicksand, and be beyond help.

Crossing the river where the ford was then marked out by stakes (rather too far apart though), and turning to the right a little after getting up the bank, they found the tents pitched under a fine banyan tree, and after a good wash, sat down to a capital breakfast; the cook and khansamah, with their department, having been among the first to start that morning.

After breakfast, lighting their cheroots and taking their guns, they went for a stroll, and had hardly entered the jungle, a gun-shot off the tents, when a spotted doe jumped up from behind a bush, and was instantly brought down by a quick shot. At that instant, a pretty little fawn dashed up to its then dead mother, and all, feeling some compunction at the doe having been shot, agreed to try and catch the fawn, which would pine and die in a few hours, unless taken care of.

Spreading themselves and the coolies all round, they tried to seize the fawn, but the little animal was so active that it took them more than half an hour before they succeeded in catching it, and then only because it would not leave its dead mother. In the course of the day this little fawn became a special favourite with them all.

Feeling very thirsty after their efforts to catch the fawn, they made for the river, and the president, forming some drinking-cups out of the leaves of the práss, they satisfied their thirst. Then, the river looking so tempting, they determined on bathing in it, and having a good swim. This last proposition, however, was nipped in the bud, by the president uttering one word—"Alligators."

On being requested to explain, he said that the Soane and the Rehund would be delightful to swim in at that time of the year, being each like a mill pond, were it not that wherever there was a sufficient depth of water, there was sure to be one or more alligators in it. In proof of his assertion, he pointed to an alligator about fifty yards off, and on the rest of the party persisting that it was only the stump of a tree, the president took his rifle, and hitting it in the neck, caused it to spring up, and fall backwards into the water with a great splash. Surprise sealed their tongues, and no more was said about swimming.

As bathing might be effected, the president sent three coolies back to the camp with the deer and fawn, and instructions to return with towels, &c., directing another man meanwhile to look out for a clean suitable place, not deep enough for alligators. The report of the rifle fired at the alligator had startled several pairs of Brahminee ducks, which kept flying about undecided where to settle.

At last one pair alighted on the edge of the water, about sixty yards off, and one of the party (Wilcox) taking his rifle up, said, out of bravado, that he was going to cut off the heads of those ducks. Getting them in a line, and taking a careful aim, he did actually cut off both their heads, to the no small astonishment of all, his own included; and, on one of the others offering to lay a wager that he could not do it a second time, he modestly declined it.

On the ducks being brought by one of the coolies, their heads were found to have been clean cut off, and the president making an incision carefully, stripped off the skins artistically, saying that it was necessary to do so quickly, otherwise they would soon be unfit to be eaten.

Some green pigeons being startled by the last shot, came flying past swiftly, but Brown taking up his double-barrel quickly, had time to fire one shot, and brought down three pigeons. The skins of these birds also, for the same reason, were at once stripped off by the president, and with the others were sent to the camp with orders for the pigeons to be grilled and the ducks stewed for dinner.

By that time the man had returned with the towels, &c., and the whole party, descending to the selected spot, stripped and had a delightful and refreshing bath. After returning to the camp, while enjoying themselves under the shade of the banyan tree, in answer to a remark, the president said, that in all deep places of these rivers, and, in fact, of every Indian river, alligators were sure to be found. There are two species of saurians common to Indian rivers, the long nose, or crocodile, called ghurial by the natives, and generally considered harmless, and the broad and flat head, or alligator, called mungur (sometimes muggur) by the natives, and as universally dreaded.

Opposite Agoree, and also at the junction of the Ghagur with the Soane, there are large and very deep pools, swarming with alligators, exciting a natural wonder how they contrive to exist. The universal law of nature, however, self-preservation, causes the fishes, on the subsidence of the waters, to congregate in these water holes, numbers of which no doubt become the prey of the alligators. Moreover, the immense number of wild animals that resort to the river to slake their thirst, yield their quota for the preservation of the saurians.

Shortly after the rains have set in, when the village tanks or ponds begin to fill, and before the river becomes a furious torrent;

the alligators disperse all over the surrounding country, so that every tank, with a sufficient depth of water in it, is sure to have one or more alligators in it. When the rains are over, and before the hot weather well sets in, unless the village pond is very deep, instinct tells these animals, the same as it does migratory birds, when to return to their proper quarters, and this they do by night, hiding in thick grass or clumps of bushes by day.

Unless this conjecture be admitted, where *do* all the village alligators go to, or what becomes of them in the hot weather, when the village ponds are dry, or nearly so? Bury themselves in the mud until the tank fills again, say you?

The writer has known of two village tanks, that had two alligators at least in each of them, that were dug out when nearly dry and deepened several feet, and being desirous of settling this very point to his own satisfaction, he made particular inquiries on the subject; but no dormant alligators were discovered in either pond; if they were in the mud, they must have buried themselves *very* deep. Moreover, the writer heard of an instance of an alligator having been discovered one morning, at the commencement of the hot weather, in some high grass far away from any pond, and evidently on his journey to the Soane.

Saurians, of course you are all aware of the fact, are amphibious animals, capable of living for a time on land, but water is their natural element. When on land, although they can make very good progress straight ahead, yet these monstrous lizards are not capable of starting off at a tangent, or of turning on their centre very quickly, so that any one chased by an alligator on land may escape by dodging it round bushes, &c., or, if in open ground, by doubling back like a hare, as instanced in the following story, told to the narrator by the planter :—

Some years ago, when residing in the neighbourhood of a village where there was a large tank, in which there were one or more alligators, a very exciting incident once occurred during the rains. One of the men employed in the indigo factory had occasion to go to the tank early one morning, but was chased away by an enormous alligator. The land round about was all laid out in small squares, having ridges about one foot high, by half a foot wide, communicating with each other and with the tank, so that they might be flooded when required, and these squares were sown with paddy (rice), and were in fact the nursery beds of the village, whence the paddy plants, when sufficiently grown, were transplanted to the larger fields. Rice grows only in swampy ground, and running across such nursery beds in the rains is no joke, especially if an open-mouthed alligator is pelting after you.

In this case, the saurian was rapidly gaining on the human, who was putting into practice all the artful dodges he could think of to save his life, hallooing like mad all the time for some one to come to his assistance. In the ardour of pursuit, and the almost certainty of catching the man, the alligator was led away farther from the tank than was consistent with his own safety, for the villagers, roused by the man's cries for help, quickly turned out, some going to the assistance of the man, while a more numerous body of them intercepted the retreat of the alligator, and hammered him to death with heavy latthées (or sticks of bamboo loaded with lead or iron).

The Soane, as regards being navigable, is of very little value, in a commercial point of view. When the river is full, in the rains and commencement of the cold weather, the natives avail themselves of the only opportunity to send down to Dinapore, a large military station on the right bank of the Ganges, large rafts of wood and bamboos, loaded with buggye grass, and the string made from it, together with such other articles as they think will fetch a better price there.

There is a great variety of fishes in the Soane, the principal being the noble mahseer (Indian salmon), rohoo (Indian cod), mullet and bhacoor. These, with others of less note, are common to and plentiful in the Soane. The superior excellence of the fishes of the Soane must be attributed to the water in which they live, and also in which they are cooked. Certainly, there is no comparison between the fishes of the Soane, and the very same species of fishes caught and eaten elsewhere.

Fly and other fishing cannot be followed by Europeans in Indian rivers as it is in Europe. Fishing in India is, at all times and in most places, more or less dangerous to Europeans. To follow the occupation *con amore*, the European must necessarily expose himself to the fierce rays of the sun, thereby running the risk of sunstroke. In his eagerness to land his fish, he will very likely enter the water, giving alligators more than half a chance of seizing him.

Should he escape this danger, and, by being clothed from top to toe in waterproof, come out of the water dry shod, he must still inhale the malaria drawn out by a hot sun from the slimy ooze in which he walks or stands, and thus sow the seeds of future fevers. Nevertheless, fishing is followed by enthusiastic lovers of the sport, who, many of them, subsequently wonder where they caught that confounded fever.

Moreover, in fishing in mountain streams whose banks are more or less thickly clothed with jungle, it is not particularly agreeable, while intent on watching your float, to have your attention drawn off by hearing a suspicious rustle or movement in the bushes behind you, and to have to lay down your rod and take up your rifle or double-barrel to defend your life from an attack in the rear by some prowling tiger or other wild beast.

CHAPTER XV.

SPECIMENS IN THE SANDS OF THE SOANE.

GARNETS, onyx, chalcedony, cornelian, blood-stone, jasper, and beautiful agates, are to be found in the sands of this river. Rubies, amethyst, and chrysoprase have also been met with. The churs, or sand-banks, formed at the moohana or junction of the Rehund with the Soane, are favourable spots in which to look for specimens, the first comers after the subsidence of the waters of course having the best chance; but, by digging up the sand a few inches, fine specimens may be got, which have escaped mere surface hunters. Particles of gold also have been found in the sands of the Rehund, but in inconsiderable quantities.

While admiring the picturesque beauty of the scenery, the president proposed sending for some dug-outs or canoes hollowed out of trees, and ascending the river to the churs (sandy islands) to look for specimens, which was at once agreed to. About three P.M., only two canoes being available, four of the party got in and set off, leaving two to mind the camp. On their way up, about half-way between the camp and the chur, on the Putwut side, the president, stopping the progress of the canoes, requested one of the party to shout, giving them an agreeable surprise in discovering a fine echo, which repeated six or eight times.

The bank, on the Putwut side, being deeply fringed with jungle, it was necessary to keep the canoes a respectable distance off, and it was well that they did so, for the stream just about there, bending off to the Chopun side, they saw in the sand a little distance ahead, the fresh footprints of a large tiger, that had been down to drink, and had returned to that very jungle. On reaching the chur the party separated, each one grubbing for himself, filling his pockets with different specimens, including some fine nodules of quartz, and then returned to camp.

During the absence of the others, the two left behind taking their guns and some coolies, went for a stroll, and were fortunate enough in shooting, one a nylghau (or neelgye, as usually pronounced by the natives, meaning blue ox or cow), the other a hog-deer, and returned, reaching the camp just as the others did.

As they were taking a rest, enjoying their cheroots or pipes, a man brought a tame mungoose, a species of ferret, for sale, showing off some little tricks he had taught it, which, amusing one of the party, the animal was bought, to be added to the general menagerie. Conversing upon the habits of such animals, the president told them the following story, current among natives:—

In a certain village there lived a poor family, consisting of the man and his wife, and several children. One day, when her husband and elder children had gone out to work and the younger ones to play, the mother put her infant son on the ground, and by his side she placed a thálee (a metal plate, of different sizes, having a deep rim of half an inch or an inch) of water to amuse himself with, while she went about some necessary household duties. Before setting about cleaning the rice and so forth in the adjoining room, as they had a tame mungoose about the house, she caught and tied it up not far from the child, thinking that if loose it might hurt the boy.

When the mother had left the room, a cobra-snake, hearing the splashing of the water, came out of its hole to have a drink. The little child, not knowing what it was, stopped playing with the water, intently watching the snake as it came up and began to drink. Having satisfied its thirst, the reptile was gliding back to its hole, when the little innocent put out his hands and caught it, thinking to amuse himself with the pretty new toy. The snake made no resistance, and in turn amused itself with twining in and

THE DEATH OF THE MUNGOOSE.

out of the boy's arms and legs, until somehow the child accidentally hurt the snake, when it turned round, and bit him in the neck. On feeling the bite, the child let go of the snake, and very soon became motionless, the snake gliding off to its hole.

The mungoose, directly the snake (which is its natural enemy) came out of its hole, began making fruitless efforts to break the string with which it was tied, and, failing in that, succeeded in biting the string through just as the snake had slipped into its hole. Having seen what the snake did to the child, the mungoose ran off quickly into the jungle to get some snake-root.

Meanwhile the mother, alarmed at his unusual silence, coming into the room at that moment, and seeing the child motionless, ran and took it up, and tried her best to restore animation, crying heartily all the time. Having found the antidote, the mungoose ran back quickly with it in its mouth into the room, and the mother, turning her head in that direction, seeing the mungoose loose, and having remarked a wound in the child's neck, immediately concluded that the mungoose had bitten and killed her little son.

Without reflecting a moment, she seized the mungoose, and, in her rage, dashed it on the ground with all her strength. After one or two convulsive motions, the pet mungoose died, and then, too late, the mother discovered something in the animal's mouth; and, examining it closer, recognized the snake-root. Intuitively divining all the circumstances, she instantly reduced the root to powder, and, administering it to the child at once, had the happiness of seeing her darling returning to consciousness. The mungoose having been a great pet with all the children, the news of its death caused general grief, to none more so than to the mother, who resolved never to let anger gain the mastery again.

The president said that he related the above story as an illustration of the implicit faith natives have in the snake-root. The natives of India have an idea that when the mungoose, in its encounter with a snake, happens to be bitten by it, it immediately runs off in search of an antidote to counteract the virulent poison of the snake. This supposed antidote, the root of a plant, hence called snake-root, is regarded by all classes of natives as a certain specific against snake-bite. That it is a foolish belief is proved by continual failure.

Several Europeans, at different times and places, have put a mungoose and a cobra into a room from which there was no escape for either, and the mungoose (always victorious), although severely bitten by the cobra, was confined in the room several hours after the battle, but no ill effects resulted from the snake's bite. Either there is great virtue in the poison of the cobra administered internally (for the mungoose, in such encounter, almost invariably eats off the head of the snake, where the poison is secreted), or else the mungoose is so constitutionally formed that the most virulent poison has no effect whatever on it.

When the president's story was finished, they all rose and sauntered about the precincts of the camp, watching the gambols of a troop of monkeys as they went down the bank of the river to drink, or noting the various precautions used by different animals in descending for their evening's drink, before retiring for the night to their several lairs or roosts. The merry note of the black partridge, the "po-ta-toe" of the grey partridge, the singular cry of the Brahminee duck, and the evening crow of the jungle-cock, were all subjects of remark. The wariness exhibited by a peacock in leading his harem to the water, excited much interest, the old fellow going down the bank so carefully, craning his neck, and at every step looking to the right and left, until he reached the water, when, giving a little cluck, his harem came trooping down confidently to him.

After a good wash, dinner having meanwhile been ordered and announced, they all sat down to it with excellent appetites, enjoying especially the stewed ducks, regretting that there were only two of them. Neelgye soup was also admired, but sambhur soup was nevertheless acknowledged to bear away the palm. The venison cutlets also had their meed of praise. While at dinner, some peculiar musical notes attracting remark, the president informed them that a flight of cranes was passing over-head, and shortly after that, a flock of wild geese was heard sailing over the river, looking for suitable night's quarters.

After dinner, while they were enjoying themselves as usual round the fire, Robinson asked if there were any lions in India. The president answered that lions were to be met with in Upper India, in the districts of Ajmere, and neighbourhood, but, generally speaking, they are not found in Lower Hindustan, although a stray one may by chance be met with there. Although he could not promise them any lion-hunting or shooting, he could tell them a story about a lion if they liked to listen to it. The offer being readily agreed to, the president said that they all might possibly have already heard or read it in an abridged, mutilated form, as he had done, but of that they would judge, and without further preamble began :—

In a certain country there was a lion and lioness, that had a beautiful male cub, which was the joy of their hearts, amusing them with his innocent tricks, and delighting them with his graceful motions. In course of time, as the cub grew up, feeling the infirmities of age coming on, and that he must soon pay the universal debt of nature, the old lion had a strong presentiment of danger impending over his son, urging him to leave to the latter some useful advice, before he himself was numbered with his ancestors.

One day, during an excursion with his family, calling a halt under some shady trees, the old lion thus addressed his son :—

"As I am about to end my reign, and join my fathers, I desire that you will give the most earnest heed to what I am about to say to you. We are the undisputed lords of the desert and the forest, and none dare claim equality with us. You have, therefore, nothing to fear from the denizens of the forest or desert. If you, however, value your own safety, attend to what I now say to you. There is one wicked monster, whose great cunning you must ever hold in dread, and therefore make it your study to carefully avoid Man."

Having made his will, the old lion died, and some months afterwards the lioness also died, but not before the young lion was able to maintain his ground before all, and provide for his wants. After his mother's death, the young lion kept himself secluded for many months, pondering over the advice of his father, which ultimately led to his ruin. At length an ungovernable desire sprang up in his breast to see this formidable creature Man, and measure his strength with him, and he resolved on taking a long journey the next day through the country, determining not to return until he had seen A MAN.

Arrived at full maturity, though not at years of discretion, there was that in his looks and mien which inspired all the denizens of the forest and desert, that he had hitherto met, with wholesome fear, causing them to clear out of his path sharp. Despising these meaner creatures (except when he was hungry), panting in his heart for glory, and anxiously desirous of meeting the terrible creature Man, that he might have an opportunity of showing his courage, and putting forth all his strength, he started early the next morning at a rapid trot, altering his pace as his feverish impatience impelled him, into a series of bounding leaps, roaring out his defiance now and then to all.

CHAPTER XVI.

THE YOUNG LION MEETS AN ELEPHANT.

HIS headlong speed soon covered some miles of ground, when, seeing a huge monster coming towards him, eating branches of trees at a mouthful, and whose legs were as thick as his own body, he stopped suddenly, pondering over the advice his old father had given him, to avoid a human being.

The huge monster, an elephant, when he saw the lion, having no desire for a closer acquaintance, was turning out of the road in another direction, until the lion, ordering him to stop in tones not to be misunderstood, asked if he were a human being.

The elephant answered, " No, I am only an elephant. Human beings are very wicked and cunning. They laid a snare for me in the jungles, as they have done for thousands of my brethren. When they had caught me, they broke my spirit by starving me for many days, until I was glad to do anything they told me, so that I might get a mouthful to eat. They put heavy loads on our backs, and getting on our necks, they make us go where they choose, or do what they like, and, if we resist or complain, they beat us with iron sticks having a sharp point at one end, which they sometimes dig into our heads. Now, when I meet my free brethren in the forest, seeing the marks of servitude on me, they all shun me, so that, having no kindred to comfort me, I return to my hard task-masters, and wait patiently for the time of my release by death."

If this huge monster were not a human being, then man must indeed be a very formidable creature, thought the young lion. Determining not to return to his den until he had seen a man, and the better to make up for lost time, the lion went bounding on his way in all the pride of his strength. After proceeding some miles at this rate, he came upon a lofty animal pulling down the topmost branches of the trees, and eating them. Making sure that he had come upon the object of his search, he thought it wisest to stop, and secure the means of retreat, should necessity compel such a course.

While thus deliberating, the lofty animal, a camel, seeing the lion, left off browsing and turned to flee, showing evident signs of fear. The lion, seeing that the other was afraid, began then to assume the bully, and, ordering him to stop, asked if he were a human being.

The camel, taken by surprise, answered—"I! No; I am only a servant, and all my kindred have been made servants by these wicked human beings. There is not a free camel now in any country. They make a hole in our noses, to which they tie a string, and the other end they fasten to the tail of another camel; then, having loaded us with heavy burdens, a child may lead us wherever he pleases. Often we do not get enough to eat, and when we complain we are only beaten. Oh! these human beings are very wicked."

The lion, wondering what a human being could be like, since he was able to conquer and subdue such huge and lofty animals, was only the more resolved not to return until he had seen a man. Irritated at his want of success, he went on his way, filling the forest with his roar, and the hearts of all inferior creatures with dread at his terrible voice. Presently he came to the edge of the forest, and, seeing a puny animal doing something at the bottom of a large tree which caused it to bleed, and pieces of it to fly off, he angrily gave a loud roar.

The puny animal, who was a man, and a carpenter by trade, engaged in felling a tree, on hearing the roar of the lion looked round for a suitable tree, and, running to it, was beginning to climb, when the lion, ordering him to stand still, spoke thus to him—"You spindle-shanked, insignificant thing, can you tell me where I may find a human being? I have long heard of their wicked acts, and am come out to avenge the cause of all creation on these monsters; so, if you do not show me a human being, that I may fight with and kill him, I will kill *you* and eat you up."

The carpenter, being quick-witted as well as clever at his trade, understanding the matter at once, soon devised in his mind a trap for the lion. Turning to the lion, he said to it, "Most undoubtedly I will, if you will have the goodness to be seated, and give me your royal word of honour not to harm me or interrupt me in my work. My master is a man, and I expect him here in about an hour, and then I will show you a human being."

Having received the lion's word of honour not to injure him, the carpenter took his axe, and selecting a tree fitted for his purpose, he soon brought it down with a thundering crash, the lion all the time wondering whether *that* puny thing could be a human being.

After bringing down the tree, he cut off several heavy logs from it, and firmly fixing four of the logs in the ground, far enough apart to admit of the fall of another one between them, he placed a fifth heavier log on two of the upright ones, in the centre of which he tied a long rope, having previously arranged shorter ropes attached to the upright logs.

When the trap was ready, holding the long cord in his hand, the carpenter said to the lion that if he would walk between the upright posts, right opposite to him, he would show him *his* master.

The lion, believing him, did as directed, and the carpenter, seeing that the lion was far enough in the trap, not giving him time to draw back, suddenly pulled the cord and let the heavy log fall on his neck; then running up quickly, he fastened all together with the other ropes.

Going then round to the front, he said to the lion, "I promised to show you a live human being, and, now that you are in a pretty fix, what do you think of him? I am a man."

The lion too late reflected, that man was not to be avoided for his strength or stature, but for his great cunning.

When the president's story was finished, the party held a council as to the proceedings of the next day, during which it was determined to visit the old fort of Agoree, and orders having been given to that effect for an early breakfast, and a slight luncheon to take with them, they all retired.

During the night one of the party (Wilcox) was awakened by a noise, made as he thought by some wild beast prowling about, and getting up without disturbing the others, he went to the door of the tent with his gun. Peering out cautiously, he saw something making off in the dark, and, raising his gun quickly, fired a chance shot, it being too dark to take any aim.

The shot had evidently told, as there was a great rustling and noise in the bushes. The report of the gun had roused some of the rest, and also some of the servants, so, taking their guns, and the servants flaming brands, they all went cautiously to the spot, and found a rascally hyena just dying, and the little fawn by its side, dead.

The hyena, it appeared, had seized the fawn, broken the string with which it was tied, without awakening any of the servants, and was making off with it. The fawn, it was supposed, made the noise which awakened Wilcox, who had so speedily avenged its death. The servants having been scolded for not taking better care of the pet, the dead fawn was given to the mehter, or sweeper, with orders to have the skin of the hyena taken off and the head cleaned; and then they retired once more to finish their nap.

The next morning, getting up early, they all had a refreshing bath in the Soane, after which breakfast was served directly on their return to camp. While bathing, the mullah (ferryman) had brought some mullets, which had half-an-hour previously been caught, and, having been cooked immediately, were enjoyed and pronounced first-rate.

After breakfast, when everything was ready, the party started for Agoree. On reaching the floating bridge over the Rehund, the elephant, on which two of them were riding, showed his sagacity, for, after trying the bridge, before trusting his whole weight on it, his instinct telling him that it would not bear him, he turned tail, and no amount of persuasion could induce the animal to try it again. Those on its back had consequently to dismount and proceed on foot, the elephant being sent back to the camp, with orders to the driver for the grooms to bring the other horses.

After reaching Agoree, and being satisfied with their inspection of the old fort, they ordered one of the pleasantest rooms to be thoroughly cleaned, and the luncheon materials to be placed in it. Then opening a case of fishing-tackle which Brown had brought, and making spare rods out of bamboos growing in the neighbourhood, after selecting shady spots each, they amused themselves for an hour or two in fishing. Having met with greater success than was anticipated, the fishing-tackle was packed up, and the fishes sent off to camp, well protected with wet grass and leaves.

Brown having deplored the loss of a fine hook and a great deal of line, "which," he said, "must have been carried away by a regular whopper," the president quietly said that the greater probability was that an alligator had seized and carried off his fish, breaking the line on his (Brown's) attempting to haul it in.

To which Brown replied with a comical look and shrug, "Well, my tackle was not exactly warranted to catch alligators; but although regretting the loss of a capital hook and so much good line, I am *not* sorry I did not land that fellow, otherwise my loss might probably have been greater. I should, however, like to give a hint to some of his tribe not to make quite so free another time."

The president thereupon pointed out at least a dozen alligators at different distances, but, not being used to see them, the rest persisted in saying that they were trunks of trees floating down. The president desired them to watch awhile, and presently Robinson saw one of the supposed trunks evidently moving *up* the stream, when, first one and then another of the party took a shot, some hitting, and others going near enough to scare the saurian out of its reverie, until not an alligator would show his nose.

Strolling then about the neighbourhood, as they were going along, Wilcox narrowly escaped being bitten by a large cobra, which managed to glide into some rubbish, the *débris* of a part of the old Fort, to which they at once gave a wide berth. Then, clambering about here and there, Smith discovered a hole, and being of an inquisitive nature, he went down on his knees to explore it, and on looking in, was greeted with a phit! and an angry growl. The hole being dark, he was unable to see what animal it was, so after calling out, "Look out!" he brought his gun to bear, and fired a random shot into the hole.

He had scarcely time to stand up, when out rushed a large wild cat, blinded by the shot, with its head and neck all bloody. Before he had time to clear out of the way, the animal blundered up against one of his legs, and in its death-throe fastened its teeth and claws in deep. Fortunately, he had on a pair of Wellingtons, otherwise he stood a chance of being lamed for some weeks. Smith's exclamation, the report of his gun, and the scrimmage, soon brought the others round him, when after some trouble he was freed from his clog. Determining to keep a memorandum of the incident, he had the brute decapitated and the skin taken off by the attendants.

CHAPTER XVII.

UTILISING THE CARCASE OF THE WILD CAT.

AS they were about leaving the spot, Robinson suggested that the carcase of the cat might be made use of as a bait for the alligators, and the idea being voted a good one, a man was ordered to bring it along, and a block of wood. On coming to a convenient place by the river's side, they tied some string round the cat's body, and the other end round the block, which was to act as a buoy.

Then getting their guns ready, one of the coolies was ordered to throw the carcase and block into the water, as far as he could, and, almost immediately, three or four alligators were seen making towards it, and fighting for it. Several balls were then fired, one of which entered the eye of one of the alligators, and the saurian was seen kicking, as if dying, as it sank out of sight.

The sun getting too powerful, it was proposed to adjourn for tiffin, which was carried without a dissentient voice. While discussing some cold venison pasty, a man came running in, saying that a tiger was coming down the opposite bank to drink. Such news caused them all to jump up quickly, and, seizing their guns, they were soon in a position to see the tiger, without being themselves seen. As it was thought a pity to lose any chance, it was arranged for the two best shots to fire first, and if they missed, or only wounded it, two of the others were to fire on the chance of hitting.

Accordingly, two of them fired, one hitting the tiger on the near hind leg, the other in the spine, breaking his back. Giving out a great roar, the tiger tried to get up, but in the effort he fell back, with one of his legs in the water. At the very moment that the other two fired, hoping to put the tiger out of his misery, an alligator showed his nose out of the water, but before he could make a grab at the tiger, a rifle ball hit him such a hard rap on his head that he thought it best to dive down again.

One of the subsequent shots, being well aimed, proved mortal, and then a consultation was held how to get possession of the dead tiger. At last, the gentlemen promising a liberal present, the coolies proposed making a raft, and so bring the tiger over, stating that the only danger was from the alligators smelling the blood of the tiger, and, in trying to get at it, they might upset the raft.

Collecting, then, a lot of dead wood, and cutting down what more was required, they soon constructed a raft capable of bearing a dozen persons, which two of them paddled across, and, placing the dead tiger on it, were on their return, when one, then another, alligator would poke his nose up, but a rifle ball admonishing them that it was not good manners to be too curious, they put their noses down again.

One brute, however, pertinaciously followed the raft, but, in such a position, behind the men on the raft, that it could not be fired at. When the alligator came too close, one of the men hit it with his pole, which seemed not to intimidate it, as it still followed, but striking it again, and hitting the brute harder, on the tip of his nose, the last of the saurians disappeared. Just then the raft struck the bank, and tiger and men were hauled up safely.

Returning to finish their tiffin, they saw a pariah dog bolting off hotfoot, with something in his mouth, and after entering the room, they missed the cold haunch of venison. It appeared that, while engaged with the tiger, the servants, being desirous of seeing what was going on, had left the tiffin to take care of itself, and the pariah dog, hungry, as all pariah dogs are, finding the coast clear, had, wisely enough, made good use of the opportunity fortune had put in his way. Although he had cleared two of the plates, and bolted with the cold haunch, he had not touched the pasty or other things; so, sitting down again, the party managed to satisfy their hunger, and while talking over the events of the day, they made the old Fort ring again with their boisterous mirth.

Before proceeding again with their tiffin, the tiger had been sent off to camp by three men, with orders for other men to be sent immediately to the Fort; those going, to remain and skin the tiger. After enjoying themselves in the shade for an hour or two, they prepared to return, and having crossed the bridge, the horses were sent on to the camp, the party strolling through the jungle to the right, till they reached the tents; one spotted deer, a couple of young pea-fowl, a hare, some partridges, and a few green pigeons giving the attendants something to carry.

While waiting for dinner, walking about listlessly, one or two carrying their guns, hoping to have a shot at something, they heard the cry of a flight of cranes, and, looking up, saw them flying high, nearly over head. The president quickly raised his gun, but some remonstrating said that they were far too high, and a long way out of shot; but, nothing daunted, he answered that he would try, and, aiming carefully, about one foot ahead of the leading bird, he fired.

Cranes, like wild geese and similar waterfowl, fly in a wedge form, like the letter V upside down, thus Λ, the leading bird forming the apex. The report caused the leader, and of course the rest, to swerve a little, and this movement probably saved the leader's life, the ball striking and breaking one of the wings of the fourth bird on the right of the wedge. A good many seconds elapsed before the crane reached the ground, dying from the effects of the fall from such a height. The shot was a remarkably long one, and caused no little surprise to all who witnessed it.

The president said that that kind of crane was uncommonly good eating, but very difficult to get a shot at, being so wary, and ten to one the remainder would take care to fly higher in future;

in fact, directly the one had been hit, the rest were noticed flying about confusedly for a time, and then mounting much higher, continued their flight. After plucking the finest feathers, the president promised them a treat for dinner next day, and giving the crane to a servant, he made him responsible for it.

During dinner, which was shortly after served, one of them remarked that it seemed they were fated not to carry away any pet in the shape of a fawn, one having been killed by the leopard, and the other by the hyena. The president said that he expected as much, and only wondered that the two dogs of Brown and Wilcox had not been carried off before then, leopards being known to have a partiality for dogs' meat, and suggested that in future they should be tied up every evening to the pole of the tent in which their owners slept.

The suggestion had hardly been made when, something attracting their attention, the two dogs rushed out into the bushes, barking furiously. Presently, on hearing a choking cry of pain from one of the dogs, their owners and the others jumped up and seized their guns, when, as the president was telling them that it was useless to go out, the leopard was far enough off by that time, one of the under servants came running to the tent, saying that a cheetah, or leopard, had carried off one of the dogs.

The dog having been a really valuable one, and to which Wilcox was much attached, he greatly regretted its loss, blaming himself for not leaving it at home, and not taking better care of it in the jungles. The other dog (Brown's) came back, its hair on end, and eyes glaring with anger, not recovering its serenity for hours; and, had it not been tied up at once, it would have bitten some one. Seeing that nothing could be done for the dog that was gone, it being dead by that time, those who had risen from their seats resumed them after Bruno had been securely tied up.

At a subsequent period of the tour, one evening the servant had omitted to tie up Bruno, and after sitting down to dinner, as they were taking soup, the dog rushed into the jungle, barking loud and angrily. Having become attached to the dog, determining to try and save it, all the party jumping up, got their guns, and ran in the direction where they heard a battle royal going on, a mob of the servants also running up, with flaming brands, to the rescue.

When they all reached the scene of the encounter, they saw the dog, Bruno (a fine, large animal, with a cross of the Newfoundland), engaged in fighting with a wolf, which it had just then seized by the throat, and was worrying. Seeing that the dog had decidedly the best of it, the gentlemen would not allow the servants to interfere, it being a fair fight between the two animals. In a short time, the dog's teeth making a hole in the wolf's windpipe, that animal, after a convulsive struggle, died, not without leaving its mark—Bruno's ears and neck being a good deal lacerated.

Directly the battle was over, the dog was caught, taken to the tents, and its wounds attended to, while some of the servants were ordered to take off the skin and head of the wolf, to be preserved as trophies of the victory. Bruno, by his gallant conduct, rose cent. per cent. in the estimation of every one, Brown saying that no money should buy the noble dog. The servant, whose duty it was to tie up Master Bruno, was then cautioned, that, if he omitted doing so on any future occasion, the dog should be set on to him. The man, having witnessed the behaviour of the dog in the fight with the wolf, never again neglected his duty.

As the dinner progressed, the conversation running upon such subjects, the president gave the following account of how another dog had once been carried off in broad daylight by a leopard :—

The village of Romph, about one mile north of Ekpowa Ghât, on the table-land, is built at the foot of the slope of a hill, rising one hundred feet or so from the plateau of the Kymore range. On the summit of Romph Hill, many years ago, the exact date of which the memory of the oldest inhabitant of the village could not satisfactorily give, a joghee, or Hindoo devotee, undertook to erect a temple.

Whether the pious man engaged to raise the fane with his own hands (as an expiatory offering, or a very meritorious act), or with extraneous aid, perhaps future archæologic researches may be able to determine. Also, whether the man began to build without counting the cost, or whether (the fervour of his devotion falling suddenly) he thought to carry his zeal to a better market, could not be ascertained.

And, on further prosecution of the inquiry, another misty haze arose—whether the man did or did not leave the place; whether he died a natural death, and buried himself, or, lastly, whether a tiger carried him off and buried him, there are absolutely no records existing to prove either hypothesis.

The only reliable traditionary record states that the reputed holy man was seen one day working at his temple, and—was not seen any more. However annoying such a result may be to patient investigation, the above is absolutely the whole sum and substance of the evidence connected with this important case. Future researches, conducted by enthusiastic members of the Antiquarian Society, may, perhaps, lead to more satisfactory results, and set at rest this hitherto much-vexed question.

At present, the only certainty connected with the affair is that the ground-plan of an edifice is evident, and that a few courses of stones had been laid. Now, there are no records in existence to prove that the quadrumana, or quadrupedal tribes, ever employ masses of stone for architectural purposes, and, as the stones themselves gave indisputable evidence of labour having been expended on them, the logical sequitur is that they must have been squared by man, and tradition declares the work to have been done by— a joghee.

CHAPTER XVIII.

A DOG CARRIED OFF BY A LEOPARD IN BROAD DAY.

BE the matter as it may, a party of gentlemen, encamped in the neighbourhood, once ascended Romph Hill, to obtain from its summit a good view of the surrounding country. After taking a look round, and examining the remains of the joghee's temple, they leisurely descended the hill, reaching the bottom a little before sunset, while it was yet broad daylight. They were accompanied by a valuable retriever, which followed them a few feet in the rear, when, a sudden noise causing them to turn round, they saw a large leopard had hold of the dog by the neck, and was in the act of springing over a boulder. Two of them had guns in their hands, but had not time to fire; they, however, started in pursuit, but the leopard had most unaccountably disappeared—where he went to, or how he could have vanished so speedily, with a large dog in his mouth, they could not imagine.

On inquiring of the villagers, they were told that that leopard was very bold, and extraordinarily cunning; that several gentlemen had tried to shoot it, but never got a chance; that the village shikari had often put himself in concealment near the animal's den, but he could never get a shot at it. That leopard may be in existence at the present moment, as far as deponent knew, he had himself gone after it more than once in vain.

After dinner, when assembled round the usual fire, it was determined upon to go the next day to inspect the cascade, a little distance below the junction of the Ghagur with the Soane, and thence to take a gallop to Kone, a market about thirteen miles from Chopun, and so see a little of the country. This being settled, Jones made a remark about the singular-looking, but, for all that, very nice eating fishes that they had for dinner, which led to general conversation on the peculiarities some fishes were gifted with.

One instanced the flying fish, which of course they all had seen; another, the shooting fish, which could bring down a passing fly with a water-bullet shot from its mouth, which some of them perhaps had not seen.

The president remarked, that the most extraordinary fishes that he had ever seen *were walking on land*. Many years ago, before the railway was dreamt of in India, he used to visit a friend's factory at Ruggoonauthpore, up Bally Khál, about ten miles from Calcutta, and spend the greater part of the day shooting in the vicinity. In those days there were there plenty of snipe, grey snippets, teal, plover, and other birds, to be had for going after them.

Going up the Khál on one occasion (khál means creek, literally an inlet from the sea or river, subject to the rise and fall of the tide), a flock of plover or other birds attracting his attention, he ordered the boatman to steer the dinghee (native boat) to the bank.

On getting out of the boat, he saw several curious animals taking somersaults down the bank into the water, and his curiosity being greatly excited, he caught some to examine, and found them to be veritable but queer-looking fishes. These fishes were two or three inches long, with thick tails, very strong in proportion to the size of the fishes.

But the chief singularity consisted in the fins, which were bulging and horny, and the manner of using them reminded him of a man, with two stiff knee-joints, using a walkingstick. When progressing, these fishes had a ludicrous appearance; the right fin, sharp at the tip, would be dug into the ground as a prop, while the left fin would be advanced, then the right fin would be raised and the body drawn forwards, the fish making a passing grab at any insect it might see near enough.

What amused him most, was seeing them take somersaults down the bank. On being alarmed, they would bend the tail down on one side, spring up, and go head over tail down about twelve to eighteen inches, then, before you could well lay your hands on them, up they would go, and down another foot or so, until they gained the water. These curious fishes were not seen more than ten, or, at most, twelve feet from the water's edge. He has subsequently read that similar fishes have been seen in Ceylon.

The conversation was at this point diverted by a great barking and jabbering among a tribe of monkeys in some of the trees surrounding the camp; and on the others wondering what could be the cause, the president said that perhaps it was a tiger passing under their trees, or most likely it was a leopard that had climbed up the tree, and seized one of their number asleep. Monkeys have a mortal antipathy to the tiger and leopard, and, when one of these animals passes within sight, they always bark and jabber at it, thus giving warning to human travellers.

One of the party then remarked that he should like to have the skeleton of a monkey, and would take the first opportunity of shooting one.

The president objecting, said "that he would not be justified in killing a monkey merely for the sake of possessing a stuffed specimen or a skeleton. Travelling as they were, dependent on their guns for the principal part of their daily food for themselves and servants, they were justified in killing certain kinds of animals, or in destroying others that were injurious to man.

" But, unless it was for a scientific object, to add to the collection of a museum, or to terrify a troop of monkeys, habitually plundering an orchard or fields of grain, or when some particular monkey was dangerous, killing monkeys was in his opinion a heartless act. Personally speaking, he had never shot at a monkey, although once he had been placed in such a position that he must have fired in self-defence, had the monkey attacked him.

" On a certain occasion, his supply of English powder ran out.

Seeing his stock of English gunpowder getting low, he had intended, day after day, sending for a fresh supply, but circumstances prevented it; he could not spare a man to go and fetch it. He was therefore reduced to the necessity of using native powder, which contains too large a proportion of saltpetre in its composition, fouling the gun so much as to require wiping out after every discharge, besides being uncertain in power.

"Well, one day he was going through the jungle, carrying his double barrel, charged with this horrid powder, on which no dependence could be placed, and a servant following. At the turn of some bushes he came to a bit of open ground, which was being crossed by a numerous troop of black-faced monkeys, or baboons. On being seen, the leader of the troop and the biggest of them all, that was then bringing up the rear, gave a loud peculiar bark, which caused the young ones and females to scuttle away over the open to the jungle.

"Three or four of the largest dog, or male, baboons only remained behind, and the leader, a very powerful brute with formidable teeth, actually advanced towards himself and servant, until it came to about twelve yards off, when it sat on its haunches, showing its teeth in a menacing manner. Not wishing to fire at the animal, which was only acting the part of a good general, covering the retreat of his troop, yet not seeing the joke of giving the *pas* to any number of baboons, he ordered his servant to throw some clods of earth at it and drive it away.

"The first two or three passing close to it, only made it grin the more, but the next one striking it, in one or two easy bounds it had reduced the distance between us to less than half. Raising the gun to his shoulder, he was on the point of firing, when some signal being given by those in the jungle (to announce their safety apparently), the leader and the others turning round, went off at a hand gallop to join the troop."

By the time the president had finished his relation of the meeting with the baboons, it had got late enough for bed;

so when he had given orders for an early breakfast, they all turned in.

The fatigue of the previous day having caused the whole party to oversleep themselves, it was unanimously agreed to postpone the visit to Kone, and inspect the cascade only. Refreshing themselves with a bath in the river, during which one of the party picked up a very pretty specimen of agate, which he determined on having made up into a brooch for a certain friend, on their return to camp they sat down to a hearty breakfast. The smoked deers' tongues, venison steaks, fried fish, curry, and jerked neelgye made into bhurta, left nothing to be desired.

The bhurta gave general satisfaction as a capital zest, and is made as follows:—Smoke-cured lean of any kind of meat, or fish, is scraped or pounded fine, young onions and green chillies, or capsicums (in quantity according to individual taste), cut up small, with a pinch of salt, is then added, and all mixed well together. The remainder of any kind of cold boiled or roast meat is frequently utilized in this way. This zest is usually eaten with curry and rice, but spread on bread and butter is not bad.

After breakfast, mounting their horses, while those who chose it were on the elephant, and having a troop of followers at their heels, they started for the cascade, and for whatever shooting they might get in going or returning. Having satisfied their curiosity with the inspection of the cascade and the scenery of both banks, as they were deliberating in which direction to go for a stroll, a pair of Brahminee ducks flew by, and settled within easy distance.

Jones, admiring the flavour of stewed duck, fired and killed one of them, which fell on a piece of low, swampy, and treacherous-looking ground, part of the bed of the river. Being a keen sportsman, not choosing to send any of the attendants for it, and not heeding any remonstrances, he must needs go and fetch the bird himself. Striding along confidently, he entered the swamp, and very soon got into a mess with the mud and water.

The duck being only a few feet further on, he thought that, as his boots had got wet, he might as well get the bird, and took another step. Then, finding some difficulty in raising his other foot, he too late judged it prudent to return without the bird. While considering the matter, he was sinking slowly but surely; and when he had determined on returning, he found that he could not move. The president, who had been watching his progress, soon understood the matter, and calling out, told him not to be alarmed, but to remain as he was, without making any further useless efforts, and simply do as he would be directed.

He then asked all the native attendants to lend their chudders, or upper garments, which he tied together and so made two long ropes, twisting the horses' head-ropes with them and making then two thick ropes. Throwing the end of one of the ropes, he directed Jones to pass it round his chest under his arms, and, making a firm knot, to slew the knot round to his back. He then threw the other rope with similar directions, and, when that was ready, informed him that he was in a quicksand, and must offer no resistance, but gently lean back and point his toes downwards, when they would do their best to extricate him.

As Jones had sunk by that time beyond his knees, it was time to do something, so, dividing all their forces, they manned the two ropes, and by a steady hard pull released him from his dangerous position. One of the ropes gave way just as Jones' feet had been extricated, and of course all that were pulling at that rope fell backwards, one on the top of the other, causing no little merriment.

The chief difficulty having been overcome, the other rope was able to drag Jones to a place of safety, but without his boots. On finding himself safe on his legs again on firm ground, his first question was how to get the duck, he intended *to have it.* The president assured him that the duck should be brought to camp, but that not satisfying he insisted on the duck being then brought.

The native attendants, however, having seen the danger, and knowing the treacherous nature of the swamp, all refused to go after it; whereupon the president told them to get a long bamboo, and when it was brought he tied a long string to one end, and made a loop at the other end of the string, with a small stone tied above it, and with this contrivance the duck was soon jerked within reach.

The president then plainly described the danger every one had incurred, and suggested their returning to camp with all speed to be physicked. Jones, who had been extricated from the swamp, was to be unreservedly in his hands, otherwise by delaying vigorous measures the tour would be at an end, as they would all be laid up with jungle fever in a few days, and most likely have to be carried to their homes in palankeens. Finding the matter to be more serious than they thought for, they were soon mounted and back into camp. On arrival, when they had changed their clothes and had a good rub down, each one was prescribed a good dose of quinine, with orders to go to bed, cover themselves with blankets, and have a good sweat. Jones, who had been in the swamp, was ordered to have a warm bath immediately, then an extra dose of quinine, to be followed by an extra blanket, to insure a profuse perspiration. The servants also had the same treatment as their employers.

CHAPTER XIX.

STRONG REMEDIES IN TIME.

WHEN they had all perspired well, until one or more of them exclaimed that there would be nothing left of them shortly, and had changed their clothes, the president prescribed a glass of warm spiced brandy and water, with half a biscuit each. He then explained that all having been exposed to the sun, and inhaling the miasma of the swamp for so long a time, powerful remedies were necessary, to eject the seeds of the fever, before they had time to be developed in the system. Of course the whole day was lost through all the bother, but it had the effect of teaching each one, and Jones especially, by his own experience, that it is as well at times to listen to good counsel.

Towards evening, mutual inquiries elicited a feeling of great lassitude on the part of some, while others complained of a sinking of the stomach, owing to their extraordinary exertions, the quinine, and not having taken any tiffin, and were clamorous for an early dinner, which was accordingly ordered and sat down to with excellent appetites, the stewed crane being completely demolished with undisguised approbation.

After dinner, allowing a reasonable time for cheroots and talk, the president prescribed a glass of hot spiced brandy and water each, and bed immediately after, with plenty of coverings to promote perspiration the night through. But before separating, Jones, who had been in the quicksand, was profuse in his thanks to all, for the assistance that they had given him, and especially to the president for caring for and doctoring him so well.

The president, disclaiming any particular merit, replied, "Nonsense, any one with two grains of sense would have done just the same."

Robinson here interposed, saying, that "in his opinion it was not nonsense, that there were lots of fellows who would not have the ready wit or experience to use their two grains of sense, and it's just that that makes all the difference."

The next morning, after a bath, a small dose of quinine, and mutual inquiries, they all declared themselves to be in excellent health, thanks to the treatment of the previous day, and promised religiously to avoid all treacherous-looking places in future. The cold bath, which they all enjoyed, notwithstanding a slight frost, the fresh air over the river, the quinine, and the healthful scent of the forest, combined to create an appetite which Brown declared to be wolfish, and accordingly the good things at breakfast were discussed with more than usual relish.

When breakfast was over, and the "fragrant weed" was sending forth its cloudy incense from the mouths of fervent devotees, the president suggested their taking a short stroll in the jungle in the forenoon, proposing their studying natural history in the afternoon, on a plan which he would explain at tiffin, or luncheon. This being agreed to, they soon got ready and started with several attendants. After they had been out two or more hours, and had bagged a fair amount of game of different sorts, Smith got accidentally separated somewhat from the rest.

On his way to rejoin them, seeing a bush covered with bean creepers, bearing plenty of nice-looking pods, he thought to give the rest of the party an agreeable surprise in a dish of beans for dinner, intending to give them to the cook secretly, with directions for none of the others to know anything about it, until they were on the table. Unfortunately, not being well up in the vernacular, he did not understand his attendant, who was trying to dissuade him from touching the beans.

Turning from him rather angrily, he determined on filling his pockets quickly, before the others came up, and grasped the creeper with both hands. He had hardly broken off two pods, when, feeling a burning sensation, he let go the creeper, and rubbed his hands on his shooting jacket, thinking that some red ants had bitten him.

Feeling temporary relief, he again rubbed his hands on his jacket, but the burning sensation increasing, he called out to the others. On coming up, and inquiring into the matter, and seeing the creeper, the president at once cautioned the rest of the party not to touch the bean, and ordered the attendants to hack the bushes and creepers to pieces. He then told Smith to rub his hands back and front, through the hair of one of the native attendants. Feeling no relief, the president asked him what he had done on feeling the pain, and on his answering that he had rubbed his hands on his jacket two or three times, he said, " Then you are in for three days' suffering."

This accident causing the whole party to return to camp at once, on their arrival the president directed Smith to dip his hands, which by that time had become considerably swollen and inflamed, into two waterpots of cold water, and keep them there for a long time, when, feeling great relief, he was not inclined to take them out, except to put them into fresh pots of cold water. After a time, a cooling ointment being rubbed in, and frequently applied, the inflammation and pain were gradually reduced.

During tiffin the president stated that this pernicious bean had the property of the English stinging nettle, but was more virulent in effect. It also differed in another respect; the nettle, when resolutely grasped, caused no pain, its thorny and poisonous hairs being neutralized by seizure, but this bean could not be touched by the *natives*, not even by villagers, whose skins were toughened by continual exposure, and whose hands were hardened by toil. The stem and runners of this bean are covered with extremely fine-pointed and delicate prickles, which become detached on the slightest touch; and, as if animated, search the skin and enter the pores, causing intense irritation, inflammation, and swelling.

There is also a caterpillar, common to gardens all over India, some being more infested than others, whose body is covered with similar fine-pointed poisonous hairs, which become detached on the slightest touch. This caterpillar, from being covered with hairs, resembling the bristles on a pig's neck, is called by the natives soor-pokur, or pig insect, and, from its qualities being known, is carefully avoided by high and low. The name of this insect has passed into a proverb, a meddlesome mischief-maker being said to be as dangerous as a soor-pokur.

In both cases, when a person has accidentally come into contact with the bean or insect, the simple remedy adopted is to rub the part touched on the head of another person, whose hair has not been oiled or greased. Rubbing the part, the hands for instance, on one's own head, strangely enough, has no effect at all. In either case, rubbing the part affected on any substance, other than the human hair, only drives the poisonous hairs deeper into the pores, rendering the irritation permanent, until the strength of the poison is exhausted.

With reference to the lesson in natural history alluded to in the morning, the president said that he proposed each one going into the jungle with one attendant, mount a tree and watch in silence the actions of any animals that may pass underneath or close by. He would recommend their not firing at any animal until close upon sunset, and then each one might act as he thought best. He would also suggest that particular notice should be taken of every animal coming within range, and that each one should give in a report after dinner, of all that he had seen. This suggestion being generally approved of, it was decided on setting out by three P.M.

While they were walking about the camp after lunch, two men came up close without speaking, but holding up to view a torn garment each, silently reminding them of help rendered the previous day. On inquiring the cost of such articles, the paymaster was requested to disburse something more than sufficient to purchase each a new garment, and also to give a gratuity to all others who had rendered assistance, and which being done, all were well satisfied.

The head of the store department then reporting that the beer and sundry other items would hold out only a fortnight longer, it was forthwith resolved to send off a trusty man that day with a letter, and instructions to return quickly with a further supply to Sulkhun.

Two men were then seen approaching the camp, each carrying something, which proved to be a pair of tiger cubs, and a large pot of fine honey. Rewarding the men liberally for the honey and the cubs, the man, who was just then starting with the letter, was ordered to take the cubs and leave them at the menagerie at Sulkhun in charge of the shikari there, with money for expenses.

These matters being settled, and it being time to start for the jungle, they all got ready and set off in different directions. Selecting suitable trees, more or less distant from the camp, and from each other, they mounted with their attendant each, and conned their respective lessons. The setting sun proclaiming their vigil at an end, first one, then another, and then other shots were heard from different points, and the forest relapsed into its usual silence. Coming into camp, one was seen bringing a peacock, another a hare, another with one end of a pole on his shoulder, helping his attendant to carry a pig, another doing ditto with a deer, while two returned empty handed.

One of the party beginning to question another as to what he had seen, the president interposed, reminding him of the agreement that each one should make his report after dinner, and so help to pass an agreeable evening. After performing the necessary ablutions, dinner being announced, they sat down to it with keen appetites, and an evident impatience on the part of one or two to repeat the lessons that they had committed to memory during the afternoon.

THE NIGHT ALARM BY A TIGER.

When dinner was nearly over, Jones, who had been extricated from the quicksand *minus* his boots, suddenly remembered that he had not seen the duck which had caused so much trouble, either at yesterday's dinner, or at breakfast, or that evening. On inquiry being made, it appeared that none of the servants either could or would tell anything about it; one of them said that he had seen it brought to camp, but what became of it afterwards he could not tell. It was then shrewdly surmised that the servants had a mind to try how Brahminee duck tasted, thinking that it would not be missed.

When dinner was over, and all were seated comfortably round a glorious fire, they were suddenly startled by the roar of a tiger, close to the camp, but in a direction opposite to where the horses were picketed. The president, knowing the danger, jumped up quickly, and roared out, in a stentorian voice, orders for the grooms to take care that the horses did not break loose, requesting all the party, almost in the same breath, to get their guns instantly, in case the tiger meant mischief.

When all were armed and around him, he requested silence, that they might ascertain whereabouts the tiger was, calling also to him one or two of the camp followers for their advice. Soon after, the tread of some large animal over dry leaves between some bushes being plainly heard advancing, the president sent a ball in the direction, judging it best to scare the brute away before any mischief happened.

CHAPTER XX.

DEFENCE OF THE CAMP.

THE report of the rifle, and the ball striking close, if not hitting it, caused the tiger to gallop off at a great rate in another direction, taking him out of earshot very quickly. The president then said that the tiger's going off was good so far, but they must move camp the next day, as the brute, having evidently smelt the horses, would not be satisfied until he got one of them. Meanwhile, it was necessary to take extra precautions that night, as the tiger was certain to return, and try for one of the horses. He therefore proposed that they should keep watch the night through, in turns of one hour each, the servants and camp followers also to be divided into similar watches, that each one might know whom to call when necessary. This being agreed to, the president then summoned all the servants and camp followers, and told them off into watches, informing them that it was necessary to keep a good watch all that night; and that one of the gentlemen, in turn, would also keep watch.

He also gave orders for the camp to be moved, early next morning, to Oobra, opposite Punnaree, the servants to pack up immediately all that was to be packed, and breakfast to be prepared at Oobra. As a great quantity of wood had been collected, good fires were ordered to be lighted round the camp, and those on watch, in turn, were to attend to and keep up the fires, special care to be taken of the horses.

These orders, and preparations for departure next morning, engrossing all their attention, the relation of their several experiences was deferred to a more suitable occasion. When each one had packed up his individual belongings, or those in his department, the watch was set, and all the rest retired, silence in the camp being strictly enjoined.

The watches were regularly relieved, and all went on well, until about half an hour before daybreak, when Smith, whose watch it was, and who was making the round of the camp, plainly heard some animal approaching the horses, which were beginning to be restless. Smith, deeming it best to frighten the animal away, whatever it might be, judging by the sound, at once fired in the direction of the footsteps.

The ball evidently struck the brute, for the tiger, as it turned out to be, giving a tremendous angry roar, came rushing towards the camp. Meanwhile, the silence of the camp being thus rudely broken by the report, and almost simultaneous roar, every one was roused, and the rest of the party jumping out of bed, seized their guns, and rushed out in their night-dresses to do battle.

As the tiger was coming, one of them fired, and hit the brute in or near the eye, which confused and caused it to stumble over the ropes of the necessary tent. When down, one or two more shots made it tumble about more, and in doing so, the brute either broke the rope, or pulled out the pegs, causing the tent to fall and cover it. This was capital, as it enabled all the party to run up close, and fire a general volley, which happily settled the matter. By the time the battle was over, day began to break, and, although half inclined to stay longer at Chopun, as the things were packed, they went to dress and get ready for starting, after ordering the tiger to be immediately skinned, and its head cut off and cleaned subsequently.

An hour or so after the whole camp equipage had left, the party, some on [horses and others on the elephant, started for their new station. On their way they managed to shoot a spotted deer, and Brown had a long shot at a bear clambering up some rocks (after a hive apparently), but without hitting it. Taking it leisurely, stopping every now and then to admire the scenery, the servants had time to pitch the tents, and get breakfast ready by the time they arrived.

A traveller's appetite made them do justice to an excellent breakfast, Robinson wondering how the servants managed to get eggs, and to cook such a superior omelette in such a place. After breakfast, a consultation being held, it was determined on taking a stroll up the sandy bed of the Rehund, on the bank of which the camp was pitched, until they came to a suitable place, when, after refreshing themselves with a bath, they would return through the jungle, in time for an early dinner, getting a shot at anything on the road.

Orders for an early dinner having been given, the party left the camp, with men carrying towels, &c., and finding a convenient place, they enjoyed a good bath, regretting only the shallowness of the water. During their walk, several specimens of agates, &c., that had attracted their attention, were picked up and pocketed. After lighting their cheroots, they left the bed of the river and entered the jungle on their return. On their way, frequently hearing the crow of the jungle-cock, but without seeing it, one of the party at last determined, if possible, to get one.

Accordingly, on hearing the next crow, he fired a ball in the direction, and by chance cut the bird's neck half through, as if done with a knife. The dying tumbles of the bird on the dry leaves guided one of the attendants, who with difficulty secured it.

Further on, they had a shot at a neelgye, which gave them a fatiguing chase over rocky ground, but, being too badly wounded, they came in sight as it fell dead down a little ravine. The chase had caused them to make a considerable detour, and the jungle being strange to every one, they were for a time lost. But, taking the bearings of the sun and the river, they soon struck out a straight course for the tents.

The long walk had made them all tired and thirsty, but a good wash and a glass of beer soon refreshed them; and as dinner was

A PAGE OF NATURAL HISTORY—WILD BOAR. 125

not ready, it was proposed to pass the time in relating their experience of the previous afternoon.

The president being called on first, said, that, after waiting patiently a very long time, without seeing bird or beast, he saw the branches of a thick bush moving, and a tolerably large boar creep out, or rather step out confidently, yet warily. Turning its head, it examined first one direction, then another, with its sharp bright eyes. Seeing no signs of danger, it came leisurely on, until it stopped directly under the branch on which he was seated, and stood perfectly still for some time, as if considering in which direction it should proceed, for either food or water.

He could not help admiring the natural grace and ease with which the animal stepped and bore itself, every sense on the alert, ready to fight or flee ; and, contrasting its appearance with that of a domesticated porker, was obliged to award the palm to its forest congener. After watching it a considerable time, in order to see how it would act in unusual circumstances, he spat down right on its back.

The action of the wild pig was admirable, and really instructive ; but its bewilderment was excessively amusing. Directly it felt the warm spittle on its back, the start of surprise it gave, on being so near danger and unconscious of it, was worth witnessing.

In a moment it was many feet from under the tree, where, turning round, it stood facing the tree, its eyes twinkling with anger, and the bristles on its back upright, while every nerve and muscle was tightly strung, and champing its tusks, ready for any comer. The animal knew it was not raining, but, as if doubtful in its mind, it looked up to the sky to convince itself. It then looked up into the branches of the tree, but not seeing anything move, it did not know what to make of the whole affair.

Feeling convinced that some great danger was lurking near, and yet utterly unable to make out from what quarter to expect it, the animal began sniffing the air all round, gradually raising its snout, until getting the scent of man from the branches, had you all been there, you would have plainly perceived the light of conviction entering its mind, so to speak.

At that moment he made a slight hish! and the next instant the free rover was out of sight, dashing through the bushes as if they presented no obstacle. Although taking so long to describe, the whole scene did not take more than two or three minutes in acting, and the serio-comic play was well worth seeing. Nothing else noteworthy happened, and the sun setting, he was thinking of getting down, when he heard a shot fired, and a moment after, seeing some animal running on the other side of some bushes, he fired, and found he had shot a fine peacock, which he brought home.

Robinson being called upon, said that, soon after mounting his tree, some small grey monkeys coming along afforded him considerable amusement, in watching their various actions and antics. A young baby monkey, engaged in drawing its sustenance, being apparently too hungry, bit or somehow hurt its mother's breast, whereupon mamma monkey, snatching it away to arms' length, gave it a hearty cuff. Then, sitting on a broken bough and placing it in her lap, she began searching it for peculiar parasites, and in this domestic occupation she in turn hurt the young one, which wriggled out of her paws, and was making off, when mamma, stretching out her long arms, caught and gave it another good cuff. Under this correction, baby monkey having been brought to a sense of the intended error of its ways, the wellsprings of the motherly nature gushing out, the young one was seized, cuddled, and put to the breast, just as any human mother would do.

He then watched a troop of young monkeys in their various gambols, which were extremely amusing. One of the young monkeys had a decided genius for fun, and, if it could have been caught and trained, would soon make the fortune of any showman. An older young monkey, a sort of hobbledehoy, neither man nor boy monkey, evidently aping the behaviour of its elders, thinking itself too big and grand to be any longer on familiar terms with young scapegrace monkeys, was walking along as sedately as it could, when young genius went behind slyly, and gently lifting the tip of the other one's tail, gave it a good bite, and then bolted.

The way hobbledehoy jumped round and started in pursuit was really laughable. Having caught young genius, and administered a good basting, he looked at him as much as to say, "*Now*, you young warmint, let me catch you at such tricks again, if you dare!" and then walked off with an air of offended dignity satisfied, young genius making snooks, or its equivalent, at him as he was going.

Altogether the scene was so comical that he could no longer help bursting out laughing, and then the dismay of the whole troop, and the grimaces and jabbering they made while scuttling off, afforded fresh merriment. About sunset he saw a hare coming along, and thinking it would make a good curry, or soup, he shot it, got down from the tree, and made for camp, very much delighted with the instruction and amusement he had derived from his study of even a single page of natural history.

CHAPTER XXI.

BROWN'S PAGE OF NATURAL HISTORY.

BROWN being then called upon, said he too was for some time up his tree without seeing anything. At last a noble peacock came into view, escorting his harem of five peahens. In the course of paying his amorous court, he would, every now and then, elevate his magnificent train, strutting about, evidently vain of his attractions, and the sight was really a beautiful one. Whenever he raised his glorious tail, the hen to which he was paying his addresses, would cease pecking, lift up her head, and appear enchanted with his beauty, until overcome at last by his many attractions, she would yield herself unresistingly to his supremacy.

Altogether the sight was worth going a considerable distance to see, and having seen the glorious beauty of the peacock in its wild free state, he would not give a rotten carrot for all the domesticated ones, with their torn, dirty, and draggled tails. Nothing else occurred, until he heard a shot fired about sundown, and a wild boar came rushing past, but thinking that a pork chop would taste nice, he had rather roughly asked it to stay. On comparing notes, it appeared that the president had shot the fine peacock which he had so much admired, while he had shot the wild boar that had amused the president so much.

Smith was then called upon, but said that no lesson had been set him. From the time of mounting his tree until close upon sunset, he had seen neither bird nor beast; the page had been entirely blank to him. Just as he was thinking of getting down, some one fired a shot, and the report startled up a spotted deer, which had apparently been lying down behind a clump of bushes right opposite his tree, and close to it, but which at that moment was flying over a bit of open ground, not fast enough, however, to prevent its being brought down by a shot from his gun. He then got down from his tree, and returned to camp.

Dinner being then announced, the further relation of the lessons of the rest was deferred to a later hour. Hare soup, roast pork, venison cutlets, haunch of venison stewed whole, and other fare, was done ample justice to ; and when assembled round the usual fire, Jones was called on to repeat his lesson.

Jones then said that a short time after ascending his tree, a pair of hoopoes flew down on some open ground in front of him, and certainly the lesson they gave him in the patience and perseverance exhibited in the pursuit of their object, was full of sound instruction. On coming to an earth-worm's hill, the bird would knock it away, and then tap on the ground with its beak.

It would then incline its head to one side, as if either peering down the hole, or listening whether any one was at home. If assured of there being a tenant, it would erect its pretty top-knot, and give utterance to its pleasant note, hoop-oo, whence its name, reminding him strongly of home-scenes in any street in London, where a man would knock at the door and sing out, " Ba-ker !"

After knocking at the door and announcing himself, if master wriggler would not answer the summons, up would go his top-knot in anger, and down would go his beak vigorously, enlarging the orifice. The worm, disturbed by the sudden influx of light into its habitation, would perhaps show a bit of his tail, when down would go the bird's bill again ; but the hole not being enlarged enough, he would miss his aim. The bird would then jerk his tail, up with his top-knot, and down would go his beak with vigorous blows, until the worm was unearthed. Seizing it with an exultant shout of hoop-oo, the bird would then fly off with it to some secluded nook to enjoy the dainty morsel in secret.

After these birds had flown away with their worms, his attention

K

was attracted to a loud tapping noise, continuously repeated. Recognizing the sound, he examined the trees around, and soon discovered a woodpecker industriously engaged in hammering away at the trunk of a tree, knocking off chips every now and then, until he succeeded in getting the grub. It was really instructive to notice his industry. Running up the bole with surprising celerity, or along the under side of a thick bough, he would nevertheless peep into every crevice that was likely to harbour any insect.

Whenever he was certain that there was something worth his trouble, he would begin tapping at the door, *i.e.*, above the bark, under which his prey was concealed, and utter his peculiar note. If the insect, alarmed at the noise, came out, it was snapped up in a moment. If it was a grub, and would *not* come out, the bird would be enraged, and would tap away with its powerful beak until it had chipped away enough of the bark to enable it to get at the grub, which it would then seize viciously and swallow. Nothing else occurred up to sunset, when, hearing several reports, he thought it best to get down, and make for camp.

The last one of the party, Wilcox, being called upon, said that after climbing his tree, which he thought he never should get up, and settling himself comfortably, he saw something shining in some grass, and then lost sight of it. After awhile it came out from behind a bush, and then he saw that it was a snake, about five feet long, beautifully marked, with bright little eyes, like two diamonds, set in its head. As the reptile was gliding slowly along, making for some bushes on the other side of a patch of open ground, he had a good opportunity of noticing it well.

The searching intelligence which gleamed from its eyes, the wonderful ease and quickness with which it moved about its forked tongue, and the general gracefulness of its motions, was a singularly apt emblem of a deceitful person, who, although blessed with wit, beauty, and accomplishments, or what not, concealed a double tongue, or showed it in such a manner that, to casual observers, it was scarcely visible. He could now understand better the beauty and appositeness of many passages in Scripture, relative both to the serpent and to deceit.

After the snake had disappeared in the bushes, a blue jay came flying up into a tree close by, where it made noise enough to prevent any other animals being heard coming. Nothing better offering, he watched the actions of the jay, and admired the bird's great industry and wonderful quick sight. Perched on a naked branch, it would chatter away, seemingly charmed with its own horrid noise, when suddenly it would fly off forty or fifty yards, pick up a grub or a grasshopper, fly back to its perch, tap the insect on the bough to kill it apparently, and then swallow it.

Remaining stationary for half a minute, it would go through the same performance, varying it slightly by changing its perch. During the time he watched it, the industrious bird must have caught about forty insects of various kinds. Taken altogether, he would not have missed his lesson for a considerable pecuniary compensation. As no other animals came by his tree, when he heard several shots fired, he got down, and came into camp.

When each one had related his experience, Robinson got up and said, speaking for himself, he thought it was a queer whim of the president's, but as the rest agreed to it, he chimed in. Nevertheless, in his secret soul, he expected to be considerably bored, perhaps bitten by confounded ants. But, to his great surprise, he had passed a most agreeable afternoon, which he would not have missed doing for anything, and he would be ready any day to repeat the experiment, taking the chance of something instructive turning up. The others, coinciding in his sentiments, a hearty vote of thanks was accorded to the mover of the suggestion.

The night being cold, Brown suggested a bowl of punch, but was reminded that there was no punch-bowl. Putting it to the vote, and finding the majority in favour of punch, he roared out to the khansamah to bring the materials and the soup-tureen, which would do as well as the best punch-bowl at any time. The night being young still, the punch duly brewed, pronounced capital, and glasses filled, the president was called upon for a story, connected in some way with or bearing upon forest life. The president, being thus called upon, considered for a few minutes, and then related sundry incidents in his own experience.

The proceedings for the next day were then deliberated upon, and it was decided to push on to Gurwhar without delay, unless there was any chance of tiger-shooting at Bilwada. The president then giving the necessary orders for the camp to be moved early next morning to Bilwada, they all retired.

The country between Punnaree and Bilwada, a distance of about twenty-six miles, being singularly deficient in water, it was necessary to engage extra men to carry several loads of water from the Rehund for drinking or other purposes. The men having been engaged the previous day, and the water dispatched under the caterer's personal superintendence, the party allowed the whole camp to precede them a couple of hours, which they took advantage of to have one more good bath in running water, and then started for the new camping-ground. Having been deceived by the drivers, who had provided very inferior camels, they overtook the camp equipage at Muggurdah, and were obliged to arrange for the camp to halt there for the night.

The name Muggurdah is given to the spot, why or wherefore even the youngest inhabitant (*Hibernice*) could not tell, as not even the poorest native ever dreamt of building a hut for living there permanently. Three or four acres, denuded of trees, on the bank of a nullah or ravine, forms the general camping-ground of all travellers on the high road to Singrowlee.

Here, as at other general camping-grounds, may be seen a singular proof that, although the caste prejudices of the natives are extremely puerile and daily infringed, yet they cannot be beaten or reasoned out of them. Many natives, in travelling, dig holes for cooking purposes, which succeeding travellers carefully shun, lest there should be any contamination in them.

Other travellers, Hindoos and Moslems, prefer using stones, on which to place their cooking-pots, putting fire underneath, and these stones succeeding travellers do not hesitate to use, although, being blackened by fire, there is evident proof of their having been repeatedly used, and by what caste travellers who could tell? These holes, stones, ends of charred wood, remnants of fodder, animal leavings, &c., are the usual signs of Indian encampments.

In the nullah, adjoining the camping-ground at Muggurdah, is a hole in the rocky bed, deep enough to accumulate, and, in most years, retain sufficient water to last from one rainy season to the commencement of the next. Taking this hole as the centre, not a drop of water can be found elsewhere within a radius of eight or more miles. Consequently, this water-hole, being the sole resort of all travellers and of all the birds, beasts, and reptiles of the surrounding jungles, is not inviting at the best of times.

CHAPTER XXII.

THE WATER-HOLE AT MUGGURDAH.

ON arrival, they found the whole of the camp equipage had halted, and on inquiring the reason the camel men said that their camels would not be able to make such a long march as to Bilwada. Knowing altercation to be useless, the president ordered the tents to be pitched, and breakfast to be got ready as soon as possible.

Meanwhile they went to inspect the water-hole, which had excited the curiosity of the rest. Some of the party on seeing it, remarking the muddy state of the water, said that it was enough to poison any human being to use it.

The president, in reply, stated that it was then in comparatively excellent condition, and further informed them that, on a certain occasion, he himself had arrived and camped there, in a very hot year, about four days before the setting in of the annual rains.

He had a little dog with him, that had doubled the actual distance of the march through running about in all directions, backwards and forwards, and had fatigued itself greatly. On arrival, the dog scented out some damp place, and following up the scent, it made for the water-hole. Being at the extreme end of the hot weather, and in that rocky, dry, and parched land, there was little better than thick mud to be seen that year, and the surface of this mud, moreover, was covered with a thick layer of flies.

The dog paddled about in the mud until it came to the footprints of some buffalo, into which water, such as it was, had percolated. After lapping once or twice, the dog actually turned away, disgusted with the filthy stuff. Although its tongue was hanging out of its mouth, and it was really suffering from thirst, in such very hot weather, the puddle could not tempt it again to go near it.

While at the water-hole, a servant came to inform them, that breakfast was waiting to be served, and ordering it to be served at once, they returned to the tents. Sitting down to a late breakfast, after a long ride through heavy jungle, and over the hills, with an appetite sharp set, the claims of nature allowed little room for conversation until the cravings of hunger had been satisfied.

After breakfast they strolled about the neighbourhood, taking their guns with them as a precaution, in the event of meeting with anything. Several beautiful peacocks—the only residents apparently, whose long familiarity with harmless travellers had emboldened them to walk about in perfect security, excited the admiration of all the party at the cleanliness and beauty of the birds in their wild state. The confidence they displayed disarmed the whole party, the birds allowing them to pass near enough to have knocked them down with a stick, had any of the party been so minded.

The neighbourhood not being suitable for any extended stroll, they soon returned, and then amused themselves with watching the different groups of travellers arriving from either direction, and noting their manners and customs in camping, and making their several arrangements for the night.

Amongst one party of travellers there was a Byrágee, a sect of Hindoo religious mendicants, who, after resting himself a little, went round the camping ground, from one group of travellers to another, begging for whatever they chose to bestow. In this occupation he appeared to be very successful, one or other of them giving a handful of rice, others a little pulse each, others a pinch or two of salt, or some curry stuff, until he had got the materials of a very comfortable meal, as far as quantity and variety were concerned.

One set of natives apparently informed the Byrágee that Europeans were on the ground, and advised him to try his luck with them. Turning round, he examined the party, and either not liking their looks, or having previous experience, he seemed doubtful at first, but, with the chance of getting something, after awhile he came up to them with a bold bearing.

On being asked why such a strong, able-bodied man went about the country living upon others, he frankly said he did not like work, and moreover had never been taught any trade; so, what could he do? He must eat, and had therefore taken up a religious profession, as the surest means of getting his food.

Robinson thereupon was very indignant, and said that "the man was a shameful impostor; that he ought to be made to give back all his collections, and then be flogged and driven away."

The president said that he could not see the man's conduct in that light. No doubt, under the garb of religion, he had deceived, and so obtained contributions. But, as the donors had been actuated by charitable, pious motives, they would never receive back what they had once given. Moreover, the donors being of different castes, and the several gifts having been mixed in the beggar's wallet, how were the several handfuls to be separated? As to flogging him, he did not see how that could be done justly; the man had not imposed on *them;* on the contrary, he had made a frank confession.

Jones then settled the matter abruptly, by telling the Byrágee that they could not encourage him in his idleness, and ordered him to be off to his own place.

Dinner being just then announced, they sat down to it with good appetites, Brown remarking during the course of it on the wonderful aptitude that the natives seemed to possess of inventing and relating stories.

To which the president replied that "the habit of story-telling appeared to be common to all ages and countries. In India, especially, where there were no Literary or Scientific Societies for the rich, or Mechanics' Institutes for the poor classes, it was the custom, at the close of the day, for neighbours to get together and pass the time in talking of various subjects, and when conversation flagged, one, and then another, would be called upon for a story. Moreover, there were professional men who went about the country, visiting great people's houses, and such professional story-tellers, especially after making a name, were always welcome, and were liberally rewarded on dismissal."

Retiring early after dinner, it was a long time before they could hope to go to sleep (two, however, had contrived to do so), owing to the native travellers keeping awake till a late hour, talking and laughing. At last everything was quiet, and they were just dropping off to sleep, when a great noise at the water-hole rousing them, they listened and recognised the noise of two bears fighting.

It being a clear moonlight, those awake determined on trying to get a shot at the bears; so, slipping on some of their clothes quickly, and getting a double-barrel each, they crept, under the cover of some bushes, to the top of the bank, above the water-hole, and close to the bears. As it was necessary to act quickly, it was determined that, having eight barrels between them, two should fire both barrels quickly at one or both of the bears as they got a chance, and the others to reserve their fire for any subsequent emergency. According to this arrangement, two of the party fired while the bears were engaged grappling with each other, and making a pretty row, one of them falling dead, but the other, although badly wounded, was able to rush up the bank, and charge the party. Those who had fired retreated to load their guns, leaving the two others to fight it out.

The bear, on ascending the bank, charged one of his supposed assailants, but the other firing caused the animal to turn round and rush towards him, when the first one fired, and made the bear turn again. This went on until the last shot was fired, and they were beginning to retreat, when the others, who had in the meantime reloaded, took up the game, giving the bear one or two more shots, which settled it.

Altogether it was a very exciting affair, and the hurry-skurry among the native travellers was not the least part of the fun. After the bears had been ¡brought to the tents, skinned, and the fat secured, they once more turned in, and slept without further adventure. The two who had gone to sleep early managed to sleep through the whole of the row, and were not a little chaffed about it on the following day, and subsequently, as being two of the seven sleepers, and so on.

The next morning, as the day began to break, the encampment was a scene of bustling activity. The native travellers loading their bullocks or themselves, and going their several ways—some towards Singrowlee, and others in the opposite direction; while the servants of our party were busy packing up, and loading the camels and coolies with tents, furniture, &c. As there was a probability of some game at Bilwada, our party, after seeing the camp started, mounted and passed on ahead.

On arrival at Bilwada, they sent for the shikari, who informed them that there was a travelling tiger that visited them now and then, doing much mischief in thieving the village herd; that the animal was not thereabouts then, but might be expected any day, and that, when favouring them with a visit, he took up his quarters in a place wholly unsuited for a hankwa. The shikari added that deer might be had for the stalking, and perhaps a pig or two; but, owing to a festival in some neighbouring village, he could not promise to procure more than half-a-dozen men and boys.

As the larder was almost bare, they determined on at once beating-up some game, so, leaving the horses and elephant with the servants, they followed the shikari, who collected a few men as they went along. The neighbourhood of Bilwada being very rocky, they found the labour of stalking rather fatiguing, but the question of a Barmecide feast, or not, for dinner, settling the matter, they manfully trudged up and down the hills, and were rewarded with a couple of spotted deer, as many young porkers, and some hill grouse, like ptarmigan.

By the time they returned, footsore, the camp had arrived, tents were pitched, and breakfast was nearly ready. After a good wash, they sat down to breakfast tired, but with frightful appetites, which precluded conversation for some time. When breakfast was over, the shikari was called, rewarded, and told to keep a good look-out for the tiger, and if it were at or near Bilwada on their return, to make the necessary arrangements for a hankwa, if possible.

As they were too tired to go for any further walk that day, they remained in the tent, talking and smoking. An hour or so having passed thus, one of the party called upon the president for a story, putting the suggestion to the vote of the rest, who unanimously declared for it. The president thus called upon being willing to oblige, reflected awhile, and then said that he would relate something of his own experience :—

Having occasion to visit, on some necessary duty, a certain Government post, not far from the top of Kowie Ghát, the head native officer reported that a well-known, one-eyed tiger, called by the natives káná bágh, or blind tiger (having lost its left eye in a fight with some other tiger, probably), had for some days past regularly taken up its station, about three P.M., on a large boulder of rock, some twelve to sixteen yards from and above the high road, and that, the report spreading, traders and travellers getting alarmed, were obliged to make a considerable detour through the jungle. As he had only a single-barrel shot-gun with him, intending to shoot some partridges on his return, he did not know what to do, knowing the folly of attacking a tiger on foot, and especially without a second barrel to meet him with on his rush, if only wounded.

Recollecting that, as a Government official, it was his duty, understood if not expressly ordered, to facilitate the traffic of the district, he determined to run some risk. Drawing the charge of shot, and ramming home a ball, he rode down to where he could see the tiger, when, dismounting, he ordered the syce (groom) to take the pony a long way back out of danger. While he was looking round for a suitable tree on which to spring up, should the tiger charge, he saw a native coming along, passing about forty feet from the tiger, without being aware of its proximity.

CHAPTER XXIII.

THE ONE-EYED TIGER SHOT.

WHEN the man came close up he stopped him, and banteringly complimented him on his bravery in passing so close to the tiger. The man stood, evidently debating in his mind whether he (the president) was mad, or only joking, until at last he said—"What tiger? I have seen no tiger." Catching him by the arm he turned him round, and pointed with his gun to where the tiger was seated comfortably, just then watching them.

Directly the man's eyes lighted on the tiger, the alarm depicted in his countenance and actions was excessively comical. Turning sharp on his heels, and uttering the universal native exclamation of surprise, bapree! (alas! my father) he trotted off at a great rate.

Sending two men up a suitable tree, about forty yards distant from the tiger, with orders to lend a hand in climbing, should the tiger be hit and charge, he rested the gun against the stem of a sapling close by, and, taking a careful aim, fired. The ball hit the tiger somewhere in the loins, on the left side, on which it was blind, making that peculiar thud which a bullet does on striking a mass of flesh, but, fortunately, the animal, instead of charging, sprang up with a slight roar, and bounded over the rocks in the rear, into some heavy jungle.

The two men that were with him disputed the fact of the ball hitting the tiger, one saying that it struck the rock, and the other that it glanced against a young tree, and he was sure he saw a splinter fly off. So, to settle the matter, after reloading the gun and allowing the tiger time to get well out of the way, he took the two men with him and examined the spot.

Now, had the bullet struck the rock it would either have been flattened and fell at the foot of it, or would have glanced off, leaving a plain mark of the lead; but no bullet, or trace of it, could be found, disposing of doubt the first. Then, carefully examining every plant near the spot, no trace of the bullet having struck either of them could be found, and so the second doubt was dispelled.

The most conclusive evidence, however, of the bullet having told was in the fact that the said one-eyed tiger was never more seen, and the natural inference is that the animal had succumbed to a fit of indigestion, induced by an ounce of lead. It was fortunate for him that the tiger was blind on the side where it was struck, otherwise he would have stood very little chance of saving himself. He then resolved that he would never do such a foolish thing again as attack a tiger on foot.

The khansamah (butler) coming then to the tent for orders for dinner, the president informed the party that he intended giving them a new dish for dinner, and took the man aside to give him the necessary secret instructions. When the president's mysterious confab was over, on his return he ordered a light tiffin to be served. Those who fancied it took a biscuit and some cheese, all, however, refreshing themselves with a glass of beer. After lighting their cheroots or pipes, in listening to the president's further relation of sundry other incidents in his experience, the time passed rapidly until nearly sunset. After having a good wash, they all walked about the precincts of the camp, until dinner was announced, when they sat down to it with their usual good appetites.

The soup was pronounced excellent, but one of the wild porkers barbecued, and stuffed with ingredients about which the president had given secret instructions, was by all declared to be admirable, and had like to have given them a surfeit. Also the curries and sweet dishes, prepared under the directions of the president, met with general praise, leaving nothing to be desired.

After dinner, while seated round the fire, as usual, smoking their cheroots, the president being seen to smile, was asked what had tickled his fancy. He answered that a certain humorous native story just then came to his remembrance, and which, if they chose to listen to it, he would relate. A ready assent being given by all, the president related the following story of a simple-minded washerman:—

A great many years ago, in a certain town, there was a simple-minded washerman, who used to take his customers' clothes in two bundles, slung across the back of his ass, to a tank some distance out of the town, and there wash them. The road to the tank leading him past a large native school, kept by a moolvie, or Moslem doctor of laws, the washerman often heard him scolding his boys for their stupidity, and, when particularly angry, he would tell them that they were asses still, although he had tried so much to make men of them.

The washerman in his simplicity understood the moolvie's words literally, and was glad to hear that asses could be made into men. Remembering that he had a little foal of one of his asses at home, he thought how much better it would be to get its form and nature altered. He thought, further, how nice it would be, as he had no children, if the foal were changed into a boy, who would run by his side, be obedient to him in all things, learn the business, and be the comfort and prop of his old age.

Full of these thoughts in his head, he went one day to the school, and, bowing himself to the feet of the learned moolvie, requested the favour of his admitting the foal into his school, and that the moolvie would change it into a nice boy.

The moolvie, seeing through the character of the man at once, determined to take advantage of his simplicity, so, telling the washerman that the work of transforming a young ass into a nice boy was very laborious, and must be paid for accordingly, he desired the man to return home, bring the young ass, and a fee of one hundred rupees (£10), and leave the rest to him.

Running home quickly, the simple washerman raked up an old pot from a corner of his hut, in which he had been in the habit of depositing his savings for many years, and counting out from it one hundred rupees, he tied them in his cummerbund, or cloth wrapped round his waist. He then went to the outhouse, and unloosing the foal took it and the money to the school. The moolvie duly received the money, and gravely told the man to fasten the foal in a place he pointed to, directing him then to come exactly on a certain day and hour, when he would find the foal changed, and ready for delivery.

The impatience of the simple washerman made him go to the moolvie several times before the appointed day, to inquire how the foal was getting on. On such occasions the moolvie used to reply, " that the foal was learning to speak fast, that it was much more civilised, or, that then it was studying the art of good manners, and that its ears having become much shorter was a certain proof that the change was going on well, and that by the appointed time the transformation would be completed."

At last, the happy day arrived for which the simple man had been looking forward to with so much anxiety, but, unfortunately, a great press of work prevented the washerman from going on that day to bring home his fondly-expected, nice boy. The next day, however, after having delivered correctly all the clothes to his various employers, the simple washerman presented himself before the moolvie, claiming his boy.

The moolvie thereupon answered, "How unfortunate it is that you were not punctual on your part to the appointed hour. Had you only come yesterday, it would have been all right; but, after I had transformed your foal, who grew rapidly into a full-grown man, and well educated, he refused submission to my authority, and would be no longer under my control. He left me yesterday, and I received information this morning that he has been appointed Cazee, or Judge, of Cawnpore."

The simple man was at first inclined to be angry, but, on second thoughts, he concluded that he had got the best of the bargain still, since his foal had been transformed into a full-grown man, instead of a boy, and was already on the highway to fortune, and would be able to do something for himself and his wife.

Thanking the moolvie for his trouble, and making a respectful obeisance, he returned to his house, and imparted the good news to his wife, who was equally simple with himself. Consulting together on the subject, they resolved to shut up their house, and go in search of their stray chattel, and either reclaim him, or make him allow them a maintenance.

With this determination they commenced their journey to Cawnpore, and, on arrival, were directed to the court in which the cazee, or judge, presided. Leaving his wife outside, the simple washerman, on entering the court, saw the cazee sitting on an elevated chaboottra, or raised platform, and in front of him was a great crowd of pleaders, plaintiffs, defendants, witnesses, and officers of the court.

The simple man had taken the precaution to bring the bridle of the foal in one hand, and a quantity of hay in the other, and as he could not approach the cazee on account of the great crowd, he at length got tired of standing and waiting so long.

Holding up, therefore, the bridle in one hand and the hay in the other, he called out loudly in open court, "Khoor! khoor! khoor!" a sound he used when calling his donkeys together, hoping thereby to attract the attention of the cazee, and induce him to come to him. Greatly, however, to his surprise and mortification, instead of the cazee, several of the officers of the court, by the cazee's order, came and turned him out without ceremony, putting him into the hájut, or lock-up, for creating a disturbance in court.

When the business of the day was over, and the court closed, the cazee, pitying the supposed madman, sent for him to learn the reason of his strange behaviour; and, on his being brought before him, the cazee asked who he was, and what he wanted.

L

The simple washerman answered, "Wah, wah," (an exclamation of wonder) "sir! You do not appear to know me, or to recognise this bridle that you have had in your mouth so many times. You seem to forget that you are the foal of one of my asses that I got transformed into a full-grown man, by paying the large sum of one hundred rupees, the savings of many years, to a learned moolvie who undertakes to change asses into men, and to teach them all sorts of learning, polite language, and good manners! You are strangely forgetful of what you once were; and I suppose you want now to refuse submission to my authority, as you did to the moolvie's when you ran away from him!"

All who heard this extraordinary speech were convulsed with merriment; but the cazee saw at once that the man had been shamefully imposed upon by the moolvie, and after much difficulty convinced the poor man of his folly. The washerman understanding the matter somewhat, but not perfectly, began beating his breast and head, bewailing his misfortune in losing one hundred rupees, the savings of so many years, and that he was a ruined man, and so on.

The generous cazee, compassionating his condition, made him a present of one hundred rupees, besides sufficient for his expenses back, advising him to remove from the town where he had hitherto carried on his business, that he might be away from the roguish moolvie, and set up in business elsewhere. Thanking the cazee for his great generosity, and placing his head at his feet in token of profound obeisance, the simple man left the place with his wife, wiser and richer than when he entered it.

When the president had finished his story, after all having a good laugh over it, the whole party being tired, through the exercise of the forenoon, they retired to rest early, the president having given orders for the camp to move next morning to Ghurwar.

CHAPTER XXIV.

VISIT TO THE JHEEL AT GHURWAR.

THE next morning being very cold and frosty, and bed very comfortable, the whole party were loth to turn out until the khansamah reported a blazing fire and hot coffee ready, when jumping up they washed and dressed quickly, and were soon round the fire, enjoying the bracing air of early dawn.

Allowing the camp equipage a good hour's start, and being a very cold morning for those parts, it was determined on by all to enjoy a good walk. Setting off at a brisk pace, the horses and elephant following, they walked as far as Beyreeádee, having been descending all the way from Bilwada to that place, which is the first village as you come into the basin of Singrowlee. Mounting their animals at that village, they proceeded thence on nearly a dead level to Ghurwar.

On arrival, finding that the tents were not all pitched, and breakfast would not be ready for an hour or two, the president, to their agreeable surprise, proposed having an hour or two's snipe and teal shooting. Delaying only long enough to get out and load their fowling-pieces, and themselves with shot-belts, &c., they set out for the rajah's jheel, or swamp.

When they got to it, the president said it would be best to divide the party, one half going to the right, and the other to the left. Acting up to this suggestion, and separating themselves some distance from each other, they succeeded in bagging some ten brace of snipe, several brace of grey snippets, and teal of three or four varieties.

Satisfied with the result for the time being, the calls of hunger being more imperative than the desire for slaughter, they made for the tents, Smith on the way vowing vengeance against a rascally eagle for feloniously conveying away the only wild duck that had been shot. He had shot it, he said, and was proceeding to get it, but when he was about a yard off, and was stooping to pick it up, a thief of an eagle swooping down like a flash of lightning, carried it off from under his very nose, brushing him with his wing while doing so.

He allowed that the robbery was neatly effected, but had his gun been loaded, which unfortunately it was not, having just then fired off both barrels, he much doubted whether he would have been a consenting party to such a barefaced act of petty larceny being committed with impunity. However, he thought he should be able to recognise the freebooter again, and, if he ever got a chance, he would remember his impudence.

A good wash and a change of clothes gave time for an ample breakfast to be laid out, to which they all sat down, nothing loth. After breakfast, inquiries were made respecting any tigers that might be in the vicinity, and learning that one had carried off and partly eaten a pony the previous night, and might be sure to come again that night for a second meal, it was agreed upon to sit up for him that night. Those of the party who had not gone after the Putwut tiger claimed their right to sit up and take their chance for this one, and arrangements were made accordingly.

The villagers also reporting that there was game to be had in the jungle close by, the temptation was too great to be resisted; so, taking their guns and some men acquainted with the jungle, they went for a stroll. Crossing an open bit of ground, Robinson saw a wild pig come out of one bush and make a rush for another, but, taking a quick aim, he stopped it half-way. This report startled some spotted deer which were making off fast, when a double report laid two of them low in the dust. After a fatiguing walk, seeing no other game excepting pea-fowl, two of which were shot, they returned to camp.

On their way back, they went to see the carcase of the pony, and what trees were suitable for sitting up in for the tiger. The only suitable trees being rather too far from the carcase to allow of the tiger being seen properly, owing to the moon's rising late, they had the carcase dragged sufficiently near the two selected trees.

When they came near the carcase, some pariah dogs were seen busy at it, but a couple of balls knocking over two of them, the rest made themselves scarce pretty sharp; and to prevent further demolition, one of the villagers was promised the all-potent bucksheesh if he guarded the carcase till their return.

Arriving at the tents, the president, who was also caterer, busied himself with sundry mysterious directions about dinner, which was ordered early to allow those who were to keep vigil to start by sundown. Whenever the caterer busied himself, holding mysterious conferences with the khansamah, it was observed that some new appetising dish was sure to be seen at dinner; so, on his return, one remarked that there would be something out of the way for dinner, and asked what it was to be, but without success—the caterer was deaf.

During the afternoon, one of them proposed their all visiting the old rajah, but the president thought that the visit would not be agreeable to either party. He said that on one occasion he came down into those parts, and on the turn of that road, pointing to it, he came suddenly upon the old rajah, who was standing in his own grounds, giving directions to some of his workpeople. He was by no means dignified in his personal appearance, nor did his dress any way betoken him to belong to the order of princes, as he had positively nothing on him in the shape of clothes excepting a very dirty *lungotee* or cloth wrapped round his loins, reaching down to his knees only.

When he saw him, the rajah was deeply engaged in sucking at a common *nariyul*, or cocoanut hubble-bubble or hookah, scarcely worth eight annas, or one shilling, removing his mouth now and then to give his orders. On seeing him, the whole posse of workpeople and attendants simultaneously surrounded the rajah, as if *they* were ashamed of their malik, or superior, being seen in such a state of nudity by an European, and were determined to hide him.

Not having taken any tiffin that day, when dinner was announced they were prepared to make a vigorous onslaught on anything and everything, and ample justice was done to the tender pork chops, trail toast, young pea-fowl roasted, with a peculiar stuffing, saddle of venison, and venison cutlets with tomato sauce, and other good things.

One of the party, admiring the sauce greatly, inadvertently asked for *the bottle*, to help himself to some more of it, but received a withering look from the caterer, who said to him, "Do you really suppose *that* sauce was concocted from any shilling cookery book, or may be *bought* ready made?" The ruffled plumes of the caterer took some time and trouble to smooth down, nor was he pacified, until the offender had made a peace-offering of an elegant little meerschaum, and something to fill it with.

Dinner being over, the president advised those who intended going, to smoke their cheroots at the camp, and not on the road, or up in the trees, in case of alarming the tiger, and preventing his approach. Towards sundown all three loaded their rifles very carefully, and borrowing a black blanket each, for warmth and concealment, they set out with two villagers, carrying spare guns while on the road, who would mount other trees near. One of the trees did not please the president (who accompanied them), the branches being too low, but as they were eager for the adventure, he trusted to their prudence and skill as marksmen.

Before leaving, and again on the spot, he warned whoever mounted that particular tree, to be very careful not to attract the attention of the tiger, and not to fire at all unless he was sure of his aim, reminding them all that the night being dark was so much in favour of the tiger, and against them. The president added that the rest would sit up all night, if need be, ready to render any assistance, and arranged a signal that, if successful, they were to fire off the three rifles almost as one report, and repeat with the spare guns.

Promising attention to all the instructions, they left the camp, and arriving at the place, dismissed the villager left on guard, who returned with the president. Mounting the selected trees, the villagers climbing others, they made themselves as comfortable as they could, two in one tree, and one in the lower one, arranging their blankets so as to completely cover them and their rifles and guns from the dew, and yet have them ready for instant use.

Waiting impatiently for hours, peering into the thick darkness until their eyes ached, about eleven o'clock they suddenly heard a footstep, and the sound of the carcase being dragged away. One of the two in the tree, being nearest the carcase, saw a gleam of white moving, and believing that he covered it well, he fired, and, as subsequently appeared, hit the tiger in the small of the belly, the ball passing through. The white face of the one in the lower tree, or some motion made by him, revealed his whereabouts in the flash of the rifle, and the tiger, making a frightful roar, sprang at him.

Fortunately, the distance was too great; as it was, however, one of the claws of the tiger caught in his trousers and boot, tearing them down as if cut with a razor, but without even grazing his skin. The companion of the one who had wounded the tiger, seeing a whitish gleam flying towards the lower tree, took a snap shot, and luckily broke the spine of the brute, which rolled on the ground roaring awfully.

The one in the lower tree, recovering his coolness and presence of mind, after the touch-and-go attack of the tiger, fired his rifle in the direction of the sound, not being able to make out the animal at all, owing to the darkness and its having got behind a bush, and the ball fortunately entered his chest, killing it at once.

All of them then reloaded quickly, listening intently meanwhile for some indication of the tiger's whereabouts, and straining their eyes almost to cracking the strings; but, after more than a quarter of an hour's waiting, they concluded that the animal was defunct. Each of them was provided with a bunch of tow dipped in oil, tied to one end of a long stick, and the one in the lower tree nearest the tiger, fearlessly striking a lucifer, soon threw a light on the subject. Seeing the tiger motionless, they all descended, and the villagers, collecting dry wood, soon had a roaring fire lighted close to the tiger.

Firing off their guns twice as agreed upon, the others soon joined them, accompanied by several men, some bearing torches. Meanwhile, the men with them had cut down a stout sapling, and made cords of the peel of a young bamboo, with which they tied the legs of the dead tiger to the pole, and when the rest arrived, the pole was hoisted on to the shoulders of two men, and so carried to the camp.

Giving the usual orders for the tiger to be skinned at once, they went to the dining tent, where a smoking tureen of punch was ready, having been thoughtfully provided by the caterer. After detailing the incidents of the adventure, and talking over it, the general opinion was, that tiger shooting on a dark night was rather too risky to be undertaken again by any of them.

The president, on his part, said that he had on several occasions sat up for tigers at night, and had a narrow escape one night. It happened at the village of Khairwah, about a mile further on. An old worn-out pony, that its heartless native owner had turned out, refusing to feed it any longer, was one morning found in a mango orchard, killed and partly eaten, evidently by a tiger.

CHAPTER XXV.

SITTING UP FOR A TIGER.

THE mango grove, where the carcase was found, was planted a few yards from the base of a natural elevation, which you will see as you pass to-morrow, on the top of which was erected a small Hindoo temple, having on one side a low hedge not quite three feet high. The pony had either been killed there, or the carcase had been dragged into the open space between the grove and the base of the mound, and directly in front of the hedge, so that a better position could not be selected than the cover afforded by the hedge.

Just before it got quite dark, on a similar very dark moonless night, he took up his position behind the hedge, with one attendant carrying a spare gun. Two or three hours passed, as you have experienced, until suddenly something whitish indistinctly appeared, apparently walking round the carcase, considering where to begin his supper.

Wishing to get a better sight, he raised his head, either too suddenly or too high, or perhaps both, utterly oblivious of the proverbial good sight, in the dark, of all the feline tribe, when, the tiger raising its head, he could see its green eyeballs glaring at him. Then, in a minute or two, there was the sound of a rush up the mound, and the next time he saw the eyeballs they were about twenty feet distant.

There is no use in disguising the fact, his heart was in his mouth (of course figuratively speaking). The two eyes were glaring at him intently, seemingly as large as dinner plates; he felt his face illuminated and flushed, but had the presence of mind to remain motionless under the ordeal.

Presently the eyes disappeared, and the next sound he heard was the tiger dragging away the carcase. Aiming as well as he could in the direction of the sound, he fired, and heard the ball strike—the carcase, as it afterwards appeared. The tiger, alarmed, gave out a short bark, woof! and bounded off at a great rate. When the sound of the brute's footsteps had died away in the distance, he lighted a small lantern, went and examined the carcase, and found that the ball had struck one of the fore legs, close to the marks of teeth, so that the tiger also had a narrow escape.

Some of you may perhaps ask, " Why did you not shoot when the tiger was so close?" For the simple reason that the night was so dark he could not see the end of his gun, and had he fired and missed, or only wounded the tiger, he, and not the pony, would have been made a supper of.

The next morning, it appeared that the tiger had returned, dragged the carcase into the grove, and had a good supper, still leaving plenty for another meal. As the carcase had been dragged immediately under one of the mango trees, and another tree, about twenty-five feet off to the windward of the carcase, being well adapted to the purpose, he determined on again sitting up, thinking that he could not fail to make out the brute at such close quarters.

When night set in he went, and getting up the tree, arranged everything comfortably, covered up with a black blanket, and the same attendant with a second gun. Hours again passed wearily, but although watching the carcase, or rather looking in the direction where the carcase was known to have been, he saw nothing, nor had heard any animal approach, and yet suddenly there certainly was some powerful animal enjoying himself, tearing the flesh and cracking the bones of the pony. No, he *could not* see anything, strain his eyes much as he might, and did. Although so close, not thirty feet off, the gloom of the thick grove added to the pitchy darkness of the night, rendered it impossible for himself or attendant to make out anything.

After a few minutes the noise of eating ceased, and then it was heard again distinctly, fully fifty yards off, the tiger having lifted the remains, and silently walked off that distance with them. Having lost the chance of a shot, he had no mind to be perched up in the tree until the tiger had finished his supper, so, firing his gun in the direction of the sound, he had the satisfaction of hearing the brute make tracks far enough off. Lighting the lantern, he and his man descended, examined the place where the carcase had been, and then where it was, and determining not to have that sort of fun any more, made for home before the tiger returned.

The president's story and the punch being both finished, and the small hours set in, the party retired, orders having been given for the camp to be moved after an early breakfast next day.

Owing to their long sederunt the night previous, it was long past sunrise before they got up. The morning toilet performed, they sat down and enjoyed a comfortable meal, orders having been given for some of the camp equipage to be packed at once, and started for Hinowtee. After breakfast, when the rest of the camp had left, sending on the animals to Khairwah, they walked to the jheel and had another hour's shooting, until the birds got wild and flew off to some other water.

Smith, who had been robbed of the duck the previous day, had the satisfaction of killing the eagle, which boldly attempted a second larceny, but without success, for, being discovered and watched, the second barrel was reserved, and the contents poured on its devoted head while in the act of swooping down for a fine teal.

Walking from the jheel to Khairwah, they all mounted and proceeded to Hinowtee, where they found the tents pitched and ready for them. After an hour's rest, they got up and strolled about the neighbourhood, one and another asking many questions by the way. The president, in reply, informed them that the village of Hinowtee was built on the bank of a nullah, as they saw, which was the border between what was then the honourable East India Company's territories and those of the Rajah of Rewah.

This border is very convenient for evil-disposed persons, and the natives do say that even to the present time people occasionally disappear unaccountably. Many years ago it was a common practice, so report went, that when a man had reason to suspect his wife, he used to take her, on pretence of a journey, into Rewah, and return without her. Every one used to go armed in those times, and a thrust or a cut with a sword, in a thick jungle, was soon given, no one being any the wiser. As for troublesome inquiries, people very soon learned, in those days and places, to mind their own business.

Walking along, they came to some huts here and there, which the president informed them constituted part of another large, straggling village, on the border, called Kotah, and that they were not far from the coal mine. Expressing a desire to see it, the president led the way, and, on reaching it, introduced the rest to the superintendent of the mine.

After a hurried inspection of the mine, they persuaded the superintendent, who was rather an eccentric character, to accompany them to dinner, and to sleep at the camp, as it would be dangerous to traverse that jungle late at night. While on their way back, the superintendent, stopping suddenly in the middle of the road, said that was the exact spot where he once met with a tiger, in broad daylight, and not at night. On being asked to relate how it occurred, he said that when he took charge of the concern, there was no house for him to live in close to the works.

The mine being newly-discovered, was bought by the then present owners, who, whether doubtful of the success of the speculation, or owing to the mismanagement of the party originally in charge, did not enter into the affair with spirit. Moreover, rregularity in payment of moneys due created a difficulty in getting people to work, and in inducing them to continue for any length of time.

There was one other drawback, the mine was situated in the heart of a dense jungle, full of wild beasts. The cleared spaces visible were then primeval forest, and the whole road they had come along was made by his direction. The danger from wild beasts for a long time prevented the workpeople from living close to the mine, and Kotah, a small hamlet then, became the head-quarters of the miners and himself, until he had built the house they saw close to the mine.

Living at such a distance, one and a-half miles from the works, and having to go through a thick jungle, was of itself another drawback to the prosperity of the concern, as, owing to the danger from wild beasts, the workpeople used to leave the mine in a body, a little more than an hour before sundown, and return to work an hour after sunrise.

The danger was not fanciful, because, one evening one of the men loitered behind doing something, thinking to catch up the rest soon, but he was never seen again, and his not returning the whole night created a panic, so that for two days not a soul would go to the works.

The mine, being deserted during the night, was frequently visited and taken possession of by wild beasts. Entering the mine one morning, the hands were alarmed at the roar of a tiger, and rushed back helter-skelter, the tiger after them, fortunately without harming any one, being as much scared by them as they were by him. On another occasion a bear had taken up its quarters in the mine, and, giving a good deal of trouble in doing battle for his new home, was obliged to be killed, the people not being so much afraid of a bear as of a tiger.

He generally went with the men in the morning, but being one day detained in his tent, drawing a plan of the present and proposed works, he did not leave camp until about eleven A.M. Not dreaming that there would be any danger at that time of the day, he was going along alone at a brisk pace, when, at that spot, he was brought to a stand by a tiger leaping over some bushes into the road a few paces ahead of him.

Here was a pretty fix! Half-way between the tent and the mine, in the heart of a thick jungle, not a soul within call, with only a foot rule in his hand, and a hungry tiger in a narrow road a few paces in front of him! He was not chicken-hearted; besides, he knew well the danger of turning his back on the tiger, as the animal would then have been on him at one bound. There was nothing else left for him to do but face the tiger, and stare him out of countenance. Keeping his eyes well on those of the brute, he shouted out, and the tiger, answering the challenge, roared out. Then, after a time, the brute would pretend to walk off, but suddenly turn round as if going to spring.

Finding that he kept his ground, the tiger began literally kicking up a dust in the road, hoping apparently, in the cloud, to get an opportunity of springing on him. That trick not answering, the brute sat upright on his haunches watching him, until, getting tired, he lazily laid himself down on his belly, but in such a manner that he could spring up instantly. How long this game would have lasted he could not tell, but not much longer, as the strain on his nerves was getting too painful. He had to stand nearly motionless, scarcely winking his eyes, for about an hour; for, if he moved hand or foot, the brute seemed on the point of springing on him.

All of a sudden, he saw the tiger cock his ears forwards and listen; then, in half a moment, he was on his legs, apparently undecided to spring on him or not. Although he did not hear, and could not turn his head to see if any one were coming up behind, yet, from the tiger's actions, he was sure some one *was* coming, so, shouting out loud for help, fortunately he was heard, and the persons answering his shout came running up quickly.

The tiger apparently could see them coming, and, thinking the opportunity gone, with one bound he was over some bushes, and soon out of sight. For himself, he felt upset for more than a week, the reaction after the release from imminent danger made him so nervous that he could not walk to the works or back without assistance.

CHAPTER XXVI.

DISCOVERY OF THE COAL MINE.

JUST as the superintendent had finished the relation of his encounter with the tiger, they reached the tents, and dinner being announced shortly after, all sat down to it with keen appetites, enjoying the society of their guest, and making a jovial night of it. During dinner, in answer to a question as to the discovery of the coal mine, the superintendent said that there were various reports current, but the most probable one was the following :—

Some brinjarries (carriers) had encamped thereabouts, and, as is the custom with many natives, some of them picked up each three black stones, as they took them to be, for their cooking-pots to rest upon; but, after putting fire between the stones and under the pots, they were greatly surprised and alarmed at finding their fire-places burning.

Superstitious in the extreme, they began to worship the burning stones, as the visible manifestation of the presence of the Goddess of Fire (*Agni*). The report soon spreading reached Mirzapore, and various gentlemen came prospecting, on the report of one of whom the present owners speculated in the purchase. He was then in Government employ, in the survey department, and shortly after the discovery of the coal came down on duty into these parts.

Dinner being over, when all had assembled round a good fire, the superintendent informed them that, in the performance of his duty while in the survey, and since then for his own pleasure, he had traversed these jungles in all directions, going into the most out-of-the-way places, entering curious caverns, and meeting with many adventures with wild beasts. In the course of his wanderings he had found a valuable deposit of corundum, and had discovered a rich lode of copper in Rewah, and, happening to have in his pocket a specimen, he showed them a piece of virgin copper.

On being asked about his adventures with wild beasts, he said that once while in the survey he had to ascend a high hill in the neighbourhood, and which he pointed out, to take an angle, and commenced the ascent, his people following, some carrying the theodolite or other instruments, while two carried his guns, one of whom he ordered to keep close behind him. Having left his pony at the bottom of the hill, he carried only a small riding-cane in his hand, as he did not expect to meet with any wild animals, and ordered one man with his rifle to keep close to him merely as a matter of precaution, useless as it turned out.

Going along he had to pass a narrow ledge about twelve feet wide, with a sheer precipice on one side of forty or fifty feet, and a wall of rock on the other side. Just as he had crossed the ledge, and had come close to the turn of the road, a rather large bear came round the corner; half turning round to take his rifle, he saw his rascally servant bolting with it, and the other cowards, seeing that one run, also skedaddled.

He had retreated to about the middle of the ledge, when the bear was on him, and, having nothing in his hand but his small riding-cane, he struck the brute a smart blow with it across the tip of his nose, making him drop on all fours, shake his head, and sneeze hard. He could not back further than a pace or two, owing to some obstruction, when the bear stood up again, and came at him with open mouth and glaring eyes. Having a good chance, he hit out fair from the shoulder, and sent Master Bruin staggering, but not without receiving an ugly claw from his right shoulder down to his elbow.

However, the beast came at him again in a moment, more savage than before, and he thought that there was very little chance for him then. The bear that time grappled with him, and in the struggle they both fell to the ground, when the idea came into his mind to get the brute to the edge of the precipice, and if he could not get free, then with his own death to ensure that of the bear.

He managed to get the brute to the edge, and then the beast, feeling himself in an unsafe position, fortunately let go his hold, and down he went with a, to him, very satisfactory thump. His clothes were in ribbons, and he had received several nasty scratches, but luckily his face escaped. When the fight was over the servants came sneaking up, and candidly confessed that they were afraid, and therefore ran away. What could he say to them? He took the first opportunity of getting better men.

After further conversation their guest said that he had several times been in imminent peril from wild beasts, tigers especially, and that on one occasion he was literally surrounded by tigers. He was traversing the jungle one day, in search of suitable trees to cut down, for the erection of a house for himself near the mine, which had been sanctioned by his employers. A man carrying his rifle was with him, to mark the trees that might be selected. As they were proceeding they came to an open space, about a hundred yards in diameter, nearly in the centre of which stood a solitary tree.

The open space was surrounded with low bushes, having an opening between them here and there; and while he was standing under the tree, making some pencil notes, his man said to him in a low voice, "Sir, there is a tiger," pointing in the direction they were to have gone.

Seizing his rifle quickly, he thought of firing at it; but reflecting on the probable consequences of missing or only wounding the tiger, having no second barrel, he determined on retreating. At that moment his man said that there was another tiger behind them, and turning his head half round, sure enough there was a tigress walking into the open space, from the very opening by which he thought of retreating.

SURROUNDED BY TIGERS.

While he was wondering what they should do, and thinking of getting up into the tree, another tiger leaped over the bushes on one side, and almost at the same time one more made its appearance on the opposite side, the last two being the nearly full-grown cubs of the first two. Here was a nice family party of four tigers, walking about, or sitting down and watching us, one or other of the younger ones now and then coming up to within fifteen or twenty yards of us!

Telling his man not to be afraid of the young tigers, but to keep an eye on the old one in one direction, he turned full round to watch the other one. He had examined the tree, but the branches were not within easy reach; and while he was thinking about assisting his man to climb, and then take his chance of being helped up by him, a noise attracted the attention of all the tigers.

Listening with them, they in a minute or two heard the lowing of a bullock, about two hundred yards off the open space, which had evidently got lost, and was calling to its companions. On the second low being distinctly heard, the tigress made a light bound over the bushes in the direction of the sound, the tiger also going off so as to head the bullock, the younger ones remaining for a time, in an uncomfortably excited state.

Presently they heard a sound which needs only to be heard once to know that it was a tiger striking his blow and breaking the neck of the animal. With that sound the young ones leaped over the bushes in beautiful style, following the tigress. Taking off their shoes, they started in the opposite direction, making a long detour back home as quickly as they could, glad enough at their escape.

One of the party asking if there were any wild dogs (dhole) in that part of India, their guest said that he was not aware of there being any in Singrowlee at that time; but that two or three years previously he had seen a tiger being chased right through the coal mine settlement by a pack of wild dogs.

These animals, he said, were small, and do not give tongue like other dogs, but they are very bold and determined. When once a pack of them put up any animal, no matter whether deer or tiger, that animal's doom is sealed; they never leave it. They will dog their prey for days, if need be, and run it down exhausted, and if it turns to fight, they go in fearlessly, and by their numbers win.

All animals dread the wild dog; others they may elude by speed, artifice, or battle, but their instinct tells them that there is no escaping the wild dog, as it hunts in packs by scent, as well as by sight, and is as brave as it is persevering.

Wonder being expressed how natives even, much less Europeans, could live in such a wild place, continually exposed to danger from wild beasts, not to speak of the climate, their guest in reply asked, if they remembered an old school copy, "Familiarity breeds contempt," adding that it was so with danger. When a man frequently encounters danger in various forms, he becomes gradually used to it, and learns to look it boldly in the face.

It is his belief that all men are schooled for the different parts that they have to play in life. If it is to be the lot of any one to encounter great danger, he is not thrown into it abruptly, but, meeting first with lesser dangers, his nerves are gradually strung so as to be able to stand the strain of greater perils. Speaking for himself, he was a bit of a fatalist, so far as this, that if he *was* to be killed and eaten by a tiger, he *would* be killed and eaten by a tiger, and no more need be said.

Talking of bravery, he said, you all noticed a fine, handsome native boy, about ten or twelve years of age, to whom he directed their attention while inspecting the mine; *that boy*, in his opinion, was the king of the jungles in those parts. Such a fearless lad he had never seen or heard of, being no more afraid of a tiger than of either of you, not so much perhaps. He has repeatedly saved the lives of his work-fellows, once in a remarkable manner.

One day a number of them had gone into the jungle, some to

cut down suitable trees for erecting or repairing their huts, and others to collect firewood, and this boy for amusement went with them and some other boys. The men were somewhat scattered over the top of a hill, and the boys playing together, when suddenly one of the men called out that a tiger was coming up the hill, and he began running away down the hill on the opposite side. Hearing the man call out, and seeing him run, struck a panic into the rest, and they began to run, joined by the other boys.

This lad alone stood his ground.

Then, catching up a stick, and calling on the men not to run away, he boldly placed himself between the advancing tiger and the men. As the tiger advanced, and came within three or four yards of him, the lad shouted and ordered it to stop, lifting up his stick, threatening to strike it.

The tiger, intimidated or not at the bold bearing of the boy, actually did stand still, and then the brave child began abusing it, ordering it to go away a long distance in another direction, and not to dare to harm or frighten any of his friends again.

As the tiger did not obey instantly, the boy advanced a step or two towards it, with his stick uplifted in a menacing attitude, and shouted to it to go, or he would beat it. The brute, awed or not by the magnificent daring of the child, turned round and went off sulkily; but this not pleasing the boy, he ordered it to be off quickly, and made as if he would run after it, and beat it, and then the tiger broke into a gallop, and was soon out of sight.

One of the men, who had managed to climb up a tree while the others were running away, witnessed the whole scene, and related it to him. That boy lives in native clover, doing what he likes with every one, and he would be a very daring man who lifted his hand to hurt him.

CHAPTER XXVII.

ROBIN HOOD ARMAMENT.

THE evening had passed so agreeably that none of them noticed the flight of time, until one of them looking at his watch, to the great surprise of all, said it was past one o'clock! Insisting on their guest remaining to breakfast with them, they all retired and were soon asleep.

The next morning, rising somewhat late, they were ashamed to find that their guest had been up, gone to the mine, given necessary instructions, and had returned before they were awake, to keep his promise of breakfasting with them, apologizingly saying that his employer's interests must be attended to. During breakfast their guest proposed taking them into the jungle, beyond the mine, where they might get some deer and bear shooting, which proposal was readily agreed to.

Breakfast being finished, the heads of departments having given their several orders, and all preparations being made, they mounted and proceeded to the coal settlement. Here they found several fine-looking men, dhángars, on whom the superintendent could depend, waiting, some carrying sharp little tangarees (wood-axes), and two carrying strong bows and arrows.

Seeing some of the party smiling at the Robin Hood armament, the superintendent asked one of them to string one of the bows, handing him one for the purpose.

To his great disgust he found that he could not manage it, while the owner, receiving it back, strung it without the least effort apparently.

The superintendent then said in vindication of such weapons, that the owner of such an axe and bow would travel through any jungle without hesitation, being able to send his arrow through any beast, except an elephant or rhinoceros.

Leaving their horses at the mine, they then proceeded on foot and soon came to thick jungle, where the axes were found very useful, and into wild-looking places at the base of precipitous rocks. One of the natives clearing some branches out of the way, was met by a bear, which he had seemingly disturbed, but before the beast could rise on his hind legs to claw him, a well-aimed blow, delivered with good-will, sent the head of the axe crashing through its skull, braining it on the spot.

The affair was over so instantaneously that most of the party knew nothing of it until they heard a noise, and, on going up, saw the last throes of the bear. Robinson, however, had seen the whole affair, and was quite eloquent over the coolness of the man, and the neatness with which he had felled the animal. As the bear, by hunter's law, belonged to the man, he and another were told to take it to his home, and return to them quickly.

As they were going on further, one of the natives ahead, seeing a spotted deer escaping, sent an arrow clean through its heart, and out in front. The gentlemen, feeling nettled, scolded the man; but in defence he said that there was no time to let them know, that he had scarcely time to fit an arrow and shoot, and that he thought it a pity that the animal should escape.

On being told to take the deer to his hut, the man said that he had not killed it for himself, but for the gentlemen; but they being piqued, refused it, saying that they could kill for themselves what they wanted. However, on second thoughts, they consented to give him a present for it, should they not be able to shoot any deer for themselves.

Just then the other men returned who had gone with the bear, and two were sent off with the deer to the mine, with orders to return quickly. Some likely caves attracting their attention, one of the natives was ordered to try if any animal were in them.

Examining two or three without success, the next one, he said, contained some animal, a bear he thought, and pelted some stones into it.

One of the stones apparently hit the animal, for while the man was stooping to pick up another stone, the bear came out, knocked the man over, rushed down the rocks, and charged the party before they were ready for it.

Two or three shots were hastily fired at close quarters without effect, the bear getting up to and seizing Jones. At that instant one of the dhángars sent an arrow cleverly through a vital part of the bear, making it let go and fall dead.

After expressing their thankfulness at the very timely deliverance of the one seized (Jones) but not harmed, they all felt vexed, saying that the niggers were having all the fun, and were inclined to return in a huff to the tents, but were persuaded to remain.

Meanwhile, the men who had taken the deer to the mine returned, and others were sent off with the second bear, with orders to return quickly, and bring some additional men. Further on they were successful in bagging a couple of deer, three peafowl, and some green and wood pigeons. Then, feeling hungry and thirsty, they returned to the coal settlement, and, persuading the superintendent to become their guest for another night, mounted their horses and soon reached the camp.

After a good wash, and refreshing themselves with a light tiffin and a glass or two of beer, when they were seated under the shade of a large tree, smoking cheroots, some remarks being made by one of the company, the president explained that a serai, or native public inn, was a large space enclosed by four walls, with only one strong gate in the centre of one of the sides.

Small lean-to rooms are built inside the enclosed space, along the sides of the quadrangle, travellers occupying one or more according to their requirements, their animals being picketed and their goods piled up within the enclosure, in front of their several rooms. The bhuttiar, or his wife the bhuttiarin, supplies rice, oil, salt, pulses, &c., to travellers, and fodder to the animals, all payments being made on delivery.

When travellers are settled in their rooms, the bhuttiar (person in charge) goes round and levies a small rent for the accommodation afforded to man and beast. In troublous times, the gate is securely fastened before night sets in, and no one obtains admission or is allowed to depart until day has well broken.

These serais are used by merchants travelling with a large assortment of goods, hawkers on a large scale, and pedlars, who are common in all eastern countries, besides casual wayfarers. It is the practice for pedlars to go about outlying villages, and dispose of their wares by barter with the villagers for the produce of their holdings or the gleanings of the forest, in the shape of gums, lac, medicinal roots, herbs and seeds, horns shed by deer, &c.

Not feeling inclined for further exercise that day, they requested the president to relate a story, who began the following one of "The Two Mendicants:"—

"On a certain annual festival a great king, magnificently attired, took his seat on the splendid throne used only on great state occasions. As was the custom, all the great officers of the kingdom, the nobility and gentry, wealthy merchants and others, arrayed in costly garments, presented themselves at the durbar, or levee, to offer their felicitations and gifts.

"Amidst the throng, two fakirs presented themselves, and blessing the king, prayed that he might live for ever. This done, they stood on one side with joined hands, waiting until it should please his highness to make them some charitable donation.

"With the view of flattering the king, one of the fakirs, who was a sycophant, said to his fellow, loud enough for the king to hear, 'Kings have all sublunary power, and they give to whom they please; what then can the Ruler of Destiny do?' The other fakir, an honest man, rebuked him, saying, 'When the Ruler of Destiny gives, what can the greatest king do?'

"Determining in his own mind to prove the truth of these

two aphorisms, the king took a green sour lime, and having extracted the pulp and seeds, inserted a valuable jewel in their place. He then gave to the flattering fakir some fine rice, best ghee (clarified butter used in cooking), good pulse, excellent vegetables, and other articles, adding the green lime last.

"To the honest fakir the king gave coarse rice, and other things corresponding thereto, adding a fine ripe whole lime. Enjoining on them to be sure to bring to him every seed that they might get from their respective limes, the king dismissed them from the presence, threatening to punish severely whoever should disobey him.

"The two fakirs having received their several presents, with profound obeisances left the palace, and went to an imaumbari, or Moslem religious house, where, as religious mendicants, they were entitled to, and received, free quarters. Selecting their separate cooking-places, they left their respective presents on the spot, and went to bathe.

"The flattering fakir, being hungry, hastily performed his ablutions, and returning to his place, unpacked his different gifts, to prepare his dinner. Then, seeing the honest fakir's ripe lime, showing at the top of the other man's bundle, moved with envy, he strongly coveted it. Arguing the matter with himself, he said, 'See the injustice of the king! He has given me everything good but this nasty green lime, which quite spoils all the rest of his gifts. Had he given me the ripe lime, one thing would have fitted in well with the rest, and the whole would have been perfect. The king must surely have given me the green lime by mistake, and I am therefore justified in making the exchange, while I have the opportunity of doing so.' Thus deciding, without examining his green lime, he hastily took the other man's ripe lime, and put his green one in its place.

"The honest fakir, having performed his ablutions properly, went to his place to prepare his dinner. On opening his bundle, he at once saw the exchange that had been effected; but being a wise, humble, and peaceable man, he did not quarrel with the other, consoling himself thus: 'If this man, who has received so many good gifts, and only one inferior one, is discontented, and has chosen to take away my good gift, let him keep it. If I can be thankful for all the other inferior articles the king gave me, surely it will be no great hardship to bear with this one green lime.' He then cooked and ate his dinner contentedly.

"After they had both taken their morning meal, the flattering fakir gathered the seeds of the ripe lime and put them into his pocket, while the honest fakir carefully secured what he had taken from his green lime. They then both laid themselves down and went to sleep.

"When the heat of the day was over, they woke up, and proceeded to the palace, to give in an account of their seeds. The king, seeing the two fakirs, called them up to him, and asking the flatterer how many seeds he had obtained, the man answered 'Ten.' Turning to the honest fakir, he asked him the same question, who said that his lime had yielded only one.

"The king, greatly surprised, then said to the honest man, 'It is quite true what you said to your companion in the morning, 'When the Ruler of Destiny gives, what can the greatest king do?' I gave your companion the green lime, in which I had concealed a jewel worth the ransom of a great prince, but the Ruler of Destiny did not intend him to have it, seeing it is in your possession. Although given to him, he did not get it, the Ruler of Destiny having meant it for you: keep it and go.'

"Turning to the flattering fakir, the king said, 'King as I am, I gave you a royal gift, but the Ruler of Destiny did not intend it for you, since, through covetousness, you must have exchanged it for a ripe lime. Learn from this that it is not in the power of frail man to overrule the least of the decrees of the wise Ruler of Destiny.'"

In commenting on the story, Brown remarked that most native stories have an excellent moral appended to them.

CHAPTER XXVIII.

CASUALTIES BY WILD BEASTS.

WHILE dressing for dinner, their guest arrived, and, in course of conversation, informed them that some of his men reported an hour ago that a tiger was in the neighbourhood, and that, expecting they would like the opportunity of shooting it, he had ordered a young buffalo to be tied up, and had arranged for a hankwa the next morning. This news, of course, put every one in good humour, and dinner being announced, no delay was made in sitting down to it. Sharp set as they were, there was a limit even to a hunter's appetite, and the good things having been discussed, and a bumper tureen of punch being ordered to be prepared, they adjourned to the fire.

On one of the company asking whether many natives were killed by wild beasts, their guest remarked, that the casualties from such causes, all over India, must be something frightful. From his many years' experience in the various positions he has occupied, to his certain knowledge many natives have disappeared unaccountably. They have left their service on leave, some to go to their homes, others to distant places on particular business, but they never reached their destinations. Their poverty was against any probability of their being murdered for gain, and the only conclusion that could be arrived at was, that, in passing through tracts of jungle, they had been killed by tigers or wolves, or, in crossing some stream, had been seized by an alligator.

The president here remarked that he remembered a case in point. It occurred at a place some distance to the west of

A YOUNG GIRL EATEN BY WOLVES.

Tilowlee, on the table-land of the Kymore, in the district of Mirzapore.

A fine young girl, about twelve years of age, resident in a certain village, had been betrothed to a young man of a neighbouring village. All the parties being in a humble station in life, there was more freedom of intercourse, and less ceremony, than between those in higher grades. The two villages were only about half-a-mile apart, and the road being considered safe enough, children used to be sent from one to the other at most hours of the day. Between the villages there was a small patch of scrubby jungle, not dense enough to form a lair for a tiger, but sufficiently so to conceal a considerable pack of marauding wolves.

One morning early, the girl was sent by her parents on some important business, to the house of her intended father-in-law. She was directed to go quickly, finish the business, and return to help her mother in some heavy household duties. The girl left her home, no doubt pleased at the prospect of seeing her intended, who happened to be agreeable to her, and to be in his society for even a short time, but—she never reached her father-in-law's house. Several hours having elapsed without the return of the girl, the mother meanwhile chafing at being left to do all the work alone, until, getting anxious, she sent one of her younger children to the field, in which her husband was working, to call him home.

While this child was gone on his errand, a man came from the intended father-in-law on the very business concerning which the girl had been sent early that morning. Greatly alarmed, the mother asked where the girl was, explaining that she had sent her daughter early that morning on that business, to her intended father-in-law's house. She had been angry at her not returning quickly, but thought that they had detained her to take her morning meal with them. The man replying that the girl had not been to the village all that day, heightened the mother's alarm and distress, and she began making loud lamentations.

Her husband coming in just then, on learning the particulars went out, and collecting several friends, started off to search all the patches of jungle, being led to do so by the fear that some accident had happened to her, remembering that some wolves had been seen about the country a day or two previous.

The first patch of jungle they came to bordered on the road along which the girl would necessarily have to go, and, searching this, they came upon a bush a good deal broken, as if some heavy body had fallen upon it, and hanging to some of the twigs were some rags, which the father recognised as forming part of his daughter's dress.

On searching further, they came upon more rags, hair, and marks of blood. Following up the trace, they disturbed three or four wolves, which fled on their approach, leaving what proved to be the head of the poor girl. Had they been a little later, even that would have disappeared, and as it was, the nose, ears, and part of the chin, with the lips, had been eaten off. No other fragment of the body being discovered, they carried off the remains of the head, and performed the funeral ceremonies over it. The girl's intended, it is said, devoted himself to a shikari's life, vowing vengeance, especially against any wolf that he should hear of in the whole country.

While on the subject of wolves, the president stated that, unless pressed by hunger, wolves were cowardly animals, and extremely suspicious, and related the following native account illustrative of his statement. Some parts of the Kymore range seem to be more infested with wolves than others, and the same may be said of different districts of India, of Upper India especially.

Two natives were once returning to their own village from Mirzapore, where they had been on some court business, and had to pass over some open ground, at the other end of which was some scrubby jungle. As they came near the jungle, they saw some dogs, as they at first took them to be, but, on getting a

A NATIVE RUSE.

better view, they found them to be wolves. Wolves, as a general rule, unless, as said before, pressed by hunger, will not attack even a single man, if he is armed with any weapon.

These men had not even the usual lathee, or walking staff, and having nothing to defend themselves with, one proposed to the other to make a wide detour, and so avoid such dangerous wayfarers. The other man, aware of the suspicious nature of wolves, told his companion not to be afraid; that he did not intend going out of his way for a parcel of sneaking wolves, but would make them get out of the road.

Then, taking off the cloth wrapped round his head as a protection from the sun, he told his companion to go a few yards to the right, and do the same, imitating him in all his movements. Unrolling the cloth, he let it trail on the ground behind him, with a waving motion, advancing cautiously towards the wolves, the other man doing the same.

The wolves watched them all the time, not knowing what to make of the long cloth trailing behind the men. Presently, one pricked up his ears, and then another, and then one sat on his haunches, examining the advancing men attentively, when, not liking the appearance of things, he got up and walked off, looking behind him over his shoulder every now and then. The other wolves, seeing the leader of the pack sneak off, began, one after the other, doing ditto.

The artful man, seeing the wolves on the march, told his companion to shout loud, and run up with him towards them. The wolves hearing the shout, and seeing the men run after them with their long cloths, didn't wait to be caught, but, putting their tails down, they broke into a long leaping gallop, and were out of sight in a very short time. The men, having effectually terrified the wolves, laughed heartily on seeing them scamper off, and readjusting their clothes, reached their village in safety.

Wilcox here said that wolves and hyenas were very numerous in many parts of Upper India, and that many children are annually carried off by these animals. Owing to the careless habits of the natives, especially in the hot weather, sleeping with their doors open, or altogether outside their dwellings, wolves or hyenas steal up quietly, seize a child by the neck, preventing its making any outcry, and make off with it, the loss only being discovered in the morning.

The reward for destroying dangerous wild beasts having been so shamefully reduced by a parsimonious government calling itself, in mockery, paternal, it is not to be wondered at if these kinds of animals should increase, and the list of casualties also increase, especially after the Gun Licence Act, disarming the natives, their poverty, that of shikaris in particular, preventing their taking out licences.

Their guest here remarked that the wonder with him was, not that there were so many known, as well as conjectured casualties from wild beasts, but that there were not many more. That there were not more human beings destroyed by tigers and other wild beasts, he attributed solely to the fear of man implanted by the Creator in all inferior animals.

Natives and Europeans deriving their subsistence in or on the borders of jungles, and traversing them in the prosecution of their various callings, must necessarily, and do frequently, meet with tigers, or other dangerous animals. Almost always a shout, and a bold front, will cause a tiger to turn out of the road, and let the traveller pass on.

But, in these degenerate times, few men have stout hearts, and, in their wisdom, they commit the greatest possible folly, seeking safety in flight; as then the tiger, no longer having the fear of man before him, follows up, and with one blow of his paw crushes in the skull, or seizes and carries off the terror-stricken traveller.

Tigers, and all other animals, have their different moods and humours, just the same as human beings, and he could relate numerous instances in point. Sometimes tigers will allow people to pass within a few yards of them without harm, while at other times they would charge a regiment.

Personally speaking, he had had so many encounters with wild beasts that he cared very little about them. To the north of his house by the mine there is a platform of rock, and about a year ago a tiger and tigress used, for several days together, to come there regularly in the afternoon, for basking in the sun and courtship.

This was in full sight of all the workpeople, and certainly not more than fifty yards distant from his house. For the first day or two the people were alarmed; but he told them that though his house was much nearer to the tigers, he was not afraid of them, and they need not be, after which no one troubled himself or herself about them.

It so happened that a party of three gentlemen came down to Singrowlee, a week or two after the tigers' first appearance, and he at once sent off a man with a letter requesting them to hasten their march, so as to arrive at his house by noon the next day, promising them some tiger shooting.

The reason why he did not fire at the tigers was because he was alone, and could not make *sure* of killing one, much less both of the tigers, at one shot; and had he fired at them, and only wounded, or even if he had killed one, he was apprehensive that the other would have made reprisals, and the works in that case might have been stopped for days, until the second brute had been killed.

And the reason why he wrote for the gentlemen to come was this: the tigers used to leave the platform a little before sundown, retiring over the rocks behind his house into the jungle, passing about fifteen yards from the house. After the first day or two seeing that was their route, every one took good care to clear out beforehand, and let them pass.

CHAPTER XXIX.

THE TIGER'S DECLARATION OF WAR.

ON the day previous to the arrival of the gentlemen, one of the tigers took it into its head to come up to the house as it was passing. While the tigers used to be about the place, he noticed that his servants deserted him, leaving him alone in the house, busy with his correspondence, accounts, or what not; and this day, having occasion to go to the bath-room, one door of which opened on to the back verandah, as he entered the room he saw the tiger about two yards off from the verandah, advancing. Shouting loud, he slammed the outer door to, hard, shot the bolt, turned quick and shut the other door, and then peeped out of the corner of the window.

The tiger, it appeared, walked up and down two sides of the house, entered some of the rooms, went again into the verandah, and not finding him, walked down the steps by which it had entered the house, and he had the satisfaction of seeing it join its mate, and the pair of them walk off. As this was a clear breach of etiquette, and a declaration of war on the part of the tiger, directly they were out of sight he sat down and wrote the letter, sending a man off post-haste with it.

The next day the three gentlemen arrived, and, after sending the horses and servants far out of the way, cautioning the gentlemen to speak only in whispers, they had tiffin with closed doors. As the gentlemen had spare guns, he having two, it was arranged to wait until the tigers should be, on their return, close by the house, when their afternoon gambols were over, and then for two to fire, with as sure an aim as they could, at separate tigers.

This plan of action being agreed to, after tiffin they placed themselves in concealment. Soon after having done so, the tigers came, but the male one was evidently in a bad humour about something, for, on the tigress offering some feline endearment, the tiger, like a brute of a husband, gave her a tremendous wallop with one of his fists, or fore-paws, sending her reeling down the rocks.

Jumping up quickly, she sprang at one bound on to the platform, in no placable humour, and they all expected to see a pretty set-to between the pair, but, seemingly admonished by a growl and an angry look, she stalked off in sullen dignity.

The tiger, however, was not inclined to let her go, and following, tried to induce her to return; but no—he had struck her, and she would not be mollified so easily. Continuing this play, they advanced to the distance agreed upon, and then a simultaneous discharge of four barrels took place. Catching up the spare guns instantly, they were just in time to receive the tigress with a volley, which sent her down the rocks.

The tiger had fallen, shot through the heart, but the tigress had been only wounded at the first discharge, although severely, and in two or three bounds she was about five yards off, when she was floored. And so the settlement was happily delivered from such neighbours.

The president said that he remembered a story of a tiger passing close by a gentleman, without offering to do him any harm, although not without receiving harm. A party of young militaires were out on leave, and were visiting some indigo planters in a neighbouring district.

One of these officers, an ensign, it so happened, had never seen a living tiger, even in a menagerie, and one day, while they were all out in the jungles, picking up what game they could get, this ensign got separated from the rest. Tramping along through the jungle, he saw a large cat-like animal, coming from the right-hand side, in a direction that would take it past him right in front over some open ground, and about twenty-five feet off.

Standing still to admire it, the thought came into his mind that he would like to have the skin of such a fine cat, and as the animal passed right in front, he raised his rifle, to have a shot behind the shoulder. The tiger, seeing the motion made in raising the rifle, stopped for an instant, turning partly round, thus presenting a full front to the ensign, who coolly took a deliberate aim, and sent a ball through its heart, dropping it on the spot.

Calling out loudly two or three times to his chums to come and see a fine cat that he had shot, he began examining the tiger, and they, on coming up, did not know which to admire most, his coolness or his greenness, thankful, nevertheless, at the narrow escape some of them had by its timely destruction.

On being told that was a tiger, and a good big one too, the ensign said that if they were all like that, he would not care for a troop of them. He got wiser in time.

The attention of every one had been so taken up with the relation of, or listening to, the several stories, that the flight of time was not noticed, until the president reminded them that if they wished to be ready for the hankwa to-morrow morning, it was quite time to think of bed; so, taking a last tumbler of punch, they all turned in, after strict orders had been given for all to be roused at daybreak.

The next morning, whether it were owing to the capital punch or not, it seemed to several of them that they had scarcely slept half an hour, and were consequently very unwilling to turn out, until the president threatened them with a cold pig, when they jumped up, and, thrusting their heads into basins of almost freezing water, soon sent the drowsy god to the right about. While they were dressing, a man came to report "a kill," and that everything was ready; so, taking a cup of hot coffee, they started for the jungle at the foot of the hills.

Taking up their positions in the several machauns, they waited impatiently a long time for the hankwa to advance. The signal had been given, and the drive had commenced; but after advancing some distance it seemed to stop. They were all naturally very anxious to know what mischance had happened, but neither they nor the rokhs, or stoppers, dared descend to inquire, not knowing where the tiger might be. It appeared afterwards that the tiger had got into a *cul de sac* of a ravine, thickly covered with jungle, and *would not* come out, until at last they had recourse to long sticks, with bundles of lighted rags at the end, which dislodged it.

The brute, however, not choosing to go the way the men wanted it to, had a mind to break back, and through the line of beaters, but luckily one of the men with a lighted stick was at hand, and pushing it right into the face of the tiger, caused it to spring round with a roar, and proceed in the proper direction. The roar of the tiger was answered with a general shout from the whole line of beaters and a horrible din from the tom-toms, or drums.

The roar of the tiger put every one in the machauns on the *qui vive*, and well it was that they were ready, for the tiger, the next moment it seemed, came galloping up. A quick shot caused it to stumble, and, before it could rise, a general volley settled its business.

Waiting until the beaters had come up, they descended from the machauns, and after examining the tiger, gave orders for it to be carried in the meantime to the tents, where the beaters should be paid.

Here, however, a friendly dispute arose between their guest and themselves, as to who should pay the expenses, he saying that having arranged for the hankwa it was his place to pay for it, and they, out of regard for his circumstances, insisting on paying expenses. Delicacy, of course, forbade their openly stating their reasons; but, to end the matter, it was resolved to toss up for it; whoever cried heads twice out of three, was to pay, and the other party to have the tiger.

Rummaging their pockets in vain for a coin (Europeans seldom carry money about with them in India), they had to borrow a copper from one of the beaters, and as it bore the same legend as the silver currency, it answered the purpose, and being thrown up, the lot fell to their guest to have the tiger.

This matter being settled, they were returning, when their guest said that not having been to the works that morning, he must decline breakfasting with them, urging the necessity of attending to the owner's interests. Under the circumstances, they could not insist on his company to breakfast, but would take no denial for dinner, and so parted. On reaching the tents the beaters were at once paid, and breakfast being ready, they sat down to it with appetites sharpened by the bracing morning air and their walk.

Breakfast being over, and the tiger sent off, while they were smoking their cheroots a man arrived from the mine, who said he had been sent by the superintendent to conduct them to a part of the jungle where they might have some good shooting, if they would like to go out again. As it was against their creed to decline a good chance, they were soon ready, and taking several men with them, they followed their native leader.

A good half-hour's walk brought them to a scrubby jungle, where they soon put up as much game as their men could carry, until they procured some men who were cutting firewood. Tired with their exercise, they were glad of a glass of beer on their return to camp. As it was to be their last day's stay at Hinowtee, the caterer was soon seen mysteriously engaged with the khansamah, and from the activity subsequently displayed by all the servants, it was surmised that there was to be something extraordinary for dinner that evening.

HUNGER IN THE CAMP.

The caterer's labours being at length over, he joined the rest at a very scanty tiffin, which called forth indignant remarks from the others, but he bore it all coolly, telling them that he intended that slight refection to serve as a whet for dinner. One of them, grumbling, warned the caterer not to come near him between that time and dinner, or perhaps a little cannibalism might be committed.

After the remains of this apology for a tiffin had been removed, the caterer recommended a glass of weak brandy and water, to settle their stomachs, but a question arising as to who was to decide upon the strength of the dilution, it was settled that each one was to qualify his brandy with water, or his water with brandy, to his own judgment.

Soon after this knotty point had been brought to a satisfactory conclusion, their guest arrived, was duly received, and complaints poured into his ears about the state of starvation their caterer kept them in, one and another asking if his larder were well stocked, and proposing, if dinner were not ready very soon, to go to the settlement for something wherewith to sustain their exhausted nature.

The complaints of one and another breaking out every now and then, mingled with threats of a raid upon the commissariat, the caterer, to pacify them, about five o'clock ordered the khitmudgar, or waiter, to hand round a thin sandwich and a glass of sherry to each.

Holding up their thin sandwiches, they all *looked* at the caterer, and if indignant looks could have annihilated him, he would soon have been nowhere; but he stood unabashed, the hardened man, and then they one and all declared that he had no conscience.

Dinner being shortly after announced, the malcontents sprang up with a shout, as if a large war party of Pawnee Loups or other American Redskins had broken into the camp with their war whoop. More than one of the party declared that they were e-nor-mous-ly hungry, and were prepared to do justice to a roast elephant even, and so proceeded to the dining tent.

The soup gave decided satisfaction, especially to their guest, and was followed by hunter's pie, hunter's stew, roast saddle of venison with tamarind sauce, deers' tongues with ham, venison cutlets with tomato sauce, and three or four kinds of curries, winding up with some peculiar Indian pies, and other sweet preparations, until the malcontents were not only satisfied, but were pleased to declare that the caterer, khansamah, and all concerned had surpassed themselves, that such a dinner would not soon be forgotten, and that they only hoped none of them might have the nightmare.

CHAPTER XXX.

THE HERDBOY'S FOLLY.

THEIR guest thought that something more than satisfaction ought to be expressed, and proposed a bumper with full cheers to the president and caterer, who, he was informed and had partly heard, had stood a good deal of badgering during the day. Filling their glasses, the toast was done justice to, according to custom, one of the party insisting on adding musical honours.

The president, in modestly returning thanks, trusted that the jungle fare they had tasted might not soon fade from their memories, was sorry that they had reached the limits of their excursion, and would have, the next day, to make a retrograde movement, but hoped that the trip would end satisfactorily to all.

When they had adjourned to the fire, their guest informed them that a herdboy had been seriously mauled by a tiger that afternoon within half-a-mile of where they were sitting, and being asked for particulars, he gave the following account :—

Some herdsmen were out in the jungle that day attending their cattle while feeding, accompanied by the son of one of them, a boy about fifteen years of age. The cattle were scattered about a good deal, some on the higher land, some in the ravines, browsing on the leaves and tender shoots of wild plants. The boy was tending some that were in a ravine, and while doing so a tiger sprang into the ravine, evidently after one of the bullocks.

All herdsmen and shepherds are held responsible for the cattle or sheep under their charge, and are made to pay for any loss, unless they can give satisfactory proof that any of the cattle died of disease, or were destroyed by wild beasts. Against the latter, they are expected to do their utmost to protect their charge, and are usually very courageous in the performance of their duty.

This boy, seeing the tiger spring into the ravine, boldly placed himself between it and the cattle, calling out loudly to the others to come and help, shouting at and abusing the tiger. The animal finding itself foiled, was turning off in a different direction, and would have gone away without doing further harm than frightening the cattle, but the foolish boy thoughtlessly struck the tiger as it was passing, thinking, it may be, to quicken its movements.

The tiger, half rising on its hind legs, struck at the boy with its right paw, and had it caught the boy, would no doubt have carried him off; but the lad stepping back quickly, the claws of the brute caught his left shoulder, and made two deep gashes right down to his elbow. At that moment the herdsmen all came up, and, by their united shouts and presence, scared the tiger away.

The boy's arm was immediately attended to, people living in the jungle generally having a rude skill in surgery and simples, and as the gashes are clean cuts, the boy will most likely recover his health, and the use of his arm in two or three months. There is however a man about these villages who was some years ago attacked by a tiger, and wounded much in the same way, who recovered his health, but not the use of his arm, which is quite shrivelled up, and a similar result may possibly be in this case.

Their guest added that he had ordered a "victim" to be tied up in case of the tiger remaining in these parts, and should it be killed, they would perhaps have no objection to start a little later next day.

The march for next day being only back to Ghurwar, the possible detention to shoot a tiger was rather agreeable than otherwise, and consequently all willingly agreed to the proposal. Tigers being the topic of conversation, their guest was asked by one of the company whether he knew of any instances of wild beasts encountering each other.

To which he answered, that no doubt in the course of roaming about for prey or food, wild beasts do encounter each other, tigers meet tigers or other wild animals. Judging from the actions of domesticated animals, we may reasonably infer that if a strange tiger is found poaching upon the manor of another the result is a row, and a jolly one too.

Also, it does happen occasionally that, in the pairing season, two male tigers will, for days together, follow about a female one, trying to win her exclusive favour, whilst she on her part, undecided which to prefer, smiles (tiger fashion) now on one, and now on the other. This sort of fun goes on until the rage of the males gets up to about boiling-over point, when one of them saying in his heart he is not going to stand that fellow's nonsense any longer, gives the other one a clout.

That is enough, the gauntlet is thrown down, taken up readily by the other one, and at it they go, tooth and claw literally, and if the two males are well matched, the fight is a grand one.

Three or four years ago, he partially witnessed just such a fight. The event came off in a small open space in the jungle, about a mile or less from the coal mine, and lasted about three hours. The tigress, the cause of the shindy (and what row is there in which a female is not openly or in secret at the bottom), was seen now reclining, now sitting on her haunches, on a small hillock, witnessing her two lovers clapperclawing each other.

When the tigers ceased awhile to draw breath, the fair one would descend from her throne, walk round them purring her encouragement, and perhaps give one of them as she passed an approving whisk of her tail, which would send the other one into fits of rage, and then the row would be awful.

Soon after the fight commenced, buffaloes, bullocks, deer, and other animals, cleared out of that neighbourhood pretty sharp, you may be sure. The affair of honour at last ended in a drawn battle, both having had enough, the tigress walking off with the one which, in her opinion, had shown the greatest valour.

The half-eaten remains of one of them was found two days afterwards, and it is supposed that the other one died of its wounds, or was killed by a third competitor for the fair one's favour; for the same tigress was seen a few days after the fight mated with a tiger without a scratch on it.

In fights with other animals, tigers are not always victorious. Some time ago, a large dead bear, and also a dead tiger, were found in the jungle close to each other, exhibiting plain enough signs of the battle having been à *outrance*, both being so mauled by each other that the natives who found them did not consider their skins worth the trouble of stripping off.

He remembered also a friend telling him that, in a belt of jungle not far from his factory, a dead tiger and an enormous dead wild boar, were found a few feet distant from each other.

Tigers are more fond of pig meat than anything else (unless they have once tasted man), and it was supposed that the tiger seeing this huge tusker, wanted to appropriate him for supper; but the tusker, not having a mind to be so cavalierly appropriated, resisted the bland advances of the feline.

A little opposition, you know, gives zest to an affair, and the coyness of the porker only led the feline to exhibit more ardour in the prosecution of his suit.

Having a decided objection to being made into pork sausages or mincemeat in any shape, the tusker resolutely maintained his right to be a free agent, and whenever the feline became too demonstrative in his suit, gave him an accolade which let daylight beneath his outward covering.

The tiger's activity, however, enabled it more than once to spring on to the boar's back, as was manifest by the marks of the teeth and claws, but it was equally evident that it could not maintain its hold. The scene of the fight showed that the battle must have lasted a considerable time, the ground being much cut up, and the bushes broken and knocked about a good deal, but how long it lasted of course no one could tell. The skin of the tiger was too much gashed about to be worth taking, but the villagers carried off the tusker, and were not long in putting it out of sight.

Tigers do not usually attack a man unless pressed by hunger. Of course, in making such a remark, those tigers that have once tasted human flesh must be put out of the question, as such brutes will leave the herd and carry off the keeper, many an unfortunate aheer, or herdsman, being thus carried off.

The president here interposed, saying that he remembered once rescuing an aheer who had been made a dead set at by a tiger. He was living then not far from the top of Ekpowa Ghât, when one night the man on guard came and reported that some traveller, he thought, had been beset by a tiger, and was calling out lustily for speedy help. Seizing one gun, and giving an orderly another, and a lighted lantern, and calling three or four men to him, he proceeded in the direction of the cries, ordering his men to shout, and let the man know that assistance was at hand.

In a few minutes he arrived at the place, and found that it was a herdsman that had been beset by a very persevering tiger. It being a dark night, the man had not taken his buffaloes into the jungle to feed, but only to the skirt of it, and was watching them as they were browsing. An hour or so had thus passed quietly, when on a sudden the herd broke away from the bushes, and made for the open ground.

Knowing that it could only have been a tiger that had alarmed them, he shouted, and was running up to collect them together again. As he was going, the tiger had seen him, and somehow got between him and the buffaloes, and kept him at bay.

He had tried all he could to circumvent the brute, but without success, for wherever he turned, the tiger turned, so that it was impossible to get to his herd. The brute took little or no notice of the buffaloes, seeming bent on having him for supper. He had been shouting for help for a long time, and had not some one come soon, he could not have held out much longer, as the tiger had been getting bolder every minute, and he was continually expecting it to make a spring on him. After firing a couple of shots in the direction that the tiger had taken, and escorting the aheer and his herd closer to the village, he and his men returned.

The president also related that once a party of gentlemen were out in the district on an official tour, one of the principal of them having a clever khansamah, in whom great trust was placed, and who, being too obese for travelling on foot, was accommodated through his master's generosity with a pony to ride on.

As the camp equipage was going along through the jungle, it came to a place where the road was very narrow, forming a long lane for three or four hundred yards. In this lane the sumpter animals, elephants, camels, ponies, bullocks, and servants of all kinds, some on foot, others on ponies, were crowded, and some obstacle ahead causing the whole procession to stop, a scene of great confusion soon arose.

The khansamah was lagging behind, taking it easy, when the stoppage commenced, but after awhile, knowing that *he* would have to bear the brunt of the wigging if breakfast should be delayed, he was hurrying to the front as fast as he could make his pony push through the crowd of animals and men.

The khansamah, it appeared, had got to about the centre of the lane when an enormous tiger sprang into the midst of the throng, scattering the animals and men to the right and left, and selecting the fat man as the choicest morsel, seized him by one of his arms and bore him off, as a cat would a mouse, into the depths of the jungle.

The panic caused by such an event made confusion worse confounded. The cattle in their terror threw their loads, and were rushing about wildly here and there trying to escape, the men shouting, some to scare the tiger, others to calm the terror of their animals, the cast-off burdens meanwhile blocking up the road to those behind, while men were hastening from the front to ascertain the cause of the confusion.

None of the servants being armed, and the jungle being very thick, when order was a little restored, and all knew what had happened, it would have been little short of madness to have pursued the tiger, which moreover had by that time got far enough off with his victim.

CHAPTER XXXI.

THE LEAN KHANSAMAH'S STORY.

THE next feasible thing proposed was, that some one should mount the khansamah's pony, which, though terribly scared, had not been touched by the tiger, and hasten forwards to the gentlemen with the news of the unfortunate occurrence. Directly the gentlemen got at the gist of the man's statement, made in a very rambling, confused manner, they turned their horses' heads, and galloped back to the scene of the disaster.

An inspection of the locality, together with the imperviousness of the jungle, convinced them of the impossibility of having a hankwa then, and the nature of their official duties preventing their making any delay, obliged them to defer avenging the death of the khansamah, hoping to be able on a future occasion to call the tiger to account for his misdeeds.

Their guest here remarked that he remembered hearing a droll incident in connection with another khansamah meeting a tiger, which ended ludicrously, but happily for the man's safety.

Three or four gentlemen had been invited to accompany a certain magistrate, on his usual cold weather official tour, through a part of his extensive district, where there was every promise of an abundance of game.

The magistrate's khansamah, in this instance, was far from being obese. On the contrary, he was of a very lean and spare habit. The man had but recently entered his new employer's service, and had done so, not so much for the pay, as the pickings he expected, and the opportunities of providing good billets for his kith and kin.

Being an atrocious coward, and having a great antipathy to tigers, he was in a state of mortal trepidation, when ordered by his master to prepare everything for a month's tour in the jungles. Pretending sudden illness, he tried to get off from going, by giving a substitute, but, on being sent for, and told in a few plain words either to get things ready or resign the service, not liking the latter alternative, he managed as suddenly to get well.

After the camp had been out three or four days, the khansamah reported to his employer that some few items, important in the culinary department, had, in the hurry of departure, been omitted, and requested orders being given for a man to proceed to a market town, a mile or two off the route, for the purpose of laying in a stock.

The magistrate, nettled at the man's negligence, ordered him personally to go at once and purchase what was necessary, to be quick about the business, and join the camp at a place about five miles distant from where they then were.

The khansamah knew that whoever went, he would have to pass through a patch of jungle to get to the market town, and through a large belt to rejoin the camp, and this order *for him* to go on the business caused beads of perspiration to break out all over his body.

Endeavouring, however, to conceal his fright, he tried to induce some of his fellow-servants to accompany him, but they, knowing his weakness, enjoyed his dilemma, and positively refusing to go with him, he was fain to set forth alone, and without delay.

He had reached the market town safely, had made his purchases, and was on his return through the larger belt of jungle, when, about two miles from the camp, a monster of a tiger, as he described it, with a light leap bounded over some bushes into the road right before him, and only a few paces distant.

The man's own relation of the matter was, that he was so overcome by fright at meeting with one of the dreadful animals which he most feared, that he did not know what to do. But being rather vain of his oratorical powers, vulgarly called the gift of the gab, he determined on trying what a little soft sawder would do.

Throwing down his bundle, and going on his knees, was the work of a moment; then, taking off his turban and placing it on the ground in front of him, he joined the palms of his hands together, in a very respectful humbly petitioning style, and began to speechify the tiger thus :—

"My lord," said he, "you see a poor fellow before you, without the slightest desire of trespassing on your domain, much less of intruding into your presence, but, compelled by the harsh order of my employer to traverse this forest, it has been my misfortune to darken your exalted excellency's presence with my insignificant shadow.

"I am a very poor man, with a wife and several small children, whom I find it exceedingly difficult to support; and as they have no one else to look to for a mouthful of food, should your excellency's highness be pleased to make a meal of me, they would be left entirely destitute.

"Trusting that these considerations may induce your sublime highness to have pity on me, and allow me to proceed on my way uninjured, I have ventured to address this humble petition to your excellency's majesty.

"Besides, if your excellency's highness will only condescend to look at me better," (and here he opened his vest, showing his ribs,) "you will perceive that I am of a very spare habit, that I am little better than a bag of bones, a walking shadow, not worthy of one moment of your exalted highness's consideration.

"Most exalted prince of the forest, I submit it to your highness's judgment, whether my lean and spare habit" (and with that he stripped off his chupkun, or coat, showing his buff,) "would afford you a single toothsome morsel." This brilliant oratorical display was mingled with incessant bows, prostrating himself at times until his forehead touched the ground.

Now, whether the tiger understood the man's speech and gestures (the man himself, the story goes, asserts that the tiger evidently perfectly understood all that he said and did), or not, is a moot point. Whether the tiger, after a fuller examination of the man (every facility being afforded by the human for that purpose), did not think the biped really worth the trouble of eating, or whether it did not know what to make of the fellow's gesticulations, or finally, whether it was tired of the incessant vociferations of the lean khansamah (for the speech was not delivered in a whisper), or not, the tiger, giving vent to a contemptuous growl of disgust, at both the pusillanimity and leanness of the biped, with a light spring bounded back over the bushes into the jungle, leaving the happily released khansamah to pursue his way, in a bath of perspiration, singing *sotto voce*, " O be joyful." Gossip says that a villager was a concealed spectator of the whole comedy, and his report, together with that of the khansamah, is embodied in the above relation.

It having by that time got late, the whole party retired for the night, after taking a last glass of punch, orders having been given for the camp to move early, and breakfast to be prepared at Ghurwar. After a sound sleep untroubled by nightmare, they were awaked early the next morning by their guest, who said he was sorry to report that the victim had not been killed.

This news caused great disappointment, as, in expectation of being detained, orders had been given for the breakfast to be prepared elsewhere, otherwise they might have had the company of their guest longer. Failing in the hankwa, they tried to persuade their guest to go and breakfast with them, promising him a horse or the elephant to return on; but he said that it would involve his being absent too long, especially as he had some very particular work in hand which must be attended to that day.

Not having a chance at another tiger, they then determined on spending an hour or two at the jheel, after the snipe, &c., and dressed accordingly. A chota hazreh, or literally small breakfast, being discussed, they bade a hearty farewell to their guest, thanking him for the assistance he had been to them, and for his agreeable company, and mounting their several animals, proceeded towards Ghurwar.

On their way they saw a large elephant, without any attendant, feeding leisurely in the fields, at the expense of the poor cultivators, destroying with his feet as much as or more than what he consumed. One of the party protesting against such wrong and oppression, declared that if he only knew who was the owner he would write to the district magistrate.

The president said that the only individual who could pretend, in those parts, to keep an elephant was the rajah, and whom they were so desirous of visiting. The man was known to be in reduced circumstances, but pride induces him to keep an elephant, as part of the state of a native prince, although unable to bear the expense of its keep. No good would come of bringing such matters to official notice. A letter might come down to the rajah on the subject, which would only cause him to take revenge in some shape.

Many iniquitous things are done in India and other countries that never come to light, and if honest English indignation were to run full tilt against every abuse, we should have Don Quixote charging the windmills every moment.

The poor in every country are oppressed, and he supposed will be to the end of the chapter, until the day of reckoning comes, and then, in the general uprising of the lower classes, the bad specimens of the upper ten thousand will meet with their deserts, many of the good ones most probably being involved, in the indiscriminating anger of the mob, in the same fate, as it was in France.

When they reached Khairwah the party dismounted, and sending the animals on to the camp, they proceeded on foot to the jheel, where an hour was spent very satisfactorily, and when they reached the camp, as breakfast was not ready, they strolled about shooting partridges, green pigeons, and a couple of peacocks.

Then returning again to the tents, they sat down to and enjoyed an excellent meal.

While enjoying their cheroots after breakfast, one of the servants came to say that a passing traveller reported that a tiger was doing much damage at Bilwadah, having killed two or three bullocks. A tiger being at the next camping-ground was good news, as it was their intention to proceed the following day to Bilwadah, where they resolved to stay two or three days rather than not shoot that tiger.

One of the party—Brown—being heard to scold some of the servants, the others went to hear what it was about, and found him very irate because the feathers of a teal had been thrown on the fire and consumed. On being chaffed about it, he said that the feathers of themselves were of course of little value, but as that kind of teal was the only one shot, he wanted the feathers to add to his collection, and then showed the rest a large bag three parts filled with all sorts of feathers.

He said further that shortly after starting, the idea came into his mind to make a unique feather pillow for himself, at a cheap rate, and had therefore ordered the soft feathers of every kind of bird shot to be daily brought to him, and added them to his collection.

The idea seeming rather a good one, Wilcox declared that he too would have a feather pillow, and so all future birds that might be shot were ordered to be carefully plucked and the feathers to be brought to the main tent. But Wilcox, being chaffed about its being rather late in the tour to begin, said that in his case quantity of each kind must make up for variety.

They next ordered the servants to put out in the sun the skins of the various animals killed during the tour, and while seeing this done, and examining the skins, the president said that he recollected a story of a tiger and tigress visiting the bungalow of an indigo planter once in the daytime, and would relate it if they adjourned to the tent. By that time tiffin was ready, and when that had been discussed, cheroots lighted, and so forth, the president proceeded with his story as follows :—

CHAPTER XXXII.

THE PLANTER VISITED BY TIGERS.

THE event, he said, happened at an indigo factory, in the Mirzapore district. A friend had come on a visit to the planter, and after inquiries concerning mutual friends, the visitor was taken over the works, and then to an out-station, where the planter purposed spending the day and sleeping; and while there his friend asked if there were any tigers about the neighbourhood, as he particularly wanted a skin for a—friend.

The planter, understanding at once, banteringly expressed his surprise that matters had gone so far, and asked when the happy day was to be, and so on, and then seriously informed him that there were two tigers about the place, and not far off either, quite unconscious of how literally true his words were.

As he was about to tell his friend where would be a good place to have a hankwa, a servant came running in to say that two tigers were coming direct towards the bungalow, and were close to it then.

Not believing the man's word, the planter got up and went to the door to see for himself, the servant meanwhile vanishing. Hardly had he looked out, when, stepping back quickly, he told his friend instantly to climb up the other side of the bungalow, get on the cross beam, and not stir for his life.

Seeing the planter climbing, the friend climbed too, and both had scarcely got seated when a large tiger showed itself in the verandah, at the door of the room. The brute gave a look in, but, not satisfied, came in half its length, and after a searching look around, and a stare aloft, it upset a stool that happened to be close to the door.

The noise that the stool made in falling startled the tiger, causing it to make a quick step back into the verandah, and this sudden action alarmed the tigress, which was close behind, causing her to spring off the verandah into the compound and walk off. The tiger, seeing its mate going away, tried to recall her by a sort of low growl, but instead of returning she broke into a trot, and the tiger after her.

When the tiger came up to its mate there was a matrimonial squabble between them, the two growling at each other, and clapper-clawing in a sort of friendly way. The noise they made showed them to be at a safe distance, and then the planter and his friend descended from their elevated positions.

Rushing to the inner room, they quickly fastened the doors and windows in case the brutes should return, and seizing their guns, they made for the other room, one door of which they also fastened. They then cautiously looked out into the verandah and round about, but not seeing anything of the tigers, one took one side of the house and the other the opposite side, and walked round to the back.

Just as they had met, the two tigers were seen in the plain, going away from the cover of some bushes, about a quarter of a mile off. The planter and his friend were in a state of intense indignation; they had never known or heard of such impudence; they had never been so tree-ed in their life, and they would make the brutes pay for their temerity.

In order to understand the story better, it should be stated that the bungalow was a small one, at an out station of the factory, visited only occasionally, and, through being seldom visited, these tigers, by the boldness they displayed, showed that they must have been there previously, and perhaps often.

The small bungalow consisted of two rooms, the doors of which looked east and west, one window north and the other south, with a door in the centre of the party wall between the rooms. The bungalow was surrounded by a verandah, about ten feet wide, and had a small bath-room at the south-east corner, with the door opening into the verandah.

The bungalow fronted the west, and the pleasantest of the two rooms was the east one, being shaded by a large tree, and was used as the sitting-room. Coats, hats, and guns were in the west, or bed-room; and the tigers coming from the east, and being close to the verandah when seen by the planter, gave no time to rush into and secure the doors of the west room, and seize their guns.

Being an out-station bungalow, seldom visited for any lengthened period, the beams and rafters were not concealed by the usual cloth serving as a ceiling, and the side posts, not being plastered over, rendered the work of climbing easy and speedy of accomplishment, and for which there was barely time.

The planter and his friend were wild at having been made to perform "'possum up a gum tree," and, summoning some of the factory people, they set one to watch that the tigers did not pay them a return visit. Another was sent to buy a victim, and a third to call the village shikari, who when he came had instructions where to tie it up for a hankwa the next day.

Determined to lose no chance, the guns and rifles were overhauled, cleaned, and carefully loaded. The factory people and servants being greatly alarmed, it was judged prudent to have dinner over before night set in, that the house might be secured, the servants taking good care of themselves.

The next morning the welcome information of "a kill," was received, and, the surrounding villagers having readily assembled, the two friends made for the appointed spot, and had the satisfaction of bagging both the tigers. In the excess of their joy at so speedily avenging their own enforced disgrace, they gave liberal largess, in addition to the usual pay distributed, to the hankwa.

The friend, on presenting the tiger-skin to his inamorata, did not fail to add that "thereby hangs a tale," and, being asked for it then and subsequently, his humorous account of how the planter

SMITH SHOOTS A YOUNG BOA-CONSTRICTOR. 201

and himself were tree-ed on the cross-beam of the bungalow, always elicited roars of laughter.

When the president had finished his story, he ordered beer to be brought, and, taking a glass each, they all went out for a short stroll before dinner. After shooting a deer and a few birds, they saw a monstrous snake, partly coiled round a young tree, engaged in swallowing a hare. A rifle-ball from Smith through its head caused it to drop the hare and uncoil itself from the tree, when such a scene of wriggling and twisting occurred, in its dying struggles, as made all the party fall back a good distance out of the way of the blood which was being spattered about in all directions.

When the last convulsive movements had ceased, and the party could have a nearer and better view, the snake turned out to be a young boa-constrictor apparently, twelve and a half feet long, as measured at the tents, where it was speedily carried by relays of men, who complained of its great weight. Directing the deer and snake to be skinned immediately, dinner was ordered, and after due attention to their toilettes, was sat down to with usual appetites.

The mysterious conference of the caterer with the khansamah resulted in the wild ducks and teal being cooked in a way that was pronounced delicious, the only regret being that there were not more shot. Dinner being over, and orders given for the camp to move early the next morning for Bilwadah, the party assembled round the fire as usual, passing the time in talking or singing, until the president and the whole party feeling tired, with the prospect of rousing early for the march, they all turned into bed.

A clear, frosty morning induced them, after awaking early, to walk a considerable part of the way, and so enjoy the bracing air. Not long after leaving Ghurwar, and after passing the camp equipage, when they had commenced the gentle ascent they noticed the perfectly fresh footprints of a large tiger in the middle of the road.*

On carefully examining them, the president gave it as his opinion that the tiger must be almost in sight, certainly it could not be many minutes ahead of them. The guns were soon taken from the hands of the servants, and, fresh caps being put on, they proceeded forwards, keeping a sharp look-out in all directions, until they came to rather an abrupt rising near Beyreeádee, where the footprints showed that the tiger had turned off to the left, down into a broken hollow covered with thick jungle.

Not thinking it advisable to run any needless risk by trying for a shot at the tiger on foot, they continued their walk until they reached the top of the rising ground at Beyreeádee. While waiting here for the horses to come up, they took a look round at the scenery, and could not help being struck with the appropriateness of the title, Basin of Singrowlee; the district of Singrowlee thereabouts being embosomed in, and environed by, a chain of hills, the whole forming as complete a basin on a large scale as could well be conceived.

The horses and elephant having come up, the whole party mounted, and soon reaching Bilwadah, a man was sent off at once for the shikari, who came quickly and gave a doleful report of his, among others, personal loss of a breeding cow carried off by the tiger. He was glad that the gentlemen had come, as he thought there could not be a better opportunity for killing the brute.

The tiger had that morning, not half an hour previous, killed a bullock, and dragged it to a place where were some trees suitable for sitting up in. After killing the bullock, the tiger had left it a few minutes ago and was then away, but might be expected to return shortly. He thought that there was time enough for all the party

---

* On one occasion, the writer well recollects having followed, at this very place, in the rear (as shown clearly by the fresh footprints) of a tiger and tigress, and a cub nearly full grown.

to get seated in the trees, if they would start at once and go quickly.

No second hint being required, they soon followed the shikari, who led them to a very lonely spot, admirably suited for a tiger's lair. Selecting their several trees, they soon climbed up and were seated in silent watchfulness for the advent of the depredator. They had not long to wait; the tiger had apparently left the bullock only to call its mate, for two, a tiger and a tigress, were seen coming along up a ravine.

Making hasty signals among themselves, they waited until the huge cats had come up to the dead bullock, when the tiger, after giving a look at its mate, as much as to say, " See ! haven't I got a nice breakfast for you, my dear?"—little dreaming of the kind of breakfast he was in reality going to have—tore open the stomach of the bullock, and had placed his mouth at the hole so made to suck out the entrails, when a general volley, half directed at the tiger, and half at the tigress, furnished them with an unexpected dish. The tigress fell dead, but the tiger, although mortally wounded, rose on its hind legs, roaring fearfully with rage and pain, and then bolted off down the ravine.

Every one was about descending from their trees when the shikari called out for them to stay where they were for a few minutes, adding that the tiger could not live many minutes, but had strength enough left to make it too dangerous to encounter him just then. After waiting a few minutes they had the satisfaction of hearing the growls of the tiger grow fainter and fainter, until the noise ceased altogether. The shikari then said that he would get down and reconnoitre, and, having done so, he returned, saying that the tiger appeared dead, but advised their being careful how they approached until they were sure.

After getting down from their trees and looking well to their guns, they followed the shikari who, when they came in sight of the tiger lying at full length on the stones, threw a stone and hit it on the head above one of its eyes, to ascertain if it were dead or not. Jumping up with an apparently expiring effort, and with its eyes glaring wildly, it was about to make a charge, when a ball aimed full at its chest dropped it without a struggle.

Sure then of its death, the shikari made a peculiar jubilant outcry, which soon brought several villagers round the party. The whole affair having been over so soon, the shikari was ordered to send four men with the tigers to the camp, and for himself and other men to attend them into the jungles for some deer shooting. In half an hour or so they had killed two deer, a pig, a magnificent peacock, and a brace of young ones. Having been so successful, they were satisfied with their morning's work, and returned to the camp, where they found breakfast waiting for them.

After having a good wash, which they all needed, they sat down to an ample meal, with appetites such as can only be got by plenty of exercise in a good bracing air. Their keen hunger having been at last satisfied, they lingered over the rest of the meal, talking over their extraordinarily good fortune that morning in having had such capital sport in such a short space of time.

CHAPTER XXXIII.

A FLOCK OF PARROTS.

WHEN breakfast was over, the paymaster was called upon to give the shikari, and the men who had been out with them and had brought in the game, a liberal present, which sent them away highly pleased, and making profound salaams, after which the party superintended skinning the tigers and deer, and breaking up the latter.

Then, as they had a long day before them, the larder being full obviating any necessity for going out again for anything to keep the pot boiling, selecting a shady place under the trees, they had camp folding-chairs brought, with a camp table and glasses put on it. When these arrangements had been completed, and the party were seated with lighted cheroots in full operation, the president entertained them with the relation of further items of his jungle experience.

In the afternoon, some of them wishing to examine closer the cultivation of some fields, they all went for a walk in that direction, and, as they were going through some growing corn, they roused such a cloud of green parrots as startled and astonished most of the party, and which cloud, by general guess, must have consisted of not less than two to three thousand birds.

As these parrots, besides immense flocks of minahs, starlings, doves, &c., live almost entirely at the expense of the cultivators, it was determined by general vote to thin the flock; so, drawing every ball but those of the rifles, and loading with No. 6, they spread themselves a good distance apart and prepared for a regular battue, the parrots meanwhile having settled again.

When they were all ready, the president, who was nearest the flock, approached cautiously until getting within shot, the parrots alarmed rose together, allowing him a good chance right and left. The rest of the party, as the flock wheeled about screaming, had each a chance of firing into the dense mass, until the parrots, thoroughly scared, flew straight off a long distance into the jungle, every now and then a wounded bird dropping to the ground.

Wishing to know the result, all were busy picking up the dead, and running after and killing the wounded birds. Collecting them into one heap, the servants counted them, and told off one hundred and sixty-three parrots as the result of ten shots only, besides many that were seen to drop as the flock flew out of distance, and those that were wounded and yet had strength enough left to fly up into the trees.

Several of the dead birds were half cut in two, and others with their heads half cut off, which, exciting wonder, Brown said that the flock approaching him edge on, he had fired his rifle, which was in his hand at the moment, and he fancied that those birds must be his.

One of the servants was then directed to take the parrots to the tents, with orders for the soft feathers to be plucked off, and the bodies given to whoever chose to have them, but a difficulty arose how to carry them. This was solved by one of the attendants going to the village, and borrowing a large grain basket, into which the parrots were tumbled and carried off. So much time had been spent in the parrot-shooting that they were obliged to return direct to the tents, picking up, however, a brace of hares and peacocks on the road.

On their way back, Smith expressed his surprise at the number of parrots they had seen, and wondered how the cultivators could secure any crop worth gathering. The president answered that he had wondered a good many times too, when he thought of the immense amount of damage that was, all the year round, done to the crops.

INGENIOUS PLAN FOR CATCHING PARROTS. 207

Directly the grain begins to sprout he had seen flocks of parrots, minahs, or other birds, picking out the young plants, and eating the grain; and when the remainder has grown a bit, deer, night or day, may continually be seen browsing on the young plants. When the crops are coming into ear, or when the different kinds of grain are forming, again deer may be seen eating their fill, or large flocks of parrots or other birds may be seen fattening themselves.

Then again, when the crops are ripening, droves of wild pigs during the night live at free quarters on them, while, during the day, parrots, minahs, &c., take their fill. If the crops are near a river, large tank, or jheel, flocks of wild ducks, geese, &c., especially on moonlight nights, must be added to the number of those that feed on both the green and ripening crops.

When all these things are considered, *it is* a wonder how any crops at all are gathered in some parts of the country, and no one could justly say that they had not done the cultivators good service by thinning that flock of parrots.

Some few cultivators do put up scarecrows, but birds and beasts soon get used to them. In some fields also there are watch-houses erected, but in jungly parts the watchmen themselves occasionally disappear, carried off by tigers.

In one or two places infested with parrots, he had seen an ingenious way of catching and destroying them. Stout stakes are planted all about the field, not too far apart, and these are connected by strings, on which lengths of bamboo, four to six inches each, are strung, the bamboos being of sufficient diameter to allow of a parrot's claws taking firm hold. A boy is also stationed to watch the field, armed with a short thick stick, like a small ruler.

The parrots alight on the corn, bite off an ear, and, seeing these bits of bamboo handy, fly on to them to enjoy the corn at their leisure. They have hardly got a firm grasp, when round goes the bamboo tube, and of course the parrot with it, underneath. Unwilling to let go the ear of corn, or his hold of the bamboo, the thief is seen and heard, fluttering and screaming, trying its best to get uppermost, when the boy runs up and gives him a knock on the head, which settles the question.

He was one day going to Kotah, by a short cut over the fields, and, putting up just such another flock of parrots as they had seen, fired only one barrel and brought down thirteen dead, and five wounded too bad to get away, besides wounding several which managed to escape. The flock was so thick, and rose in such a cloud, so near, that almost every shot must have told.

On arriving at the tents, they saw several syces and others busy stripping the parrots, and evidently pleased at the prospect of a good feed before them. Some of the party expressing a wish to taste parrot flesh, a few were ordered to be grilled for dinner. After attending to their toilettes they found the shikari waiting, who asked what was to be done with the victim he had been ordered to purchase.

It should have been stated before this, that too many male buffaloes, or bulls, in a herd, are no profit to their owners, consequently they are glad to dispose of superfluous stock to gentlemen requiring them, as a "victim" is always a young male buffalo, or a bull calf.

The president here explained to the rest, that he had sent on a man the day previous to have a victim tied up, but it had been saved by the tiger killing some other animal. He then informed the shikari that in the morning they had traced a tiger nearly to Beyreeádee, which possibly might come on that night, and therefore he was to tie the victim up again on the chance, and if killed they would spend one more day at Bilwadah; if not, they would leave after breakfast.

With this understanding the shikari took his leave, and dinner being announced, they all sat down to it with good appetites, not having had any lunch that day. When the edge of their appetite had been taken off by the substantial good cheer, those who wished tried the parrots, and said that on a pinch a man might do very well with enough of them, but they thought that if made into soup or stew they would be more palatable.

Assembling then around the usual fire, some general conversation followed, until, feeling tired, they all retired for the night, after the president had ordered an early start for such of the camp equipage as was not wanted.

The next morning early, the shikari came and reported "no kill," which was a disappointment; but, as they were all dressed, they went out for a walk, as well as to get whatever might come in their way. Having bagged a deer, a porker, and a few partridges, they returned to camp, where breakfast was waiting, to which they sat down with great good-will.

During the meal it was proposed that as the shikari had been useful to them, and had suffered a recent loss by one of the tigers killed, the "victim" should be presented to him, as a reward extra for his zealous exertions on their behalf, which accordingly was done.

After breakfast the whole party mounted their several animals, and returned to Muggurdah, passing through Molayun Sote, a small, straggling village in a cheerless part of the hills. Being the first to reach the camping-ground, above the water-hole, they found that the servants had selected a better position for the tents, giving them an opportunity of witnessing to better advantage the various preparations for camping of successive parties of native traders and travellers.

Not being inclined for further exercise that day, they ordered a servant to bring plenty of hot water, and occupied themselves in thoroughly washing out and cleaning all their guns, &c., until there was only just enough time left to wash themselves and dress, when dinner was announced.

While busily engaged in discussing the good things provided, they were disturbed and somewhat annoyed at a great outcry raised by different parties of travellers, in which they heard sundry not over-complimentary references to themselves.

P

A servant having been sent out to inquire into the cause of the disturbance, and why they were mixed up in it, on his return he reported that the elephant and one of the camels had got loose ; that the camel had bitten one of a party of brinjarries (goods' carriers), who were very angry ; that the elephant had walked about the camping place of several parties of travellers, upsetting their cooking-pots, eating up rice, vegetables or chuppattees (hand bread) wherever he could get them ; and, on one man trying to drive him away, the elephant gave him a blow with its trunk, and had hurt him considerably ; and that a good number of the travellers had come to the tents to complain.

Here was a nice kettle of fish ! Ordering the servant to request the people to wait for a few minutes, the party hurriedly finished their dinner, and then went out to inquire more particularly into the cause of the hubbub.

When dinner was over, and plenty of wood had been heaped on the fire to throw a good light on the scene, which would have afforded an admirable subject for Salvator Rosa, or any celebrated painter of night scenes, partially relieved by strong light, the gentlemen having summoned the elephant and camel drivers, took their seats by the fire, and commenced their investigation into what threatened to be a troublesome affair.

Inquiring first if the men who had been hurt by the elephant and camel severally were present, and learning that they were, examination proved that they were more frightened than hurt, that their hurts were nothing more than simple bruises ; the man knocked down by the elephant having received his bruise by falling on a large brass cooking vessel, and the man seized by the camel having been almost instantly released by some other man striking the camel sharply on the nose.

So far matters were greatly simplified, the affair resulting in a charge of assault and battery against the elephant and camel severally, or their owners and employers, and against the elephant for felony in addition.

On interrogating the mahout, or elephant driver, as to the cause of the elephant's being loose, he said that he had been gone just a few minutes to see if he could buy any vegetables from any of the travellers, and that during his absence the under-keeper had somehow neglected his duty, and the elephant had got loose; that directly he heard the uproar he ran and secured the animal, leading it back to its place, and himself properly fastening it.

CHAPTER XXXIV.

THE UNDER-KEEPER'S STATEMENT.

HERE the under-keeper noisily interrupted the proceedings by saying that the fault was *not* his; he had gone into the bushes for a necessary purpose, leaving the mahout sitting by the elephant smoking his hookah; that, on his return neither driver nor elephant was to be seen; that thinking it possible that the driver had taken the elephant to the water-hole to drink, he was looking out his rice for his evening meal, when, hearing a great noise, he turned round and saw the elephant among the traders; that *he* ran up and brought the elephant back, and not the mahout, as many men could prove; that the mahout, after the elephant had been secured, had returned, abused him greatly, and also beaten him; that the mahout never attended to the elephant, leaving all the work to be done by the under-keeper, and that all that the mahout did was to drive the elephant, and when that was done, smoke his hookah.

The last remark tickled every one so much that a burst of laughter was the result, which so angered the mahout as to cause him to fly at the under-keeper, and a pretty little row would have been the result, had not the other servants interfered and restrained the violence of the angry man.

Other parties having been examined, and the under-keeper's statement corroborated in every particular, the president, addressing the mahout, said that, according to his own admission, this was the second time in which he had been absent from his post, that he alone should be fined this time, and at the end of the journey, unless there were a marked improvement in his conduct, be dismissed from the employ; that a native punchayet, or jury, of five should assess the damages, and that he was at liberty to name two of the jury.

On asking the camel-driver how his camel got loose, he at once confessed that the rope with which the animal was tied was rather rotten, and had broken, but that directly the camel was observed to be loose he had run after and secured it, just as a man had made it release the person seized.

All the evidence being heard, the president said that it would be more satisfactory to allow the men to settle the matter of compensation among themselves, which, being agreed to by the rest, he ordered another punchayet in the affair of the camel, informing the driver that he might choose two jurymen. The crowd of natives having dispersed to hold the two courts, the caterer busied himself in brewing a tureen of punch, which on trial appeared to give general satisfaction.

During the interval of the absence of the natives, elephants, wild and tame, being the topic of conversation, the president remarked that his brother had informed him of sundry pranks performed by a dangerous wild elephant, in the district of Goruckpore, that had been expelled from elephant society in general for conduct derogatory to elephant morals. This brute, in course of time, was cunning enough to waylay the natives as they returned from making their purchases of rice, sugar, vegetables, or sugar-cane.

It seldom molested a man or woman without a bundle, but those who carried bundles were surprised, and subsequently terrified, at finding their heads relieved suddenly of their burdens, and, on turning round, seeing the wild elephant within a yard of them. Those who knew the animal soon gave it a wide berth, for if they hesitated the elephant settled the matter by settling them.

Strangers sometimes remonstrated, and tried to regain their property, but the elephant put its veto on that, and its feet on the bodies, after knocking the man or woman down, or else put its tusks through the bodies.

One native had apparently roused the anger of the brute, as it was seen by others, not content with simply killing the man, but vented its rage in pounding and pressing the dead body until it was an undistinguishable mass of smashed bones, flesh, blood, and mud mixed up together.

Things went on so until the people were afraid of going even to the next village alone. When they were obliged to go to market, they used to go in companies, but, as the elephant learned not to fear one man, so in time it came not to fear a dozen, and on their return it always made one or more pay toll by leaving their bundles behind, glad if they escaped with their lives.

The brute once overtook a man resting by the wayside with his two pitchers of native liquor, but, seeing the elephant approach, he vanished, leaving the grog behind, which the brute tasted and approved of so much, that it kept a special watch on all spirit carriers, waiting until it saw them resting themselves, when it would rush up, scare them away, and then enjoy itself.

An indigo planter once had a narrow escape from the brute. Going on a visit to another factory ten or twelve miles off, he had to pass through a part of the country ranged over by this wild, mad elephant, and had got rather more than half-way on his journey when, at a sharp turn of the road round some rocks, he came right upon the elephant standing a few paces off the road, evidently on the watch for travellers.

Fortunately, he was mounted on a swift Arab, and was an excellent horseman, otherwise he would, to a certainty, have been spilled by the spring-round which his horse made.

There was no need to apply whip or spur, the horse flew along at its utmost speed, terrified at the sight and the snort, together with the rush of the elephant, which tore along after horse and rider, getting, at times, just close enough to pull a hair or two out of the horse's streaming tail, causing it to bound off with fresh terror.

The running made by horse and elephant was excellent, the

race leading over about one mile of country, some of which was very broken, so much so, that, had he his choice, he would never have risked his horse's legs or his own neck by a gallop over such ground. The elephant at last seemed to think that it had had sufficient exercise for that day, and so gave up the chase.

The planter declared that he had never ridden so fast before in his life, and never wanted to again ; that he backed himself thereafter against any known or unknown jockey ; that a race for life with a mad, wild elephant pelting after you, nibbling at your horse's tail, was first-rate exercise, and a fine thing to teach a man a proper seat.

This mad brute was too cunning to be caught in any pitfall or other trap, and too dangerous to be boldly attacked and shot ; but after many natives had been killed, and after having been fired at without effect from an ambush, with large-bore rifles, by several European gentlemen, the elephant was at last destroyed by a poisoned arrow shot into its eye by a shikari, who was concealed in the branches of a tree, under which the brute came one day, decoyed there by a trained female elephant.

Further conversation was here interrupted by the return of the crowd of natives to report the decision of the two punchayets, or juries. That held on the camel gave in a verdict of one rupee (two shillings) damages, to be paid by the driver to the man bitten by the camel.

As no other loss or damage had been caused by the camel, the amount of fine was considered by all to have been very justly assessed, and being respectfully submitted to by the camel-driver, the paymaster was requested to pay it for him, the man himself being warned to take better care of his camels.

The jury held on the elephant gave in their verdict for five rupees (ten shillings) damages, to be apportioned thus : two rupees (four shillings) to be given to the man who had been knocked down and his life endangered by the elephant, and three rupees (six shillings) to be divided amongst those whose property had been either destroyed or eaten up by the elephant, and which damages were to be paid by the driver. In this case also the gentlemen agreed that the amount of damages had been very justly assessed.

The verdict having been communicated to the mahout, or elephant driver, caused that respectable individual to be very irate, and to break out forthwith into a torrent of the vilest native abuse, levelled at all and sundry around him, not excepting even the gentlemen.

The Saxon temperament being nowhere noted for patient submission to vile personal abuse, the president ordered him to be seized, and, bringing out a riding-cane from the tent, he administered to him a sound and well-merited castigation for his foul language, which was wholly uncalled for, as he had been treated, together with the rest of the servants, with great consideration.

After being released and getting beyond the reach of the president's arm, he could not restrain his unruly member, but began threatening the president and the rest of the party with actions for assault and battery, ending with hurling at the president an epithet of gross personal abuse.

As such conduct was an aggravation of his offence, the order was given to *puckerlao*, or catch and bring him, whereupon he showed a clean pair of heels, followed by a posse of servants and travellers. Having been caught and brought back, the man suddenly altered his tone, begging humbly for forgiveness, declaring that the president was his father, *mother*, uncle, *aunt*, and all the rest of his relations, male and female put together, and that if the president visited with severity the petulance of his *own* son, to whom could he go, and so forth.

The man's volubility of tongue was so great that it was in vain to try to stop him without forcibly gagging him, so, waiting patiently until he had exhausted himself, the president told him very politely that it was *his* turn to speak, and the man's duty to isten. He then said that he and the rest of the party were quite prepared to meet the consequences of taking the law into their own hands, but that neither of them was prepared to put up with a repetition of personal abuse.

The full amount of damages, as assessed by the jury, together with a fine of two rupees (four shillings), should be levied from his pay, and if he absconded on the road he should be prosecuted. He (the president) had no intention of chastising him again, that proceeding taking little effect; he therefore intended to punish him further in another and more effectual way—he was to be tied up to a tree in the jungle for the night.

Great fear is said to work an extraordinary change in the subject of it, and this saying was verified in this case. The announcement of the sentence seemed to freeze the man's blood in his veins; his whole frame was so shaken that he could scarcely stand, while, in a scarcely audible voice, he begged for mercy. The president, seeing the effect produced that he had intended, pretended to relent, and, on the man's promising better behaviour for the future, he let him go once more.

The effect of the threat was such that there could not be a better servant of his class; the elephant ever after was well attended to, and his whole bearing towards his fellow-servants was completely altered; for, where he formerly bullied, he subsequently used the most conciliatory language. The alteration in his conduct was so much approved of, that his fine and the damages were at a later period remitted.

One of the party here remarked on the extreme terror exhibited by the mahout at the mere threat of being exposed to the chance visitation of a tiger or other wild animal, contrasting his behaviour with that of natives living out in the district, where the possibility of meeting with a tiger is no unusual occurrence.

The president replied that, suspecting the man to be a mere bully, he judged rightly that such a threat would take all the bounce out of him; not that he, for a moment, would think of putting his threat into execution. With regard to the difference in the behaviour of two classes of men, the citizen and the countryman, it is to be attributed to the enervating effects of a city or town life. He thought, however, that even the boldest countryman's courage would not be proof against such a threat.

Education properly conducted would, in course of time, create a factitious courage in even a previous arrant coward, that is, by degrees he might be brought to face the greatest dangers, which, without the education, he would no more have thought of doing than he would of flying. Some persons are naturally endowed with such an amount of fearless courage, that it, so to speak, crops out in their nature.

Others have a sufficient stock of latent courage, which, like heat, lies dormant in them until occasion arises, and then it bursts into refreshing and vigorous activity. Courage is an attribute of great minds, and a man or woman, boy or girl, may rise to the height of this moral greatness by progressive steps, or, *per saltum*, on an emergency. What is called the courage of despair is in many, if not most instances, simply suicide under another name. In illustration of this, he would relate a sad and affecting incident, which was credibly reported to him as a fact.

CHAPTER XXXV.

THE OLD WOMAN'S SAD LOT.

IN a village not far from a certain place on the Kymore plateau where he was once stationed, there lived a poor old woman, whose husband, children, and other relations had all died, leaving her alone in the world. The poor creature struggled on for several years, gaining a scanty pittance, on which she barely supported life.

The time, however, came when she could no longer work, and then she took to soliciting charity, but her strength failing at length, she could no longer go even to the village nearest to her own on a begging expedition, and then she became chargeable and troublesome to her neighbours.

The poor in England lead a hard enough life, but the poor in India—God help them!—theirs *is* a hard lot indeed. " Man's inhumanity to man" is only too forcibly exemplified in the latter country.

Driven from door to door, sometimes getting a scanty meal, oftener going without, abused by all, jeered at by the young, and taunted with living so long, she one night went to the jungle purposely to be killed by some wild beast. Several nights she repeated her visit, but no wild beast would touch her!

She informed the villagers before her death that on three or four nights a tiger had come up to her, and she was rejoicing to think that her trouble would soon be over, but the animal passed by, and although she had tried to anger it (by throwing stones or clods of earth at it), she did not succeed in inducing it to kill her.

The exposure to the night dews and chilly air, added to her

otherwise hard lot, soon brought on that death which she had sought, but which even savage beasts would not give her.

By the time the story was finished it had got very late, so, after the president had given orders for an early start the next day, and breakfast to be prepared at Oobra, they all retired for the night.

Early in the morning they were wakened by the noise of the various parties of native travellers and traders packing up and setting out for their several destinations, some towards Singrowlee, and others in the same direction as themselves. A cup of hot coffee, chuppattees, and cold meat having been partaken of, and the camp equipage all started, the party amused themselves for some time in watching the pea-fowl issuing from the jungle, and strutting about over the deserted camping-ground, picking up the remains of the numerous meals of the previous night—rice, bits of hand bread, or grain spilled.

As the morning was cold, a walk for a few miles was generally agreed to, and on starting they all passed between peacocks so close that they might have struck them with their riding-whips or canes.

Two or three miles of ground were soon gone over, when the attention of the rest was suddenly attracted to a spotted deer, which one of them pointed out as coming at a great rate from the jungle on the right hand, making for the opposite jungle. Although it was fleeing for its life, being evidently chased by a tiger or leopard, yet hunters' necessity, the larder needing replenishing, could not spare it, and therefore a well-directed shot dropped it almost on the road while crossing.

Here one of the party, who was anxious for it, had the opportunity of trying his skill in skinning, disembowelling, and breaking up the deer, and so lightening the load for the syces (grooms) to carry, the party then mounting their horses. Those who chose the elephant could not help remarking the altered behaviour of the mahout (driver), and the already improved appearance of the elephant.

A SINGULAR-LOOKING BUTTERFLY.

On arriving at Oobra they found that the delay on starting, and on the road in breaking up the deer, which, being a first attempt, had been very fairly done, had enabled the tents to be pitched and breakfast to be got ready. The necessary alteration being made in their toilettes, breakfast was sat down to with keen appetites.

The meal being over, and all being refreshed with a couple of hours' rest, as they had not had a comfortable bath for several days, they determined on a double expedition, shooting their way up through the jungle to the place where they had bathed once before, and picking up what game they could on their return.

Ordering such of the camp followers as had taken their morning meal to follow, they started, and succeeded in shooting a nylgye on the way to the bathing-place, which they reached without further adventure. A good bath having set them up again, those who chose collected sundry specimens, and then lighting their cheroots they retraced their steps, without a chance of shooting anything, bird or beast.

The deer of the morning having been killed so late necessitated a later dinner than usual, and after most of the nylgye had been distributed to the camp followers, the party amused themselves in various ways, until, towards evening, when they went out for a stroll, and while out walking, one of the party saw, and tried in vain to catch, a very singular butterfly. Its wings were so shaped that, when settled on a flower sipping the nectar, it had the exact appearance of a double butterfly—a smaller one perched on the tips of the wings of a larger one.

Here another remarked that he, and no doubt the rest, had seen a curious insect, a kind of beetle, coming out of the ground. It was only seen in the morning, and was like a soft pad of bright scarlet velvet or plush. The president said that he had once collected a considerable quantity of them, intending to try what sort of a dye they would yield; but other avocations prevented his doing so. Another of the party remarked that the island of Ceylon was noted for its butterflies and insects of various kinds.

The president, however, thought that the Himalaya range was unequalled in the world, for not only the stupendous height, grandeur, and picturesque scenery of its mountains, hills, and valleys, but for the immense as well as the diminutive size, infinite variety and beauty of its butterflies, moths, beetles, insects of all kinds, mosses, ferns, and parasitical plants.

No conception can be formed of the various attributes of the Himalayas, and actual inspection only amazes, while it delights and instructs. A dozen geniuses placed fifty miles apart, blessed with a liberal competency, and possessed of indomitable patience, courage, hardness, artistical talent of a high order, and devoted to the calling from love of it, would not in a long life exhaust the boundless stores of beauty lavishly scattered over the Himalayas.

Returning from their walk without a chance of a shot at anything, they sat down to dinner, which was shortly after announced, and when that had been discussed they adjourned to the fire, where an hour was agreeably passed, until, feeling tired, they retired for the night, orders having been given for the camp to start early, and breakfast to be prepared at Chopun.

At daybreak the next morning one of the servants hurriedly awoke two or three of the party, saying that two wild animals were then fighting in the jungle close to the camp, but that none of them could make out what they were. Dressing hastily they took their guns and went out, but they also could not make out the sounds, except that a noise now and then seemed as if coming from a pig. Before it had got light enough to follow, the sounds gradually receded, until all was silent.

The sounds had been so undefined that the president confessed himself to be fairly at fault; he could not say to a certainty what the animals were that had been fighting, but he was strongly of opinion that it was either a tiger or a leopard overcoming a pig, and which subsequently proved to be the case by the footprints.

The larder being reported empty, the starting of the camp equipage was hastened, and the party then mounting rode on ahead, ordering some men to keep up with them, as they intended taking what game they could get into camp with them.

They had ridden scarcely a mile when a sounder of wild pigs burst out of the jungle to the right, close in front, but on seeing the party the pigs stood for a few moments confused, and then suddenly wheeling round, were bolting off back into the bush, when a quick shot from those who were prepared brought down three of their number. The camp equipage being almost in sight, it was determined on to wait and see the pigs properly bestowed before proceeding on.

While waiting, one of the party remarked on the uselessness of killing so much game, to which the president demurred, saying that so far from being useless, they were doing the cultivators of the land substantial service in killing all kinds of wild animals, even if they could not consume one-tenth of what was killed.

Moreover, it was good policy to have an abundance of meat in a large camp, for, were the different followers to live on their usual meagre diet they would not be so content, nor would the camp move as it had done. These classes of men, when out on a tour, look to having an abundant flesh diet, and those who are wise enough to provide it reap the benefit in good and willing service.

Already all the servants and camp followers, although marching ten to twenty miles per day, when moving camp, besides doing their own several regular work, show a considerable improvement in their personal appearance. When a charge of powder and a ball will bring down a deer that will feed ten or twenty men, it is not good policy to save it because your own larder happens to contain sufficient for personal wants.

Although, during the tour thus far, much game had been killed, there was not a single instance of wanton waste of life; of those animals that were eatable the prime parts had been reserved for themselves, and all the rest had been accounted for by the servants and followers, sharing equably among themselves, those whose prejudice (such as Moslems) would not allow them to eat pig's meat, taking deer's meat as their share.

As to dangerous animals, such as tigers, &c., he thought that no one could say a word against any number of them being killed. Were it not for Europeans destroying comparatively so many tigers, &c., the country would soon be overrun with wild beasts, and many villages would be depopulated.

In the remote eastern part of the district they were then in (Mirzapore), the site of more than one village could be pointed out, that had been depopulated by tigers, the few remaining inhabitants deserting the place as no longer tenable, except at the imminent risk of their lives.

During the above conversation the camels came up, and the pigs having been blooded and disembowelled on being shot, were stowed away, and the party set forward once more. When about one mile from Chopun they dismounted, sending the horses and elephant on by the road while they went through the jungle.

As they were going along, three spotted deer were roused, two of which were brought down in first-rate style by one gun, right and left barrel, the other one escaping, no one else happening to be ready. Another pig, a couple of pea-fowl and a hare being bagged, they were by that time close to the camping ground, which was reached just as the camp equipage came up. After resting awhile and getting cool, they took a change of clothes, with towels, &c., and went and had a refreshing bath in the delightful Soane.

When dressed, two couple of Brahminee ducks settled within ball range, and as there had been a controversy respecting the individual superiority of aim of some of them, it was suggested that a better opportunity could not offer for deciding the point; and being agreed to, it was resolved that the four competitors should select his particular duck, and fire at a signal given by the president, who, with the disengaged member, was to watch the result of each shot.

When all were ready, at the drop of the handkerchief the several guns went off with almost one report, and three of the ducks remained on the sand, the fourth one flying off too much scared to make a single quack. Two of the ducks were found to be skilfully decapitated, the third having a groove across its back, barely saving the credit of the marksman. The fourth shot, admitted to be the farthest, was pronounced a good one at such a small mark, barely missing the duck, and striking the sand beyond.

CHAPTER XXXVI.

A MÚST ELEPHANT.

ON returning to the tents they found the khansamah waiting to announce breakfast, to which they all sat down with no small appetites, and the way in which the eatables vanished showed the necessity of keeping the larder well supplied. Their wolfish nature having been somewhat appeased, one of the party remarked that, living as he had done lately, he thought that bazaar beef and mutton would prove rather insipid on his return to town.

As all reference to city life had been mutually interdicted at the commencement of the tour, " a fine !" was called out by two or three, and the offender being immediately tried, was amerced in a three dozen chest of Bass.

Breakfast being over, they all adjourned to the shade of the trees, watching a squad of monkeys, and engaging in general talk. In the course of conversation, the president being asked if he had ever personally seen either a wild or a domesticated múst elephant, said, that he had seen neither, but for about a week he had, on one occasion, been kept in a state of great anxiety as to the possibility of meeting with a domesticated one which had gone mad for the time.

Here it is necessary to explain that the term *múst* is applied only to male elephants in a certain state. All adult wild and domesticated male elephants, in the pairing season, are liable to become ungovernable through animal passion, and such domesticated males especially, unless well secured and physicked on the first symptoms of the disorder, are liable to break out, and literally

A DISSIPATED MAHOUT.

run amuck at all and sundry in their way, and then, while in that state, they are exceedingly dangerous.

Some years ago a party of officials, with the wives and children of some of them, went on the usual cold weather tour to the eastern extremity of this district (Mirzapore). Being in want of two or three more elephants, one or other of them wrote to the rajah of a neighbouring district for the loan of some, and he, like natives in general, only too glad of the opportunity of laying official gentlemen under an obligation, sent as many as were asked for. One of the elephants sent was the finest animal in the rajah's stud, a huge male, said to be valued at 3,000 rupees or £300.

The mahout, or driver of this animal, was soon perceived to be an ill-tempered, dissipated brute, who constantly ill-treated the elephant, so much so that the gentlemen repeatedly reprimanded him, and warned him that his ill-treatment of the elephant would surely be the cause of his own death by the animal some day. Instead of taking warning, the interference of the gentlemen only caused this savage to vent his spite all the more on the elephant whenever they were out of sight.

Things went on thus until one evening one of the gentlemen, and several of the other mahouts, noticing the state of the large elephant, warned the driver to give it the usual medicine, and to secure it at once with double chains. The gentlemen also told the driver that they would dispense with the services of the elephant for a few days, until it had cooled down again. The man, however, was obstinate, denying the alleged state of the elephant, saying that he had been with the animal for years, and knew the signs better than any one else, and would neither physic the animal nor secure it.

The next evening, the symptoms being too evident to be longer denied, the man was ordered to separate and take his animal to a distance, to secure it well and give it medicine at once, and if he did not obey instantly, the magistrate would hand him over to the police and put another man in charge. After leaving the presence of the gentlemen, although he knew the excited state of the animal, the surly driver could not refrain from ill-using it while leading it away.

When he had taken the elephant to a grove of trees some distance off, while he and the under-keeper were engaged in securing the feet of the animal, the surly mahout hurt the elephant beyond endurance. This was the last straw. The enraged elephant seized the driver with its trunk, dashed him to the ground, and then pounded the body to a jelly with its tusks and kneeling upon him.

While this was going on, the under-keeper escaped and gave the alarm. The other elephants were ordered to be driven away instantly to a considerable distance, as the gentlemen knew that the mad one would, when tired of venting its wrath on the body of the mahout, join the others.

The next thing was to secure the ladies and children, and for this purpose, while some of the servants ran to the village for charpoys (native bedsteads), others quickly made rude ladders, and the charpoys being placed in different large trees out of the elephant's reach, the ladies and children were soon placed out of harm's way, an abundance of blankets and other things being handed up to make them comfortable.

When the ladies and children had been provided for, the gentlemen took up a position with their guns between the tents, and in the road by which the elephant might be expected to come. These preparations had scarcely been made when the elephant was seen charging down on the camp, and although six or eight shots well directed were fired at it, yet the brute could not be stopped, but charged right on, scattering the gentlemen, upsetting the tents, and making its way straight for the place where the other elephants had been picketed. Here the animal was at a nonplus; it stood still awhile, seeming to consider, and then discovering the road the rest had taken, or it may be hearing some of them trumpeting, it made a straight road towards them.

Ordering the other elephants away was a great mistake, for had they remained, the other drivers might have surrounded the excited one with the rest of the elephants, and by placing heavy double chains round its legs, could easily have secured and prevented it from doing the harm it subsequently did.

Firing on it when it charged was the second mistake. Excited by nature, and goaded to frenzy while in that state by a brutal driver; excited further in venting its wrath, then hurt by the balls fired at it, when it missed its companions, its anger was roused, and it was then wholly ungovernable. Charging into the midst of the other elephants, it made them clear out in all directions, hurting two or three of them, one subsequently dying through the further hurts received from the monster's tusks.

As there were several gentlemen in the party, and a large retinue of servants, it was determined upon to tell the latter off into watches; so when they had been mustered they were divided into watches, under two gentlemen for each watch, and their duties explained to them; and as the night promised to be very dark, large fires were ordered to be lighted and kept burning during the night by the watch on duty in turn, all round the camp a few yards apart, and the wood for them to be collected immediately.

The people of the village near which the camp was pitched, well understanding the common danger, lent willing assistance to any scheme devised by the officials, and were of material service in acting as messengers to various places, spreading the information rapidly, and so warning the whole country.

Of course in such a posture of affairs, when the enemy in the shape of a huge mad elephant might at any moment be expected to charge through the camp, there could be no thought of getting the ladies and children down out of the trees, and dining together as usual in peace and comfort.

They were, however, made as comfortable as could be done under the circumstances, food and other things being passed up to them in the trees. One lady and children had to run the risk of meeting with the elephant, while being shifted from one tree to another, being driven away by a colony of red ants, whose persuasive arguments could not be resisted any longer.

When the ladies and children had been attended to, the gentlemen determined to rest themselves a little and dine together, notwithstanding the elephant being loose in the neighbourhood, and accordingly sat down to dinner, but had not got half through when a servant came running into the tent, saying, "Saheb! saheb! hathée aiyàn hi!" or, "Sir! sir! the elephant has come!"

Jumping up and seizing their rifles and guns, they were out of the tent in a few seconds, but were first inclined to think that it was a false alarm, until their eyes becoming gradually used to the darkness after coming out of the bright light in the tent, they saw the huge animal looming large in the gloom a few yards beyond the circle of fires, and standing perfectly still like a statue.

The oldest and most experienced sportsman in the company, a veritable Nestor, remarked that that was a bad sign, for whenever an elephant in that state stands quite still, it means that it is meditating deeply over some cunning bit of mischief, and warned all to be on their guard, adding that if they did not succeed in driving the animal into the open country, some disaster might be expected to happen in the camp during the night.

Then, ordering several of the servants to arm themselves with two suitable brands each from the fires, they were directed to advance sufficiently near to the elephant, and each to throw one brand at it, retaining the other for their own defence in case the elephant charged. They were instructed further, that if the elephant turned tail on the first brand being hurled at it, they were then to throw the second, shout together, and retreat quickly to the fires; while, if the elephant charged, the gentlemen would cover them with their guns, and drive the brute back with balls.

This scheme was resorted to, because all animals are known to be terribly afraid of fire, and it happily proved successful; for the elephant seeing the fires approaching did not wait for the brands to be thrown, but literally sounded a retreat with its trunk; one brand from each was nevertheless thrown, to expedite its movements.

The elephant having been driven away, the gentlemen returned to the tent and finished their dinner, after quieting the apprehensions of the ladies and children. Having been considerably fatigued in attending to a multiplicity of things in such a sudden and untoward emergency, after the first watch had been set, the others went to sleep. During the night, two or three false alarms were raised, but the captains of the watch took care not to disturb the sleepers needlessly.

The next morning, after inquiries were made as to the whereabouts of the mad elephant, a consultation was held, at which it was determined upon to try to give the brute the slip; so ordering everything to be packed up speedily, and breakfast being over, one portion of the camp equipage was directed to march by a road leading down a steep ghát, or pass, in the hills to a certain village, a long day's journey, while the main body, with the gentlemen, ladies, and children, would take another route for the same place.

The whole camp equipage having reached the appointed place without seeing or hearing anything of the mad brute, they all congratulated themselves upon the success of the stratagem; but, about two hours after their arrival, the alarm was raised that the elephant was coming.

In case of such an occurrence, precautions had been taken to have bedsteads placed up in some trees, and ladders all ready, so that when the gentlemen rushed out of the tents and saw that it was no false alarm, the ladies and children were soon put out of harm's way.

CHAPTER XXXVII.

NARROW ESCAPE OF ONE OF THE PARTY.

THE guns having been well looked to, the gentlemen determined to take careful aim and try to kill the elephant. When they had stationed themselves in front of the camp, they watched the course of the elephant, which was then at the top of the steep ghát, seemingly at a loss which way to go.

Unfortunately, one of the camp elephants just then trumpeted, and the mad elephant was seen to raise its head for a moment, as if to assure itself of the right direction, and then set off at a tremendous pace down the steep hill, everybody expecting and hoping to see it roll over. The brute, however, managed somehow to keep its legs, and, without slackening speed, it made straight for the camp.

Waiting until it came within twenty yards, most of the party fired at its eyes and the top of its head, the Nestor of the party reserving his fire until the brute came about five yards off, when, taking a steady aim, he gave the brute a two-ounce rifle ball in the direction of the most vulnerable part of its head.

The balls that did hit it appeared not to have the slightest effect (a careful aim being impossible, owing to the speed with which such a rolling mountain of flesh came on), the elephant rushing on as if nothing had happened, the Nestor of the party having a narrow escape in getting out of its way.

After upsetting the tent in which the ladies and children had been, and doing sundry damage in the culinary department, the mad brute tore its way through everything, until it came to where the other elephants had been, when, seeing only the most seriously wounded elephant of the previous day, it rushed at it full-butt with its tusks (grievously wounding it further, so that it died), and knocking it over, made off into the open country after the other elephants.

The other drivers had received previous orders that if the mad elephant should at any time be seen making for the camp, they were to unloose and drive off the other elephants, each in a different direction, so as to confuse the mad brute, and accordingly all but the wounded one had been driven away.

When the official gentlemen of the party found that their duties were liable to be seriously interfered with, and their travelling and camping arrangements interrupted, as well as their lives endangered by the mad elephant, it was resolved on returning to Mirzapore by forced marches, place the ladies and children in safety, and then return and make arrangements for the destruction of the troublesome brute.

Meanwhile, a considerable body of villagers were ordered to act, some as scouts to bring information of the elephant's movements, others as guards to relieve the camp retinue, who had been much harassed the last two days. Dinner being ordered early and partaken of, arrangements were made for passing the night in safety, so far as might be possible ; and after orders had been given for an early and rapid march the next day, all retired to rest except the captains of the watch.

Early the next morning the whole camp started on their return, leaving strict orders to the villagers on the route to prevent the elephant from following them, and, by long and forced marches, reached Mirzapore in safety. Previous to leaving, the villagers had not only permission but instructions to destroy the elephant by any means if they could not capture it, and a good reward was offered for either its death or capture.

The rajah, the owner of the elephant, was also informed of all that had happened; and as he highly valued the elephant, he also offered a handsome reward for its capture only, not destruction. Various schemes were therefore tried, matchlocks were fired at it, poisoned food was laid in its way, and pitfalls were dug, but all were ineffectual, balls somehow took no effect, and the brute's cunning defeated all traps.

Various reports were current all over the district, and the inhabitants were in a state of general terror, for, when the mad elephant missed its companions and its usual food, it took to racing about the country, waylaying people and robbing them of whatever eatables they were carrying, and killing those that offered any resistance.

Before the brute went mad it had been engaged (being a staunch tiger hunter) in several tiger hunts, wherein the tigers had been bagged, and brought to the tents on his back; and after the camp had returned to the station, while the elephant was roaming about, one day it overtook a man carrying a bundle.

The man, hearing the elephant coming, dropped the bundle and made off hot-foot, leaving the elephant busy undoing the package, but when it found only skins, and tiger-skins withal, it gave a shriek of disgust, pitched them right and left, and went after something more profitable.

Living at its ease, plundering the growing crops and sugar-cane fields, visiting villages and stealing the pumpkins growing on the roofs of the huts, the brute rather enjoyed its freedom.

During one of its marauding visits it managed to set a village on fire. The report was that the mad brute came to the village in the dusk of the evening, and seeing some fine pumpkins on one of the huts, it began helping itself, and the inmates hearing it, getting terrified, fled for their lives. In pulling off the pumpkins, it appeared that the elephant had pulled off a quantity of the thatch, some of which fell into the fire inside the hut, and, as usual, the fireplace being close to the side of the hut, the fire soon caught it, and, the straw blazing up, the flames spread to the roof and thence to the adjoining cottages.

The villagers, knowing the mad elephant to be about the place,

THE MAD ELEPHANT KILLS A RANEE. 235

were afraid to render each other assistance, and so the greater part of the village got burnt down. After roaming about and appearing at most unexpected places, killing several people, and doing great damage wherever it went, baffling all attempts to ensnare or destroy it, the brute's last exploit was to kill a native princess.

The report went that a ranee (princess) was on her return to her own domain at Sirgoojah, beyond Singrowlee, from a pilgrimage to Benares, and stopped for the night at a certain village near the high road.

Travelling in state, with a large retinue, her encampment occupied a considerable space. Her own immediate tent was surrounded with a canvas wall, to secure for herself strict seclusion from the gaze of the vulgar.

All natives being excessively fond of sweetmeats, the ranee had laid in a good store of delicacies at Benares, and was carrying them with her. The fame of the exploits of the mad elephant having spread far and wide, when it was seen approaching the encampment at a rapid pace the only thought of each one was to save himself; consequently, the poor ranee and her female kindred, prohibited by their order and custom from appearing in public, were left to take their chance.

The ranee and her relatives, at the moment of the alarm, were refreshing themselves with the sweetmeats, which were being handed round on several trays by the female attendants, but which were speedily dropped when the elephant was heard close to the screen, the girls and women hiding wherever they could.

The ranee escaped to her palanquin, and might have saved her life but for her curiosity, for, when the elephant had knocked down the canvas wall, like so much paper, seeing lots of sweetmeats scattered about, it very wisely and deliberately set-to picking them up, and disposing of them in its capacious receptacle for such-like good things.

The ranee, not hearing any further noise for some time, thinking that the elephant had gone elsewhere, pushed open one of the doors of the palanquin, and unfortunately discovered herself.

The elephant, hearing the noise made by the door being opened, and seeing some individual, rushed up and knocked over the palanquin, smashing it to pieces, and pulling out the princess, whom it speedily put out of misery.

By the time that the last feat of the mad brute had been performed, a bold mahout had agreed with the rajah, the owner of it, to undertake the capture of the elephant, on the condition that if he succeeded he was to be the elephant's mahout (driver) on sixteen rupees a month (double wages), together with any donation that the rajah might be pleased to give; while, if he should be killed in the attempt, his family were to have a pension of half that amount.

Receiving information of the whereabouts of the elephant, this mahout, mounted on a well-trained female decoy elephant, went after the mad brute, and succeeded in enticing it into a caravanserai, or native traveller's inn, when, giving a signal, he immediately had the gate quietly closed and strongly fastened.

Having prepared beforehand a quantity of sweetmeat balls, medicated with opium, he got off the decoy's neck on passing through the gateway, and turned to making an ample allowance of chuppattees, or hand-bread, and while these were preparing (the decoy artfully caressing the mad one all the time), he supplied the two elephants with a liberal quantity of fodder and sugarcanes.

When the bread was ready, he first showed one to the mad elephant to see how it would act, and, when he found the animal rushing to get it, he threw it to the brute. All elephants in a domesticated state have a daily allowance of bread, and the mad one having been so long without any, quickly disposed of the first chuppattee.

Allowing it to come nearer, he gave it another, and so on until it came up close, and then he gave it one of the medicated balls wrapped up in the bread, the decoy at its side watchfully interposing to prevent its doing violence to the man.

This medicated sweetmeat in the bread pleased the mad elephant still more, and the man, seeing how matters stood, gave it all the bread and sweetmeats, patting it now and again, and then, seeing the effect of the opium, he prepared for his next move.

Leaving the male elephant to toy with the female, which decoyed it back to where the fodder was, he carefully prepared the strong leg-chains with which he was provided (and which had been deposited in the serai beforehand) by covering them with cloth, and, having thrown more sugar-canes to the two elephants, he got behind the male one while it was caressing the decoy, and quietly fastened its hind legs together.

He then watched his opportunity and fastened chains on its fore legs, and with another chain fastened its hind legs to a large tree, under which the elephants were enjoying themselves. The mahout then slipping away, unfastened the gate and called to the female elephant, which at once obeyed, and on coming out the gate was again securely fastened, leaving the mad elephant to its meditations.

Not knowing exactly what to make of the decoy's leaving, it tried to follow, but found itself in a fix. The animal then made a few fruitless efforts to break loose, but the large allowance of bread and other food, together with the medicated sweetmeats, soon took effect in inducing drowsiness and lethargy, in which state it passed the remainder of the day and night.

After keeping it confined, and physicking it daily, the animal was gradually brought to its senses. It is supposed that thirty or forty balls were fired at it without taking any effect, except causing ulcerations, some of which were troublesome to heal. Also it is said that from first to last the elephant, while in its mad state, killed twenty-one individuals.

The president here said that he would not vouch for the accuracy of any part of the above account; he merely related it as it was reported to him by various parties. That the elephant did go mad, or must, and while in that state did much harm, killing several individuals, is a matter of fact, and could be attested by some of the parties yet living who were out on the official tour.

The shades of evening drawing on, they prepared for dinner, which, being announced shortly after, they were about commencing, when the agreeable information was received of the safe arrival, at Sulkhun, of the supplies ordered. The shikari who brought the information reported the messenger's being unable to come himself further that day, but that he would the next. He also reported the menagerie all well, excepting that one of the young leopards had escaped, but that it had been recaptured.

The shikari was then dismissed, and dinner having been heartily enjoyed, when the others were assembled round the fire, the caterer superintended the preparation of a tureen of punch, which on trial proved to be eminently satisfactory. The good news of fresh supplies at hand caused them to pass a jovial evening, until being warned that it was getting late, after filling a last glass each, they turned into bed.

CHAPTER XXXVIII.

JONES HAS A WEAKNESS FOR BRAHMINEE DUCKS.

IT being the intention of the party again to remain a few days at Chopun, their rising somewhat late the next morning was of little consequence; they were, however, obliged to turn out, when the khansamah reported that breakfast was ready, and waiting to be ordered. Deferring their bath, they sat down to an appetizing breakfast, consisting of fresh fish from the Soane, khichiree, country captain, curries, and other Indian delicacies, which so satisfied them that one of the party, who had not been long from aboard ship, remarked that if they were to live much longer as they had been doing, he for one would have to engage the services of a tailor to let out a reef in his clothes.

Breakfast being over, while smoking their cheroots they made a general inspection of the camp, listened to various reports, passed sundry orders, and finally consulted with the Sulkhun shikari. The multifarious necessary details having been attended to and disposed of, towels, &c., were consigned to some of the servants, and all taking their guns, they went to their usual bathing-place. After having a refreshing bath, when they were dressed, Jones, seeing some Brahminee ducks flying about wildly, remarked that he had a weakness for those birds stewed nicely, and would try and persuade one of them at least to stop.

Seeing that he was about to take a flying ball-shot, two or three of the rest remonstrated with him, saying that he would never hit either of them while flying about so wildly; but he answered that he rather thought he could bring one of them down, or at any rate he meant to try, and, taking a steady aim with his rifle, he brought his bird down, to the no little astonishment of the native attendants.

When one of the servants brought the duck, to the great disappointment of the marksman, it was found to be shot right through the body, and torn too much to be worth cooking, and was about being thrown away, when one of the servants said that it was good enough for them, and took it.

Not feeling inclined to go out for any game that day, when they returned to the tents they asked the president to favour them with a short story. After considering awhile, he began the following story of a Brahmin and some trees :—

It is the custom throughout the length and breadth of India, in all orthodox Hindoo societies, to invite the sacerdotal order represented by the Brahmin (priest) to take a prominent part in every event and every step in life taken by a Hindoo. Domestic or public events of any kind, among the great Aryan family, without Brahmins taking part in them would be as water without air in it.

Hindooism is so thoroughly permeated by the Brahmin that he may be likened to the linch-pin of a coach, as without *it*, or without *him*, some disaster might reasonably be expected to follow in a short time. Consequently, at the birth, naming, marriage, death, burial, and a thousand other occasions, the inevitable Brahmin is sure to be present. Indeed, the tax paid by the orthodox Hindoo for the support of his idolatrous and impure religion might well shame Christians of every sect and denomination.

Western civilization, together with the degeneracy of the modern Brahminical class, has so far enlightened the Hindoo mind, that the priesthood is not nowadays venerated, or held in anything like the esteem it had in ancient times.

Tradition hands down legends among the Hindoos of Brahmins who dwelt in the densest forests, holding wild beasts in subjection, and who were able to understand and interpret the various languages of inferior animate and inanimate creation, and who, by their superior wisdom and holy life, were more than a match for even celestial beings, good or evil.

The Moslem also, copying the Hindoo, ascribes to the fakirs and other reputed holy men of his fanatical religion, *in former times*, supernatural and, so to term it, supercelestial powers.

In former times, then, there was a certain Brahmin who, although held in great repute for sanctity of life and other ascribed virtues and powers, was not co-equal with his confreres of still more ancient times. On the occurrence of a domestic event of a happy nature, this reputed holy Brahmin was invited, with many more of his class, by the rajah of the country in which he lived, to be present at a sumptuous entertainment to be given in honour of the felicitous event.

On the day previous to the appointed day, the Brahmin set off on his road to the town where was the palace of the rajah, and where the feast was to be held, hoping to obtain quarters for the night with a friend; but having to pass through a belt of jungle, he saw a large tiger basking in the sun, stretched at full length on a patch of soft green grass, in rather too close proximity to the path along which he had to pass.

By good fortune, the Brahmin perceived the tiger, which was apparently dozing, while yet a good distance separated them. Now, whether it were owing to his philosophy not being proof against danger, or that there was some constitutional defect in his temperament, certain it is that the holy man thought discretion to be the better part of valour, and so, stepping very lightly and cautiously, he backed out of the immediate view of the animal.

Unfortunately for the equanimity of the Brahmin, although the tiger had not seen him, yet the wind being from him to the beast, there was wafted through the air a delicious smell of human flesh, and the olfactory nerves of such animals being very acute, this one moreover having acquired a taste for such diet, it sprang up and hurried into the path, to ascertain, by another sense, in which direction its anticipated feast was coming.

Seeing each other simultaneously, the tiger sprang forward in pursuit, while the Brahmin, turning round, quickly ran in the direction of some trees, hoping to be in time to climb up one out of reach of the tiger. The animal, however, going faster on four legs than the man on two, would certainly have caught him, were it not that the Brahmin, passing a large tree, the trunk of which was hollowed out with age,* and availing himself of the cavity, there not being time to reach a tree up which he might climb, was suddenly lost to view.

This tree being a sandal, its fragrance overpowered that emanating from the human, and thus the tiger was baffled of its prey by both its senses.

Not daring to quit his friendly retreat, the Brahmin was forced to remain where he was all night, hungry and shivering, as the tiger, unable to account for the sudden disappearance of the man, and having a confused idea in its brain that he must be somewhere near, continued for hours to pace backwards and forwards in the neighbourhood of the tree.

Unable to solve the difficulty, and beginning to feel ravenous, the tiger at last seemed to think it useless to waste more time, and so towards morning went off in search of some other prey. The Brahmin, meanwhile, although he no longer heard the footsteps of the tiger, being a wise man and acquainted with the many wiles of animals, thought it more prudent to continue in his retreat until it was broad day, when travellers might be expected to be journeying about.

In accordance with this prudent resolve, he waited until he heard the voices of some men, when, stepping out of the cavity, and seeing that the men came from the direction he wished to go,

* There is a little exaggeration here in this native story. The sandal-tree never grows large enough to conceal a man in its hollow trunk. But this one, being a mythical tree, growing *in former times*, may possibly be excepted.

he concluded that the tiger had vacated that part of the forest; and, proceeding boldly along, he arrived in safety at the palace of the rajah.

Far from being a proud, arrogant man, like the generality of Brahmins, he placed himself among the humbler of the many guests, until, being recognised, he was desired to occupy a more honourable position. Having passed the whole night in the heart of a sandal tree, his clothes and person had been so strongly imbued with its fragrance, that whether he sat or moved among the humbler or nobler of the guests, the whole air was impregnated with the perfume of the sandal.

When the rajah and his principal visitors entered the hall of entertainment, the perfume of sandal so pervaded the air as to render it very refreshing, and on the rajah's inquiring whence the scent was emitted, the other guests denying all knowledge, the Brahmin stepped forward, and modestly related the events of his journey and of the night.

After condoling with him on his cheerless night, and admiring his prudence in availing himself of the cavity, the rajah inquired very particularly as to the locality of the valuable tree.

Having obtained precise information, after excusing himself to his guests for a few minutes, the rajah retired, and gave orders for a large party of men, with carts and a responsible officer, to go immediately, cut down and bring to the palace every scrap of the sandal-tree, not leaving even the smallest rootlet behind.

Knowing that the feast would continue for many days, several of the palace attendants took advantage of the occasion, and went with the men to gather a load each of branches of wild flowering bushes, to adorn and perfume the hall of entertainment.

Before the men had started, the rajah, who was very anxious to secure the wood of the sandal-tree before any one else found it, reflecting on the possibility of his people missing the place, notwithstanding the precise instructions given to them, sent for the Brahmin, and politely asked the favour of his going to the forest with the men, as he feared that they would not be able to find the tree.

The Brahmin, knowing that the requests of rulers, however politely worded, are to be considered in the light of commands, expressed himself as delighted at being favoured with an opportunity of rendering even the smallest service to such a beneficent ruler, and accordingly went with the men.

On arriving at the place, while the Brahmin was resting himself and watching the operations of the woodcutters as they were busily engaged in felling the noble tree that had preserved his life, and possibly the lives of other men or animals, he insensibly went off into a meditation upon things in general, and particularly upon the apparently accidental and strange manner in which misfortune overtakes the good of the earth and overwhelms them.

In the midst of his reverie, as he was standing by two bushes, he was suddenly conscious of the commencement of a conversation between them, and being acquainted with the language of trees, he was desirous of making good use of the opportunity, and therefore roused himself to pay the closest attention, although without apparently doing so.

CHAPTER XXXIX.

PRETENDED HUMILITY OF THE USELESS BUSHES.

NOW, these bushes were of a kind that were utterly useless to man, not even making good firewood, and the only use that they seemed to be capable of, in the scheme of creation, was to afford a slight shelter and a scanty supply of little berries to small tribes of the feathered race.

Like all base and ignoble minds, they were incapable of conceiving a generous sentiment, and were filled with envy and hatred towards all useful and noble trees, blooming plants whose perfume was diffused around lavishly, or whose varied colours attracted and pleased the eye of the wayfarer.

The sandal-tree, and all sweet-scented or gaily-painted flowering shrubs that were in their immediate vicinity, were the objects of the special antipathy of these almost useless plants, and when they saw the rajah's woodmen and other servants ruthlessly cutting down or despoiling them, their hearts were filled with malignant joy and satisfaction.

After beholding with peculiar pleasure the work of destruction and spoliation going on for some time, the one useless plant, with a semblance of humility, thankfulness, and resignation to its lot, said to the other, " Neighbour, we have all our lives long wondered at the condition of all these showy trees and plants around us.

" We have also been envious of the notice which their meretricious attractions have gained for them from ill-judging wayfarers or visitors, and have naturally felt hurt at our own humble merits being wholly overlooked. We now see that their false charms and imputed virtues have only proved their ruin. When we saw inconsiderate wayfarers smelling at some of our neighbours, admiring the gay blossoms of others, or carrying away with them some of the fragments of the sandal, ignoring us altogether, we were foolishly angry.

"But now where is the towering lordly sandal that used to mock at our birth and condition? Level with the dust and doomed to be utterly rooted out, we already feel the benefit of its removal. The genial warmth of the sun and the increased circulation of the air, so long impeded by its baleful shade, already send such vigour through my system that I am prepared to burst on all sides with increased vitality."

"Very true," answered the other useless plant, and added, "what now is the condition of our neighbours whose perfumes or painted faces attracted such unfair notice? Stripped, wounded, and bleeding at many a broken and jagged end, we see their unsightly mournful state, and are thankful that no ruthless hand spoils the symmetry of our humble growth.

"When we think of the numerous feathered tribes that obtain their sustenance from us during the day, repaying us with their grateful songs, or that resort to us for shelter when night casts its mantle over the earth, thanking us with gentle voices, does not a glow of satisfaction pervade our veins in being conscious of the benefits we confer?

"Would we now desire their lot to be ours? Although looked down upon by our proud neighbours, and taunted with our imperfections, far happier is our lot in spending a life of usefulness, in the enjoyment of health, and freedom from mutilation. Let us be thankful that righteous justice has at length overtaken the scorners, and laid their pride low."

A chip of the sandal-wood, which had been overlooked by the woodcutters of the rajah, while exhaling a delightful fragrance around, took upon itself to answer the self-gratulatory speeches of the useless plants, and said, "Now that the good and noble ones

THE BRAHMIN REBUKES THE BUSHES.

of the earth are laid low, or have been despoiled of their blooming treasures, you dare to lift up your insignificant heads. A few short minutes have scarcely elapsed when you were humble, and held your peace before noble worth.

"Your exulting over what you deem the misfortunes of your superiors only exhibits more clearly the baseness of your hearts. You are not capable of conceiving the nobility of their condition, nor have you learned to appreciate the dignity there is in, even with our latest breath, diffusing a grateful perfume around.

"In contributing to the enjoyment of others, who are the lords of all, we fulfil the highest objects of creation in a manner and degree of which you can never be sensible, and the very act of our destruction is crowned with a fragrant or pleasant remembrance."

The Brahmin, having listened patiently to the conversation, here interposed his voice, and, in rebuking the nearly useless plants, spoke thus: "In the pride and arrogancy of your hearts, though in pretended humility and thankfulness, you have dared to rejoice over what has befallen your nobler and more worthy neighbours. Know, in future, that the wise and beneficent Creator made all things subservient to the good of man, some in a greater, others in a less degree.

"You that are not of the least direct use to man, yet serve him indirectly by affording sustenance and shelter to the meaner feathered tribes, who, in their degree, contribute to his happiness; learn now, that it is more dignified to be maimed, or even to die, for the benefit of others, than to live in ignoble security and self-preservation."

The Brahmin then, taking up the chip of sandal-wood, placed it on one of the carts, and returned with the rajah's people to the palace, leaving the useless plants to digest the rebuke, and the lessons of wisdom that they had received.

The president's story being ended sooner than was expected, they all, changing their minds, went for a short stroll in the neighbouring jungle, and after they had bagged a spotted deer, and some green and wood pigeons, as they were going along further, Jones called out, "Hallo! here's a curious rat;" but, with almost incredible celerity, certainly to his vast astonishment, the animal disappeared into the ground.

On the others coming up, and hearing the description of it, as well as seeing the crumbling earth, the president said it was only a mole, and not a rat. Being desirous of examining the animal, two or three of the party got out their hunting-knives, and began enlarging the hole; but, after a good deal of time and labour wasted in useless efforts, they were compelled to give it up, the mole digging faster than they could.

A couple of curlews being then seen flying towards them, two of the party determined on trying their skill with ball at a flying shot, engaging to bring down each his bird, and succeeded in cleverly redeeming their word. These birds, stewed under the directions of the president, were the next morning at breakfast pronounced very desirable eating.

Returning to camp, they had scarcely time to prepare, when the khansamah reported dinner on the table. While discussing the good things provided by the caterer's thoughtful care and skill, the President was asked if he knew of any natives who had been in danger from chance encounters with wild beasts.

His reply was that there were few adult natives, in the more distant villages especially, who could not recount one or more hairbreadth escapes from tigers, bears, &c., while many could show scars received in the encounter. He had come across several such men, and had heard details of various narrow escapes, and had himself been in considerable danger more than once.

He remembered an instance where the man adopted the ruse, said to have been practised by more than one individual in similar circumstances of danger. The man had gone to cut coarse grass for repairing his hut, and, having cut sufficient for a good load, he stood up to rest himself for awhile. He had hardly assumed an upright position, when he saw, at a few yards' distance, the standing grass moving in a suspicious manner towards him.

Having previous experience to judge from, he knew that a tiger was trying to surprise him, and, as it was not possible for him to hope to escape by running away, as his motion through the grass would betray him, he instantly drove his latthée or staff into the ground, and after arranging his waistcloth on the top in the form of a turban, he crouched down close by it between the tiger and his staff, and silently waited the result.

After waiting a few minutes, which seemed to him hours, he saw the tiger taking a flying leap over him, upset his staff, and carry away his waistcloth. The tiger, finding out the mistake it had made, gave a roar of disgust and disappointment, and then sneaked off into the jungle.

Waiting until he thought that the tiger had gone away to a safe distance, after looking carefully around, the man recovered his cloth, tied up his grass, and returned by a different road to his village, where he related with great glee how he had done the tiger.

Dinner being over, and the caterer having personally superintended the brewing of a tureen of punch, the parties took their places as usual around a blazing fire. When all were comfortable, the president being called upon to recount more of his jungle experience, said that he remembered a native telling him of how the sharpness of his tangaree (wood-axe) had once done him good service.

The man had been engaged with some others by a zemindar (farmer) to fell some trees, and while busy hewing away at the trunk of a large tree, a large bear had managed to creep up from some bushes behind him, without being perceived by any one.

Just as the animal had stood up to seize him, one of his comrades saw it, and shouted to the man in danger, who, turning round quickly, saw the bear just at arm's length. When startled, the man had his hands uplifted, about to deliver a blow, but, on seeing his danger, quick as thought he let his axe fall, with good aim, on the skull of the bear, through which it went crashing up to the head. Leaping quickly aside, he had the satisfaction of seeing the bear writhing in its death-throes.

There was another man, the president said, who narrowly escaped from being overtaken by the vengeance of a she-bear robbed of her cubs. The man had been in the jungle, cutting grass for thatching, and, on his return, while passing a cave, he heard some sounds which he recognised as being the cries of bear's cubs.

Thinking it would be a good day's work to secure the young bears, and sell them to some European, he instantly formed his plan, and, throwing down his load of grass, he returned into the jungle for another load, making also some string of buggye grass. Returning to the place, he deposited his second load of grass, and then mounted a tree at hand to watch.

Presently, he saw the she-bear come home and enter the cave, and after remaining for about an hour, apparently suckling her cubs, she again left the cave. Now was his opportunity. After watching for a long distance until he lost sight of her, the man got down out of the tree, entered the cave, and, after some trouble, succeeded in tying up the mouths and feet of three cubs. Taking them outside, he blocked up the entrance of the cave with loads of grass, and rolled heavy pieces of rock against them, also putting others on top of them. He then made off as fast as he could.

Unfortunately for his complete success, either he had taken a very long time in doing what he did, or the maternal instincts of the bear, warning her of danger to her young, caused her to return sooner than the man expected. From the road he took, by looking back occasionally, the man could see when the bear returned, and what it did. On the bear's return, it did not seem to know at first what had become of its domicile, but feeling sure at length that it had not come to the wrong house, a sudden feeling of alarm for its young ones caused it to make frantic efforts to remove the obstacles.

Having cleared away the rocks and grass, it rushed into the cave, and, not finding its young ones, the animal rushed out again, roaring furiously. · Just as it had stood still, considering what road to take in pursuit, one of the young ones managed to get its mouth free and set up a cry.

Although a long distance off, the mother evidently heard it, for she came at a tremendous pace in the direction of the sound. Directly the man saw the bear start in pursuit, he knew what he would get if caught by it, and, seeing that it was time to be off, he waited merely long enough to tie up securely the mouth of the young one once more, and then set off at a good hard trot.

CHAPTER XL.

THE PARLIAMENT OF ALL CREATED THINGS.

LOOKING back now and then, he saw that the bear was gaining too fast on him, and that he would not be able to carry off all three of the cubs, so, after dropping one in the middle of the road, where the bear would be sure to see it, he made off again hot-foot. Gaining a considerable distance, and an eminence in the road ahead, he turned round and saw that the bear had just come up to it, and was busy in trying to release the young one from its bandages. Thinking it best to lose no more time, he once more went off at full speed, and succeeded in getting the other two young ones in safety to his village.

After refreshing themselves with a sip of punch and a fresh cheroot, the president said that, on thinking over some native stories, there had occurred to his remembrance a tale, current in native society, concerning a general parliament of all created things, and, if they were pleased to listen to it, he would have no objection to become a *raconteur*.

When all had given their willing assent, by a general holding up of hands, the president thought that he might as well adopt the time-honoured English formulary in commencing his story, and thus began :—

Once upon a time, many ages ago, a great disturbance had been raised among all created things, animate with life in some form; and although many plans had been resorted to, with the view of adjusting the unhappy difference, not one had succeeded. Affairs had come to such a pass in those days, that all created animate things looked askance at each other, and amicable relationship was entirely discontinued.

In such a crisis, it was agreed upon, by mutual consent, to hold a general parliament, at which two representatives of each class were to be present. The place of meeting was fixed to be in a large plain, conveniently situated for all parties, being bounded on one side by the sea, into which from another side rushed a mighty river, the third side being a dense forest, while the fourth was open country.

Anxiously looked forward to by all, the appointed day at length came round, and, with the day, there came into the vast plain two representatives of each class of created animate things. Of birds, there came two of each of the classes that prey on quadrupeds, with deputies of those that prey on smaller birds or fishes; all songsters, together with birds noted for the beauty of their plumage, and all birds which did not come within either category, and, not to be behind the rest, all domesticated birds sent their deputies.

Of four-footed or four-handed animals, wild or domesticated, there was a similar gathering. The seashore was crowded with the representatives of the deep, while the waters of the mighty river were alive with the deputies of all fresh-water classes of animals. Last of all came the trees, all whose wood, bark, fibres, fruit, flowers, seeds or leaves were in any way useful, and all plants of every kind, sweet-scented, gaily-painted, or whose roots were medicinal, or that in any way had any virtue, sent their representatives. Grasses, mosses, and lichens, with confervæ of every description, possessed of the lowest degree of animation, also sent their deputies, together with snakes, and all creeping and crawling creatures, and amphibious animals, as well as insects.

At the various entrances to the place of assembly, heralds were stationed, who continually proclaimed with a loud voice that in the parliament about to meet all rancour and animosity between the several classes of representatives must for the time being be laid aside.

When all the deputies had assembled, the Trumpeter Crane was requested to blow a call for silence, and the hum of voices having been hushed, the Lion, ascending a hillock, addressed the expectant multitude thus :—

"Whereas, for a long period, unhappy dissensions having existed among all classes of animated beings, respecting their individual merits as a class, and the rank and precedence they ought to hold in the scale of creation, it was determined to convene a general council of created beings, at which two representatives of each class were requested to be present, when the whole subject might be debated, and it was hoped that a rule, or scale, of precedence might be amicably adjusted, and the subject be finally disposed of:

"He was informed that representatives from every class summoned were then assembled, and he proposed that one deputy of each class should give his reasons for claiming precedence over his neighbour, taking care, owing to the number of representatives, to condense his opinions into as concise a form as possible, after which the parliament would decide on each one's merits."

The lion having thus opened the parliament, then retired with dignity down the side of the hillock. As there had not been, nor could be, under the circumstances, any method in pre-arranging the various classes, so there could be no order settled in which the various classes could be heard; consequently, when the lion ceased speaking, and had descended from his exalted station, a scene of uproar commenced which has no parallel.

Birds of the air flew about screaming and screeching; quadrupeds roaring, bellowing, grunting, howling, or barking; monkeys, of all kinds, jabbering; snakes hissing; trees and plants waving their branches, or otherwise exhibiting their impatience; while the ocean and the river were boiling with the anxiety of their inhabitants—all eager to be heard. In the general commotion,

THE LION'S SECOND SPEECH. 255

much jostling necessarily occurred, and matters began to assume such a serious aspect, that the lion was once more obliged to ascend the hillock.

When the vast heaving multitude saw the lion once more on the eminence, and evidently about to speak, silence was gradually restored. The lion, then, addressing the multitude, said, "As each representative present seemed to claim precedence over every one else, in their eagerness to speak first, there was no possibility of the claims of each class being fairly heard and discussed.

"In his opinion it made little difference who spoke first, or who last, so long as each class was heard, but, unless some order was maintained in the proceedings, there could be no prospect of an amicable result being arrived at, and this plain would shortly become a battle-field and charnel-house. The cause of dissension was this : which class of created beings best served the purpose of their existence, by being most subservient to the good of man, their superior lord, and consequently entitled in their degree to precedence over others?

"Although they all knew the grounds of *his* title to precedence, he would for the present waive his claim, and suggest that the domesticated animals should speak first." Having said this, the lion laid himself at full length on the hillock, until the representative of one of the domesticated classes should advance to be heard.

At this point an impertinent Jackal interrupted the proceedings by saying, "The lion is evidently afraid, and *therefore* gives place to the bull."

Stung to the quick by this biting taunt, the lion sprang up with a mighty roar, and lashing his sides furiously with his spiked tail, he said, " If the majesty of the congress were to be insulted with gross personalities, he would take it upon himself to chastise all offenders, and bade them take warning."

When the lion had ceased speaking, the rascally jackal, after giving vent to a taunting "Ha! ha!" stealthily slipped away between the legs of several of the larger quadrupeds. Making his way among the multitude, he came to the fox, wolf, hyena, tiger, vultures of kinds, and such-like scavengers, and, taking a hint from the lion's second speech, he artfully suggested to each one, that the parliament was all a humbug—that he foresaw no good would come of the meeting, and that each one ought to be left to decide on his own and his neighbour's merits.

When he had interested each one so far, he further suggested that, to create a little diversion, they should all go round and foment jealousy between the representatives, and so setting them by the ears should break up the stupid assembly. Quickly divining the scheme of the jackal, they all heartily engaged in it, and the result was very soon evident.

When the lion had calmed down, the Horse, mounting the hillock, set forth his claims to precedence by saying, " It will, he supposed, be allowed that his class rendered the greatest assistance to man in dragging his ploughs, in cultivating the land, carrying or dragging goods of all kinds to various places, and in administering to his pleasures in many ways, especially in enabling him to overtake and subdue other animals,"—here the horse could no longer be heard. Cries of all descriptions—hisses, groans, grunts, bellows, barks, screams, and screeches, from indignant deputies interrupting his harangue, he was obliged to vacate his proud position, which he did with a scornful neigh.

The Bull, then mounting the hillock, said he did not intend to trespass long on their time. Indeed, he thought it unnecessary to delay the proceedings by recapitulating claims, which were almost universally acknowledged. For himself, he was quite satisfied with the position of his class in many countries ; his class there being, by man himself, held in such high esteem as to have divine honours accorded it.

He would merely mention a few of the principal grounds of the claim to precedence which his class justly put forward. It was well known that his class also did all that was required of the horse, except in overtaking others. His class, however, far surpassed the horse in not only labouring for man, but in contributing to his sustenance, both while living, as may be verified by travellers in Africa, and after death. In fact, the bodies of his class were so valuable that every part was turned into some use.

After death their flesh was eaten with great relish, while their hide was prepared and dressed in various ways, sometimes being formed into clothing, or cut up into strips for many different purposes, such as whips, snares, and nooses. Here commenced a fresh outburst of indignant cries of all kinds, so that the bull, finding that it was useless to continue his speech, left the hillock with an angry toss of his head.

Next came the Ass, but he appeared so inflated with silly vanity at the honour of addressing such an august assemblage, and behaved himself in such a ridiculous manner, that when he began to bray out the claims of his class, he was interrupted by such bursts of derisive laughter as covered him with confusion, and compelled him to descend with shame.

A Ram then mounted the hillock, and was just beginning to speak, when a he-Goat, that he had a special antipathy to, lowered his head, as he thought, in a defiant, menacing manner.

As this ram was somewhat bellicose he at once accepted the implied challenge, and, forgetting the proprieties of the place, and the injunctions of the heralds, rushed down the hillock full-butt against his hateful adversary.

All the animals that were nearest the scene, especially the larger ones, were convulsed with merriment at the suddenness and strangeness of the onset; but after a few butts had been interchanged between the wrathful combatants they were separated, and inquiry made on the spot into the cause of this unseemly breach of the peace.

When the ram had stated his case the he-goat was asked what he meant by such behaviour. Gravely stroking his beard with one of his forelegs the he-goat replied that, he could not account

S

for the temporary fit of lunacy under which the ram was apparently labouring, unless by supposing that he had a maggot in his brain, to which disease it was well known animals of his class (the ram's) were subject; that when the ram ascended the hillock, he (the he-goat) had bowed his head to him in respectful salute, and was perfectly astonished at finding his act of courtesy replied to by a personal attack, and to which it was not to be supposed that a he-goat of his spirit would submit with impunity.

The explanation of the he-goat being deemed satisfactory, the ram was chided for his unseemly martial disposition, and was requested to ascend the hillock again and state his claim, but, having been so publicly rebuked in the presence of his adversary, he sheepishly refused. The he-goat was then called upon to ascend; but, his temper having been ruffled, he bowed solemnly to the assembly, and said that he would defer stating his claim to a later period.

CHAPTER XLI.

THE MASTIFF'S SPEECH.

A FINE Mastiff Dog standing near was then requested to ascend the hillock, to state the claims of his class, and while about doing so, he was asked to become spokesman for the lesser domesticated animals, whose timidity caused them to shrink from public display.

When he had ascended the hillock, the mastiff said he had been honoured by being requested to undertake the office of deputies' deputy for certain classes of animals whose natural timidity caused them, at the last moment, to shrink from putting in a personal appearance. Having a duty to perform, it was incumbent on him to discharge that first, before stating the claims of his own class.

They almost all knew that domesticated animals in general gave themselves up entirely for the benefit of man. They were made use of in every possible way, both when living and after death. Many of them were used as beasts of burden while living, and when dead the flesh of most of them was eaten to sustain man's life; and where their flesh was not eaten, and also in many instances where it was consumed, their hides, horns, hair, fur, feathers, &c., were all converted to some useful purpose. So that, speaking as the deputy of others, he thought that domesticated animals were entitled to take precedence of all others.

Here there were many dissentient voices raised, and objections taken to the mastiff's presuming to prejudge the question before any of the wild animals had been heard. After silence had been again restored, the mastiff continued.

He would now refer briefly to the claims of his own class. They too were frequently used as beasts of burden, and also in many countries, after their death, they contributed to the sustenance of man's life. Where their flesh was not eaten, their skins or other parts were utilized. His own, and other kindred species, were principally used as watchdogs to defend man's house or property from the midnight robber or marauding prowlers.—Here a gaunt Wolf rushed half-way up the hillock, and demanded what the mastiff meant by such a base accusation, and whether it were intended as a personal affront?

Owing to the hubbub that immediately ensued, tradition does not hand down the reply, but says that the mastiff, descending from the top of the hillock, met the wolf, and that a battle royal followed, which lasted for some time, and would have ended in the death of the wolf, had he not escaped with the loss of one ear.

The mastiff having spoken to the satisfaction of the assembly in general, was pressed on all sides to ascend the hillock again, and continue his speech, but, his dignity having been offended, he doggedly persisted in refusing to say any more.

After the Elephant, the Camel, and some other domesticated animals had spoken, many wild animals declared that they ought then to be heard, and were preparing to struggle, if need be, for the possession of the hillock, when the Gorilla, making himself heard, and felt by some of them, was seen marching up the hill.

Beating his breast, and otherwise demanding attention from the cowed multitude, he said his object in ascending the hillock was simply to ascertain who had dared to submit him to such an indignity as to summon *him* to an assemblage of inferior creatures. Related as he was to man, being in fact his first cousin, he scorned the idea of being subservient to him in any way. Indeed, he would like to receive a visit from any man daring enough to demand service of any kind at his hands; he would soon try conclusions with him. An accident which had happened to his great progenitor a few thousand years ago had caused a depression of the brain and a defect in the lingual organs, which unfortunately became inherent in his descendants, otherwise he (the gorilla), and not weak man, would have been lord of creation. He refused to take part in any of their proceedings, and now only waited to learn who had dared to summon *him* to such a motley meeting.

As most of the animals knew that the anger of the gorilla was no joke, a dead silence prevailed around. At last the elephant ventured to offer a humble apology, saying that the Secretary bird had, through ignorance or the multiplicity of business, committed the almost unpardonable mistake. He trusted, however, that the gorilla would be magnanimous enough to overlook the offence, which should not be repeated on any future occasion.

The gorilla thereupon calling the elephant a great oaf, ordered him to get out of the way, and not being obeyed quick enough, lifting up his walking-stick (a sapling oak of a few years' growth and a few inches diameter), he gave him a sounding thwack across his haunch with it, which caused the elephant to bellow and trumpet lustily. Seeing the mood that the gorilla was in, the vast multitude, by common consent, receded to the right and left, leaving a wide lane for the deposed lord of creation to pass through.

When the much-dreaded gorilla had taken his departure, there ensued a scene of pushing and struggling for the possession of the hillock, until the larger animals declared that they would punish instantly any further disorderly conduct, and so peace, or at least passive quietness, was once more restored. Many wild animals in succession then ascended the eminence and asserted their claims to precedence, demolishing in their opinion the claims set up by domesticated animals, and so impertinently advocated by the mastiff.

They plausibly enough declared that, without their destruction, man himself, much less the domesticated animals (which seem to have forgotten that they were once wild), could not exist. It is, one and another said, *we* who are justly entitled to precedence. Did we not yield our bodies for sustenance, our hides for various purposes, what could man do for clothing and other necessaries? Did not the trees yield their wood, where would man's house be, or how could he cook his food, or cure himself of many diseases when sick?

The subject having been thoroughly debated, the matter of precedence between wild and domesticated animals was then put to the vote, and (the wild animals being greatly superior in numbers) was carried by a large majority in favour of the wild animals. Then came the more knotty point of discussion, that of adjudging precedence among themselves, and herein the wild animals took the lead.

After a few representatives had spoken, there arose a scene of tumult and confusion which baffles description, each class denouncing his neighbour, and showing up to public reprobation the petty tricks and meannesses to which they were severally obliged to resort for a bare living.

Recrimination led to personal affronts, terminating in fierce encounters, which becoming contagious, the plain was in a short time converted into a general battle-field, over which, as well as on which, an apparently exterminating war raged.

Meanwhile the jackal, and the other conspirators, seeing how matters were progressing, slipped away out of the *mêlée*, laughing at the fools, and chuckling among themselves at the glorious feast in prospect. Exhausted at length with the fight, the victorious representatives once more proceeded to the discussion of class precedence, and the elephant being noted for his sagacity, was elected judge.

Before entering on his office, a commotion being observed in the sea and river, the attention of all was attracted thereto, when a Porpoise sprang out of the sea with a snort, and standing half out of the water, he addressed the multitude thus:—

"You snarling quarrelsome land-lubbers, you have summoned

THE PORPOISE'S SPEECH.

shoals of us to be present at a general parliament, but have taken up the whole day in wrangling among yourselves, and for the last two hours have only been fighting and killing each other. We have waited patiently the whole day, but not a mother's son of us has had an opportunity of spinning a yarn. We have listened while one and another have reeled off their logs, and now, tired and hungry, we are determined to stay no longer, and so leave you to fight it out among yourselves." Saying which, the porpoise turned a somersault, and disappeared with all the other representatives of the finny and amphibious tribes.

The elephant then, ascending the hillock, desired to say a few words before the discussion proceeded any further. Reviewing the plain before him, he said, pointing with his proboscis to the numerous dead bodies, " Instead of this plain being handed down by tradition as the 'Field of Parliament,' he feared it would only be known as the 'Field of the Slain.'

"He had witnessed with much sorrow the many conflicts that had taken place, and had even been compelled to defend himself against a brutal assault by the unmannerly rhinoceros. With reference to the matter under discussion, he thought that where opinions were so conflicting, there could be no possibility of arriving at any universally satisfactory conclusion.

"He thought that all classes were more or less dependent on each other, that each in his degree was useful and necessary to his neighbour, and to man, and that none, but He who created them, could apportion justly the degree of merit, and the position in precedence, which each should occupy in the great scheme of creation. He thought that the prolongation of the discussion, and of the meeting, would not be attended with any good result, and would therefore suggest that the parliament be dissolved amicably."

Assembling in congenial groups, the proposal of the elephant was taken into consideration, and met with universal approval, except from the rascally jackal and his confederates, who hoped that more animals would be killed, or die of exhaustion, if the meeting were prolonged.

The proposal was then formally put to the vote, and carried by general acclamation, the jackal, wolf, &c., then hypocritically assenting, in order to hasten the departure of the living representatives.

When the great parliament broke up, the jackal and other conspirators contrived to remain behind, and passed a merry night in feasting on the carcases of the vanquished representatives.

The president having finished his story, which had been frequently interrupted with bursts of laughter, a vote of thanks was unanimously accorded to him, and they all retired to bed.

Rousing the others early the next morning, the president made them get up and go out to enjoy the early morning air, which in the neighbourhood of the Soane at that time of the year is very delightful. Each one as a matter of course took his gun or rifle, and the president having ordered several men to accompany them, they set out for a ramble, and were fortunate enough to bag two deer, as they were going to the river to drink apparently.

The deer having been shot a few hundred yards from the camp, the men soon returned, after leaving them with the servants. After bagging several brace of partridges and pigeons, they struck deeper into the jungle, and Smith spying some animal moving off among some bushes, fired a snap shot, and evidently wounded it severely.

CHAPTER XLII.

FOLLOWING UP THE TRAIL.

ON going up to the place they soon saw spots of blood, and following the trace slowly, they saw a large sambhur lying down under a bushy tree. The president advised their retiring some distance, still keeping the deer in sight, which had a hind leg broken ; otherwise, if they roused him just then, he would be able to limp away into some thick jungle or ravine, where probably they would lose him. He said further that, if they waited a few minutes longer, the animal's leg would stiffen, besides the deer becoming more exhausted from the loss of blood. He also proposed that they should separate, and surrounding it, whoever got first within shot should give the deer the *coup de grace.*

Unfortunately for the success of the scheme, the deer perceiving them, rose and continued its flight. Determined not to lose it, they reunited and followed up the trace, which led them a weary walk. Gradually gaining on the animal, they suddenly lost sight of it, and going up to where it had last been seen, they found that it had fallen into a gully, and was lying there unable to rise.

While looking for an easy descent, Brown saw a tiger coming up the gully, when signalling for silence, he pointed it out to the others as it was coming along, plainly intent on carrying off the deer, and as such appropriation by no means met with their approval, it was quickly decided for three of them to take careful aim, and fire directly the tiger stopped to lift the deer.

Accordingly the supposed three best shots waited half a minute until the tiger came up to the·deer, when the latter made a stroke at it with its antlers, which caused the tiger to spring back a little, presenting a full broadside for a moment, which was instantly taken advantage of, and a general report following, the tiger rolled over almost on the deer. With a great effort the sambhur got up on its legs, but the next moment fell, no more to rise, a ball having entered its heart.

In the ardour of the pursuit they had not observed the course taken, and could not tell where they were, or how far from camp, nor could any of the men tell them. After loading their guns again and wishing, as is usually the case in such circumstances, for something unattainable, such as a bottle of beer each to quench their thirst, they sat down to rest while the camp followers were cutting stakes, and otherwise preparing to sling the deer and tiger. When all was ready, they found that all the game was too much for the men, so two of the gentlemen had to lend their shoulders, the others relieving in turn.

A long and weary trudge at last brought them back to the camp, where they arrived considerably out of sorts, tired, hungry, and thirsty. After refreshing themselves with a good wash while breakfast was being put on the table, they sat down to it with two appetites each, as one of them declared, for himself at least. Their frightful hunger having been satisfied, to the astonishment of the servants at the general clearance effected, they made themselves comfortable under the shade of some trees, commanding a view of the river towards the east. Here they sat smoking their cheroots or pipes, now one and then another grumbling at the tremendous walk of the morning, or expressing disgust at the weight, first of the tiger, but more especially of the sambhur, the president meantime quietly withdrawing.

By the time the president had finished overseeing the skinning of the tiger and deer, and superintending the preparations for the sambhur soup, the others had somewhat recovered their serenity, when, at his suggestion, they all prepared for a bath, as the best refresher after great fatigue. On their return, although greatly refreshed by their bath in the Soane, the majority were not inclined for any more walking that day, and called upon the president to favour them with a story, as they were pleased to say, he was such a good *raconteur*.

After thinking for a few minutes, the president said that he would relate to them one or two fables, the first being called—

THE TWO JACKALS. A FABLE.

Two jackals once, of solemn face,
Sat on their haunches with a grace,
Discussing a matrimonial scheme;
    Said one, "A son I have of parts,
    Well qualified by many arts
To be a good match for your lass, I deem.

"With him a portion, too, I'll give
(In this my simple word believe).
Hard by a patrol's well-stock'd henroost lies.
    The noonday watch is lax at best,
    And yields full oft a luscious feast
To him that's fearless, or who cunning tries."

With bow polite the other said,
" My daughter's young and tender bred,
Her accomplishments cost no small expense.
    But let me, sir, your portion view;
    If then I find your words prove true,
No trifle shall part two jackals of sense."

So saying, they both left the brake;
Reaching the place, the first one spake,
"'Mongst human kind, they say, who sees, believes,"—
    Just then the patrol saw them run,
    And, seizing quick his double gun,
He summary justice dealt the two thieves.

MORAL.

The moral is, be not too sure
    Of goods your neighbour lawful claims;
    Temptation's often but a lure,
And justice soon may blight your names.

N.B.—Shooting a jackal in some parts of India, *where they may be hunted*, is looked upon in the same light as shooting a fox is in England. But, on the borders of the jungle, where hunting is *not* practicable, a person will soon find how many enemies he has, the artful jackal among them, if he attempts to establish a *poultry-yard*.

Some having been inattentive at first requested the president to repeat the fable, who having done so, they had the conscience to cry "Encore," until he complied. When silence had been restored, the president was requested to relate his second fable, in the hope that it would be as good as the first. Of that, he said they must judge, and then gave them—

THE WILD DUCKS. A Fable.

A flock of ducks, on Beylan's stream,
    As wild as ducks could be,
Once council held, and this the theme—
    Not want, or scarcity—

But change of scene as well as air;
    "A change of food is good,"
A half-grown drake stood up and spake
    (Young ducks, you know, are rude).

The old birds star'd, their heads did shake
    At thought of speech so pert.
At length, one rose, and loud did squake,
    "It grieves me to the heart

"To think young ducks should be so rude
    As not to hesitate
To foremost speak (although 'twas good).
    Methinks they yet should wait.

"Such haste to speak, I much do quake,
    Bodes lack of sense to act."
Flapping her wings, an old duck spake,
    "Young ducks have not your tact.

"You must allow you cannot find
    Old heads on young roots grow:
Our greatest foes, the human kind,
    That truth full well they know.

"His speech yourself allow was good;
    No doubt it was well meant.
What wait we for, since change of food
    Is but our sole intent?"

Quack! quack! the whole flock joyful hied,
  And took a lofty flight.
A sportsman from afar them spied,
  And mark'd their chosen site.

With eager steps and body bent,
  Breathless with haste he came;
A friendly ant-hill shelter lent
  From which to take an aim.

His aim was sure, and two birds lay
  ('Twas sitting shot he took).
As the flock fled in haste away,
  Two more he brought to book.

Loading again, he looked round,
  And saw two yet retain'd
Their place; raising his gun, he found
  Our pert young drake remain'd.

His mate flew off, but circling came
  To take a sad farewell.
But sure and quick the sportman's aim,
  And by the drake she fell.

MORAL.

In this a moral you may see,
  Good folks, if so inclin'd:
Wherever danger 's like to be,
  Ne'er useless stay behind.
Whatever else my fable show,
  Read, mark, and well digest:
A forward spirit all eschew—
  Humility is best.

Just as the president had finished his second apologue, the mullah, or ferryman, brought some fine fishes, which he said he had caught a few minutes previously. Ordering them to be prepared for dinner, the fisherman was rewarded and dismissed, and then, being somewhat refreshed, they all went for a short stroll, during which they amused themselves in watching the gambols of a tribe of monkeys in some trees near the encampment.

Returning to the tents with two brace of partridges, they

attended to their toilettes, and then sat down to dinner. The sambhur soup, venison cutlets, and other things, having been pronounced excellent, and ample justice having been as usual done to all the dishes, the party gathered, according to custom, around the fire.

Reverting to the tricks of the monkeys, one of the party expressed himself as having been long desirous to know for a certainty whether monkeys could swim or not, and as the president knew a good deal of jungle life, he appealed to him for information on the subject. The president, in answer to the appeal, said that he would relate what he himself once saw, and then they might judge for themselves whether monkeys could swim or not.

CHAPTER XLIII.

THE MONKEYS EACH TAKE A HEADER.

WHILE living with a friend, who was commencing an indigo factory in a certain part of the Kymore plateau, his friend, himself, and another party used to go out for a walk in the afternoon inspecting different parts of the zemindary. One day they extended their walk to the extreme end of the estate, bordered by a hill-stream, irregular in depth, but in one place about twenty feet deep for a quarter of a mile in length, and the resort of several alligators.

We were sauntering along the top of the bank of the nullah, looking out for a shot at the alligators, which was the main object of the walk, when we came upon a colony of monkeys, which were apparently annoyed at our presence, resenting the intrusion into their domain by the usual jabbering and grimaces.

The monkeys were of the small kind, and were on a large tree, some of whose branches overhung the water, and their retreat to any other tree inland being cut off by our close approach, without any hesitation they went, one after another, to the end of one of the branches, and took a header in splendid style, as if well used to the performance.

Waiting to see the result of such an extraordinary new fact to them all, they saw the monkeys come up just at the edge of the water on the opposite side, and scuttle up the bank in double quick time. The nullah, or watercourse, there, was about forty yards wide, and as the monkeys were not seen from the moment of their diving down until they came up on the other side, it was clear that instinct and practice had taught them how to escape all their foes, imaginary and real.

The imaginary ones (ourselves) they escaped by swimming to the other side of the nullah, and the real foes (the alligators) they escaped by diving down like a shot, swimming a good depth under the surface of the water, and emerging from it on reaching the opposite bank, up which they scuttled in an amusingly hasty manner. Their actions altogether showed that they knew that alligators were in the nullah, and instinct, or experience, or both, had taught them that if they swam at the surface they would surely be seized by an alligator.

The monkeys could not have walked along the bottom of the nullah, because alligators, when not floating or swimming on the surface, or basking on the bank at the edge, are always at the bottom of the water they may frequent, and monkeys would not be likely to risk touching one of their mortal foes.

The president then proceeded to relate another remarkable fact in natural history, and that was, that a monkey, when taken very young from its mother, can be so domesticated as to prefer human society to that of its own species. Previous to going to live with him, the same friend had received from some natives a young monkey, of the small species, only a few hours old.

One of his friend's sluts having pupped the day before, when he found that the young monkey refused cow's or goat's milk, the idea struck him to put it to the bitch, which he did. The bitch at first did not like it at all, but after a time she took to it very kindly, seeming to like it more than its own offspring. As the young monkey took very readily to its foster-mother and sucked heartily, his friend had all the other pups destroyed, leaving only two black ones to be suckled with the stranger.

While the interesting family were growing up, their various comical tricks and gambols afforded an endless fund of amusement. When the young ones grew up sufficiently to be able to run out of the room, it was curious and instructive to watch the fierce fondness of the bitch for the young stranger.

It soon became an understood thing with all the other dogs,

that it was not safe to meddle with the monkey, the foster-mother having given two or three of them a lesson to that effect. In course of time, however, the fierce fondness of the foster-mother spread to all the other dogs, or else its own engaging manners had so won their regard, that, when the young monkey's voice was heard in any danger, the whole pack, some eight or ten dogs, would make common cause in its defence.

Sometimes a pariah dog would enter the premises, and on seeing the monkey would make a chase after it, thinking to have a little dinner, but the monkey's cry for help would bring every dog to the rescue, and then there would be a pretty little row. One day a large pariah dog had almost got Master Jacky, as he was called, but the shriek that he gave brought all the dogs full pelt up to the spot, and then ensued a battle royal, which would have ended in the death of the pariah, if he had not bolted in time with his tail between his legs, and all the dogs chasing him for half a mile.

As Jacky grew bigger and stronger, when getting the worst of it in play he used to bite pretty sharply, and when the bitten dog turned to punish him he would scamper off for protection to some other dog, on whose back he would spring or climb, and then sit perfectly at ease, feeling sure of being quite safe.

When we used to take the dogs out for sport, hunting pigs, &c., Jacky would be left at home tied up, and the lamentable cries he used then to utter often made us alter our mind, so that one of us would go back for him. Jacky disliked the native servants, but us Europeans the little monkey appeared really to love, for he would make as free with us as with the dogs. When we went out for a walk only, Jacky would be let loose, not even a collar round his neck, and then he was in the height of his enjoyment.

When tired of walking he would mount one of the dogs, or, if none were near, he would climb up our walking-sticks and clothes to our shoulders, on which he would stand or sit until some other fit took him. Sometimes he would get only halfway up one of our walking-

T

sticks, and then make a little cry, which we soon found out meant that he wanted a swing.

We had no fear of Jacky's ever voluntarily leaving us, as the poor little mannikin was too much attached to us for such a thought ever to enter his noddle. Instead of deserting us, he was always unhappy if he could not see or hear that we were near him, especially when we took him into the jungle; and many a time we tricked him, by watching when he had run a little ahead, when we would suddenly get round a bush and crouch down. When he really could not find us his cries were pitiable, and then, showing ourselves, Jacky would exhibit unmistakeable signs of pleasure.

We frequently, in our walks in the jungle, came across troops of monkeys, and then it was amusing to see how the wild ones would try to get Jacky to join them, and equally amusing was Jacky's terror of his own species. We repeatedly tried whether Jacky would join his own kindred, but without success.

He has been often thrown on to a tree, on which were wild monkeys of his own kind, and we have run away purposely, but on such occasions his terror was too extreme to suffer him even to cry out; he would, however, quickly descend the tree and scamper after us, and whichever of us he first came up to, he would climb up and nestle in his bosom, looking at us in such a piteous and supplicating manner that at last we left off the experiment.

Poor little Jacky was at last lost! We went out one afternoon for what proved to be a very long walk, too far for safety, and night came on when we were a good hour's walk from the house. Now, although we had traversed the ground repeatedly by daylight, knew, so to speak, every stick and stone, and thought that either of us could find the way blindfold, yet the woods, at dusk and after dark, put on such a totally different appearance, that we three Europeans unmistakeably got lost.

Not intending when we started to go any great distance from the house, we took only one gun between us, which, when night came on, we much regretted, as tigers, bears, &c., were known to be in the jungle, and we might come across any one of them at any moment, which, to say the least, was not a pleasant prospect. After walking about a long time, making, as we thought, a direct course for the south of the house, we came out in the end at the north-east of it.

We had for some time given up all idea as to the whereabouts of the house, and were looking out for the light of some fire at any village, so as to be able, as sailors say, to get the proper bearings, and a pilot or guide. After some further time, we saw a fire at a long distance off, and a welcome sight it was.

Quickening our pace as much as we could, tired as we were, we in time came up to it, and found that the servants had sense enough to surmise that we had lost the way, and had lighted a fire to guide us. But for this fire, where we should have gone to there is no knowing. When we flung ourselves on chairs, finding ourselves safe, we thought of the dogs and monkey.

A whistle soon brought all the dogs round us, but no monkey. In our excusable anxiety for our own safety, we did not take so much care of the monkey as at other times; besides, when night came on we each of us made sure that the monkey was with one or other of us. Early next morning, two of us, with several servants, traversed the back road for hours and miles, searching every place and calling for Jacky, but we never saw any more of him. Not only ourselves, but all the dogs, for a long time after, seemed sadly to miss the monkey.

Having finished his story, the president abruptly said, "Good night," and went off to bed, and the rest were not long in following such a good example. The next morning the president was up and about very early, giving certain directions, and when all was ready he commenced making a great clatter in the tents, effectually awakening the sleepers and making them get up.

When dressed, they saw the elephant and horses all ready, and, their curiosity being excited, they were informed that word had been brought of three nylgye having been seen at daybreak in the

Putwut jungle, and the president thought that they could not do better than go after them before breakfast. Mounting their animals, they were soon across the Soane and on the Putwut side, where they dismounted and entered the jungle to the west of Putwut, with a lot of men that the shikari had collected.

The jungle being thick and much intersected with ravines and hillocks, the president called a halt soon, and dividing the beaters equally, recommended their separating about twenty yards apart, and each one to do the best for himself, arranging a signal in case of assistance being required, should a tiger or bear be put up.

Proceeding in this way for some time, a shot was heard at the right end of the line, and word was soon passed along that one nylgye had been brought down. The president then directed the line to close up to the right, and, having heard the particulars, he suggested their wheeling to the right, in extended order as before, taking what might come in their way, as there was no use trying any longer after either of the other nylgyes.

On their return they could get only one spotted deer and a brace of peacocks, and mounting again they got back comfortably to the camp, having enjoyed their morning's walk. During their absence the ferry-man had brought a fine mahseer, which was a welcome addition to the morning meal. Making themselves clean, they sat down to breakfast with hearty appetites.

When the meal was over, the president proposed their all paying a second visit to Agoree, and returning to an early dinner, which being agreed to, the necessary orders were given. A basketful of lunch being given to one of the camp followers, and the fishing-tackle to another, they all started on horseback, leaving the elephant behind this time, as it would not cross the pontoon bridge over the Rehund.

After arrival at the old fort, they amused themselves with fishing and shooting at alligators until they were tired, and then, as the sun was getting too hot, they retired into the fort, where they soon made a clearance of the luncheon basket, this time without the help of any roving pariah dog.

CHAPTER XLIV.

A PARODY.

WHILE lounging about after tiffin (lunch), one and another enlivened the old fort with songs, and, calling upon the president, he gave them the following parody on the "Last Rose of Summer:"—

THE TOPER'S LAMENT.

'Tis the last bottle of beer
   Left standing alone,
All its mellow companions
   Are empty'd and gone;
No equal of such brewing,
   No trader is near,
To replenish my boxes
   And add to my cheer.

I'll not leave thee, thou lone one,
   To spoil in thy prime,
Where thy fellows are resting
   Thou'lt join them in time;
Myself I still flatter
   My tick is not dead,
From the batch whence thou camest
   May others be led.

As soon would I follow
   When plague leads the way,
As prove a base deserter
   From Allsopp away.
When the chest is empty,
   And credit is gone,
Oh! what shall I then do
   Without even one?

When the merriment which succeeded had subsided, the president was asked if he had any more, and then gave the following parody on "He's Gone:"—

THE BANKER'S LAMENT.

He's gone! and I shall never see
   His smiling face again.
My cash has now forsaken me!
   From fears I can't refrain.
On taking leave this early morn,
   He left me cash without;
Although he swore he'd ne'er forget,
   I now begin to doubt.

Should he forget how oft he swore
   To pay no one but me,
I'll send a writ the wide world o'er,
   Ere lose my lov'd money.
He said that to his banker dear
   He ever would prove true,
And hop'd no thought would cross my mind
   That *he* would prove *a do*.

He often said when last we met
   He'd ease my aching heart,
And grieved that unpropitious fate
   Should ever us two part.
He shortly would be back again,
   And pay without delay.
Oh! when I see him here remain
   'Twill be a happy day.

Nothing less than repeating both being insisted upon, the president was obliged to comply, and the noise that succeeded having once more subsided, he suggested that they should all return to camp. The horses being then saddled, they rode into camp leisurely, enjoying the scenery on the way. After making over to the servants the fishes that they had caught, with orders to prepare some for dinner and the rest for breakfast, they amused themselves with watching the actions of various birds and animals, and listening to the last notes of the day-birds retiring to roost.

THE TIGER'S AGILITY.

Dinner being at length announced, was done ample justice to as usual, and then all assembled once more around the fire, where the president informed them that a man during dinner had come and reported that there were some sambhur and other deer seen in another part of the Putwut jungle, and as they would most likely remain there during the night, he proposed that they should start very early the next morning and try for them, which was at once agreed to.

The conversation then turning upon tigers, one of the party asked if it were true that a tiger's joint made a cracking noise in walking, and that the animal could be smelt far enough off to permit of escape.

The president answered that a tiger's joints did make a cracking sound in walking, but that was only after the animal had made a heavy meal; that if its joints invariably made such a noise, it would have to go with many a hungry stomach; that a tiger might certainly be smelt at some distance, if the wind set from him, but as for allowing time to escape, that was quite another question. The place that a tiger habitually haunts, or in other words its lair, or den, may be discovered at a good distance by the smell, but he did not think that the common opinion was right about tigers being smelt far enough or soon enough to allow of escape from them.

Alluding to the tiger's agility, he said further, "You all have seen a house cat run up a wall five or six feet high; well, a tiger at a certain hankwa at the Jherria was seen to escape by springing up the precipitous side of the hill there, which is sixteen to twenty feet high. Another tiger was seen springing lightly over some bushes some feet higher than a man's head.

"A tiger when hungry or chasing after any animal is not easily eluded, as it has been known to gain rapidly in a chase after a leopard, fleet as that animal is. The tiger belonging to the feline tribe, is intended by nature to procure its prey by stealth and stratagem, not so much by fleetness of pursuit, and if its joints always made a noise in walking, it would seldom be able to come unawares upon any other animal."

The president then recited the following poem :—

THE TIGER.

Hush'd is the air, and night its darkest gloom
O'erspreads, when, noiseless through the silent wood,
Quitting his noonday lair umbrageous,
Conscious of mastery, the lórdly brute
Majestic takes his undisputed way.
The village tank his goal, his thirst he slakes;
Thence, peering oft through darkness' self with eye
Horrific, scanning wide with ardent gaze
The mead around, anon he spies the steer,
That truant, hapless, from the nightly fold,
Giddy refus'd the herdsman's guarding care.

* * * *

With fearful crash the drowsy ear of watch
Is sudden rous'd; the cause unask'd, by fear
His limbs all agitate, he trembling wakes
His slumbering mate, and, whispering low,
Imparts the dread-inspiring, fearful news;
Confirm'd too well by life's departing groan,
Which, long pent up, bursting at length all bonds,
Proclaims in death the savage monster's might.
With easy strength the victim now he lifts,
Quick drags it thence to some secluded spot;
The timid hinds the while with distant shout,
To scare the hungry brute in vain they strive,
Whose roar approximate, with creeping fear
Causes the stoutest frame to inward quail.

* * * *

With rasped tongue the oozing gore he licks,
His fangs to whet; anon, the pond'rous thigh
He quickly bares, and wakes the gloomy wood
With horrid scrunch. Again the pool he seeks,
And thence return'd, full oft renews his feast,
Till, gorged full, his cracking ankles warn
Th' unwary wight of danger fell too near,
As pacing slow, with visage grimly dy'd,
He seeks, 'mid thickest wood, his darksome den.

In answer to a question, the president said that the poem was written by himself, on an incident of actual occurrence, to which he was an ear-witness. He never remembered such an intensely dark night, and although not more than fifty yards off when he fired four balls unsuccessfully (judging by ear alone, for he could not see even the sight at the end of his gun) at the tiger as it was passing, the brute did not stop a moment, but dragged off the bullock almost at a trot.

The president then demanding a spell of rest, called upon one of the others for a song, which was duly given, and the rest having answered the call in turn, the president was called upon, who said that he would not sing for fear of frightening the owls, but would recite another little poem.

PRUDENCE COUNSELLING YOUTH.

As through this wilderness one day I roam'd,
A modest flow'ret caught my wand'ring eyes,
Whose half-op'd petals but display'd a grace
That augur'd well for future loveliness.
Although full many a fairer blossom
My transient eyes had rested on while I
This troublous wilderness was passing through,
None had the charm like this my weary steps
To stay; from it an unknown something rare
Seemed diffus'd around, which, like a snare,
Made surer still with fragrance thickly spread,
Barr'd my way; and, as a willing captive,
My steps arrested thus, my time I fill'd
With oft-repeated ardent longing gaze.
Its charms were not in gaudy colours dressed;
Its native hue was sombre, yet it had
Nameless graces, which I wondering saw
Diffusing "sweetness on the desert air."
I look'd around if haply I might see
Some other flower that had shed abroad
This pleasing fragrance, or whose dress might vie
With this; but no, this one alone my gaze
Recall'd; others there were, but this alone
Me captive held.
         Sweetness like this to see

Running to waste on desert air alone,
Caused surprise, inducing me to stoop
At once to pluck and place this op'ning bud
Next to my inmost secret heart, when lo!
My eager hand as sudden was restrain'd
By unseen power, greater still than mine,
While chilling Prudence, passing by that way,
Thus sagely spake :—
      "A shelter first provide,"
She said, "lest rudely plucking now, this bud,
Half form'd, through chilling blasts, should early droop
And fade away; let be, again I say,
Your pressing want a shelter to provide,
Successful, then, with tender care, transplant
This floral gem; thereafter, guarding still
With watchful thought solicitous, nourish
The secret charms which day to day matures,
Till envious Death the bond between you break."
With sadden'd soul I turn'd my wistful gaze
The flow'ret's modest face to read once more.
To my delighted eyes it seem'd to smile,
And something bade my longing heart to hope.
With courage fresh, my way with leaden steps
I took, cheered in heart by Mem'ry's sign.

When the poem was ended, Smith jokingly asked whether the homily were intended to be personal, to which the president replied, "By no means; but if any one thought that the cap fitted, they might use their discretion as to wearing it."

CHAPTER XLV.

AFTER THE SAMBHUR AT PUTWUT.

THE president then suggested their all retiring early, as they would have to be up before daybreak the next morning, and accordingly, after the necessary orders had been given to the servants, they turned in to bed. An hour before daybreak the next morning the president roused up the others of the party, and, while they were dressing, he ordered the servants to bring the chota hazree (small breakfast), taking this precaution in case of being out longer than they expected. By the time the small breakfast was over the day had well broken, and the elephant and horses being ready, they all started for Putwut, where they found the Sulkhun shikari and a good number of beaters waiting for them.

Leaving directions for the animals to wait their return at Putwut, the party set out under the guidance of the shikari, and were well satisfied with their success, two sambhur, one spotted deer, three hares, and two peacocks being their morning's work. Getting tired at last, one of the villagers was sent off with orders for the elephant and horses to be brought along the road to a certain point which they would make for. The last deer that was shot having been slung, they took the nearest way for the road, where they found the animals waiting, and giving orders for the shikari and beaters to come along, they mounted and soon returned to the tents.

After having a good wash and a change of clothes, they sat down to an abundant meal, with genuine hunter's appetites. When breakfast was over, the paymaster was requested to give the shikari and the beaters their reward, which being done and the caterer having given orders about the game, they variously disposed of themselves for an hour or so. After they were sufficiently cool and rested, the waters of the Soane again refreshed them with a delightful bath.

While returning from bathing, the president called the attention of the others to the singular politeness of a small species of owl, which he pointed out on the branch of a large tree. No sooner did the eye of each one catch that of the funny little owl, than it bowed and made a noise so much like "How do do!" that it made them all burst out laughing at the comical seriousness of the bird.

When they had got back to the tents and made themselves comfortable, the president challenged Brown to a game of chess, while the rest amused themselves in other ways. Just as the president had finished his game with Brown, checkmating him cleverly, the shikari came to announce that there were some tigers at the Jherria, and wished to know if he should tie up a victim.

This information caused them to alter a previous determination of staying one day longer at Chopun, and consequently the president ordered the shikari to have everything in readiness, and tie up the victim, the next evening, as on the following day they would leave for Sulkhun.

By this time it was getting dusk, and after giving the various servants directions to prepare to leave Chopun early the next morning, they all got ready for dinner, which was announced shortly afterwards. The sambhur soup, venison pie, and other dishes had justice done to them, and were pronounced excellent; after which they all assembled for the last time around the fire at Chopun.

After much general conversation about their several sporting adventures, the president was called upon for a story; who, after some consideration, said that, instead of a story, he would recite to them a poetical dream, which would perhaps take them, in imagination, back to old times and scenes; and then proceeded to recite—

A FLORAL DREAM.

All under a budding tree one day,
As, soundly sleeping, a gladsome fay,
New cloth'd in a suit of spider's loom,
But recent dy'd in fresh peaches' bloom,
With dewdrops bright pendant from each ear,
And deck'd with gems that man may not wear,
Appear'd to my enraptured gaze,
Enthralling my sense in deep amaze.
Form'd was her figure of loveliness,
And in her gait was true beauty's grace; 10
Pactolian streams would scarce compare
With such elfin locks of auburn hair,
That truant over her shoulders lay,
Inviting sweet zephyrs by the way.
And in her velvet tiny right hand,
She gracefully bore an opal wand,
Tipp'd with a diamond bright and clear,
That made e'en the darkness light appear;
And in it there lay such magic spell
As wisest fairies alone can tell. 20
Slow waving it thrice, she touch'd my e'ne,
And caused such sights as seld' are seen.
Waving once more her magical wand,
In silvery tones she 'gan command—
"Ye gamesome elves, and all spirits leal,
Who joyous attend our only weal,
Where'er ye be now, come featly forth,
And let your deeds straiten thanks of worth.
Whether in air soft floating around,
Dark hidden in caves, or deep in ground, 30
Embower'd low in sweet sylvan shades,
Or gently tripping o'er moonlit glades,
Our need now summons the aid of all,
Come, instant attend our queenly call."
Ere her final words had faintly died,
From unknown space there seemed to glide
Troops upon troops of beautiful elves:
Wild with mad joy, they seem'd lost themselves.
Vain were the task to number the throng
That, thicker still, came buzzing along. 40

PAST DAYS IN INDIA.

Some filled the branches that were spread,
O'erladen before, over my head;
Some, balanc'd in air; some, squat on ground;
While multitudes throng'd the grass around,
As you may have seen a hive disturb'd,
Their eager desire could scarce be curb'd,
Longing to fly on wings of the wind,
And leave all dull laggards far behind.
Some, chafing, fretted and fum'd the while;
Some preened their wings to time beguile;
Till, waving around her potent wand,
The bonny wee queen thus gave command:—
" Ye gentle elves, now let it be seen
The love that ye boast ye bear your queen.
This bidding do as well as ye may,
So shall we see which is the best fay.
We have a mortal under our charm:
Drown him in sweets, in flowers embalm;
Go, search England's isle—ransack each nook—
Bring here the best by hook or by crook.
The rarest ye find, quick hither bring,
Both those that bloom in winter and spring.
Leave not the homely ones all behind:
Bring hither some of every kind."
They scarcely were gone, ere back some came,
Loaded with flowers of unknown name.
Some, beautiful daisies fresh and fair,
Moss roses others brought, rich and rare,
Lilies of vale and violets sweet;
Some, bright buds of May laid at her feet.
Snowdrops and cowslips, and blue harebell,
And some lapfulls brought of pimpernel;
Ranuncule gay, auricula sweet;
With fairest camellia then did meet;
Dozens were bringing one peony;
Hundreds supported Victor. Regi.;
Tulips some brought, some memory's sign,
Clematis sweet some, some eglantine,
Carnations some, wallflowers a lot,
And dog-roses, too, were not forgot.
Loaded with holly some bending low,
Others bore branches of mistletoe.
Primroses, lilac, broom and briar,
Jessamine stars and flowers of fire,
Heartseases, too, and holyoak tall,
With Michaelmas daisies, came at call.

A FLORAL DREAM.

Dear buttercups, corncockle beside,
Neat-growing thrift, and true London pride,
Sweet mignionette, pink apple-tree bloom,
Fuchsia globosa was brought by some.
Some passion-flower, flaming Turk's cap,
Canterbury bells empty'd from lap.
Love bleeding lies, and fair columbine,
Peas, honeysuckle, foxglove, lupine,
Jonquil, laburnum, blue cyclamen,
Crocus, and lavender, mingled then.
Snapdragon and anemone gay
Were brought by a neat little old fay.
Pinks, piccotees, and hyacinths sweet,
Did then my enraptur'd senses greet.
Heaps upon heaps of others they brought,
Of names unknown, or else are forgot.
At length, the fay queen said, with a smile,—
" Now, little elves, come help us awhile.
Under this tree (and see him ye can)
Lies haply asleep a mortal man.
His trespass so clear deserves its doom,
We'll mortals show now how to presume.
Drown him in fragrance—such is our will ;
Smother'd with flowers, with sweetness kill."
Scarce cold were her words, ere some began
With sweet-smelling leaves my face to fan.
Some irises brought, others a rose,
And with their petals tickled my nose.
Scores upon scores came buzzing about,
Sounding in ear my funeral note.
Thousands oft went and came in a breath,
Busy engaged bringing my death.
Repassing oft, the busiest some
Higher and higher builded my tomb.
Raising a pæan, some began then
Closing the top with peony, when
I heard the queen say, " Now let us dance."
(Like as when one deep lies in a trance,
Odours delightful I smell'd around,
Saw lovely flowers strewing the ground,
And heard the queen's lips my death distil,
And felt the wee elves obey her will ;
I, seeming to sweat, mightily strove,
Yet power had none a muscle to move.)
Bury'd in bliss—nigh passing away—
An envious ant, by no means gay

(Sure crossed in love, or hap in fight
Worsted by emmet), it out of spite,
Deep drove its venomous fangs within
The tenderest part close to my shin.
Smarting with pain, mid memory's gleam,
I, sadly awaking, found it—a dream.

When the president had finished relating his dream, he said that, as there was still plenty of time, he would tell them a story which had just come into his mind, if they were inclined to listen. While they were expressing their approval, a servant came with a tray containing glasses of punch, which necessarily caused a little delay. After refreshing themselves, the president proceeded to relate the story found in the following chapter.

CHAPTER XLVI.

THE LAZY RIVER.

IN a certain country there was a River that was very lazy and discontented with its lot, continually murmuring against Fate. This river was so sluggish in its movements, that all that had anything to do with it were ever bitterly reproaching it for not moving on faster.

One day, when they could no longer bear it, the fishes, frogs, efts, newts, and other water animals, sent up a cry to Fate, that unless the river moved along faster they could not live in it. To this complaint Fate answered, that although the River was lazy, it was their own fault if they chose to live in it. You have fins or feet, why do not you swim or go away to more agreeable water? Thanking Fate for the suggestion, they all acted upon it, and in a body left the Lazy River.

The next day the herons, king-fishers, and other aquatic birds, sent up a cry to Fate, that owing to the perverse conduct of the Lazy River all the fishes and other animals that used to live in it had left, and they had nothing to eat. Fate answered, " It is your own fault if you choose to starve. You have legs and wings, why do you not go away to some other water?" These also, thanking Fate for the suggestion, flew away in a body from the Lazy River.

The Lazy River, meanwhile, was rather glad at getting rid of the fidgetty fishes and troublesome birds, and, as there was now no one in it to find fault, it crawled along more sleepily than ever. After a few days of such stagnant life, all the aquatic plants sent up a cry to Fate, that since the fishes and birds had left, insects of all kinds had increased so much, that unless the River moved on faster they would all be eaten up and die.

To this complaint Fate answered, "that the Lazy River was only preparing its own punishment; that they were helpless, and must abide by their lot. But why do you not drop your seeds, or otherwise prepare for your deaths?" These, too, thanked Fate; and acting according to the advice given, dropped their seeds or secured their roots, and then died down or were eaten up.

When the water plants had all died, the stench that arose from decaying vegetable matter so poisoned the air and water, that all the plants and trees growing on the banks sent up a cry to Fate, that owing to the extreme laziness of the River they could never obtain nourishment enough, but only just managed to exist; that since the departure of the fishes and birds there was no vitality in the water; and that since the death of their relations, the water plants, the air and water had become so foul that they could no longer live. Fate answered these as the water plants were answered, and advised them to exhibit patience and resignation to their lot. Thanking Fate for the advice, they sorrowfully hung their heads, dropped their seeds, or made other preparations, and then, one after another, died.

The plants and trees on the banks having all died, was rather a matter of rejoicing over than otherwise, as now, the Lazy River said to itself, it would be able to enjoy more of the rays of the sun, which had been so long intercepted by the bushy plants and trees. The leaves and branches of the dead land plants falling into the River, choked it a great deal, but, as it hardly moved half-a-mile an hour, it was too sluggish to carry them away; consequently they rotted, and added to the malaria.

Meanwhile the Sun, having full power on the River, called into life innumerable myriads of insects of many kinds, and many kinds of flies, in vast hosts, taking advantage of the still water, settled on its bosom and completely hid it from sight, while tainting the water still further.

THE LAZY RIVER'S COMPLAINT. 291

Things having come to this pass, all the land animals and birds that used to drink of the water sent up a cry to Fate, that owing to the extreme laziness of the River, its water had become so putrid that they could not drink it, and were all dying of thirst. To these Fate answered, "It is your own fault if you die. You have legs or wings, why do not you go elsewhere to drink?" Thanking Fate for the suggestion, all the land animals and birds entirely deserted the lazy, foul River, going to pleasanter waters to drink.

By this time, owing to the mass of decaying vegetable matter, and the enormous increase of insects and flies of all kinds, the Lazy River was so choked that it could no longer move even as slowly as it had been delighting in. Feeling itself dying gradually, the Lazy River at last sent up a cry to Fate, complaining of the barren country in which its lot had been placed; that there were no fishes or birds frequenting its stream, that no plants would live in its bosom or on its banks, that no ainmals came to drink of its waters, and that it was being killed by swarms of insects of all kinds.

This complaint being unjust in every particular, Fate took no notice of it. The Lazy River then sent up a murmuring cry for help, complaining against Fate for not at once attending to its call. To this also Fate gave no reply. The Lazy River then sent up a despairing cry, humbly asking for advice, if help would not be given. Fate then answered, "The fault is entirely your own. You have that in your bosom, the Boulder of Sloth, that will inevitably destroy you unless you rouse yourself, and make strong and persevering efforts to cast it from you entirely."

Thanking Fate for the advice given, and not liking to be choked to death, the Lazy River determined to make an effort against all enemies, and overcome them. Resolving to begin with the hosts of insects, it suddenly began to move. This, for some time, unusual occurrence caused a great commotion among the numerous tribes of insects, that began swimming, sliding, crawling, or flying in all directions, all of them unanimously resenting the motion of the water.

Having striven in vain for many days against the hosts of its enemies, the weary River sent up another cry to Fate, asking for help; saying that of itself it could not overcome its many enemies, and entreating assistance; and Fate, having witnessed the efforts of the River, advised it to ask the Wind and Rain for help.

Once more thanking Fate for the advice, the River sent up a prayer: "O Wind! give me heart of grace against my enemies. O Rain! refresh me with thy sweet drops." Wind and Rain having both witnessed the useless efforts of the once Lazy River, pitying its foul condition, gave their much-needed help.

Wind first came along as a gentle zephyr, which the innumerable flying insects rather liked, but as it gradually increased in force they were all obliged to take flight. The Wind blowing stronger and raising a ripple on the surface, Rain came along, and so refreshed the River that, gathering up all its energies, it made a mighty effort, and in one day cleared its hitherto choked and sluggish stream of all the decaying vegetable matter, and all the immense hosts of insects that had crowded its waters and impeded its progress.

The River then sent up another humble cry to Fate, requesting to know where the great Boulder was, and how it was to be removed. To this prayer Fate answered, that the Boulder of Sloth was embedded in the Sands of Inaction, and surrounded by the Pebbles of Discontent; and the only way to remove the Boulder was by ploughing furrows through the sand. The Pebbles of Discontent being then loosened, and the Boulder undermined, it was by main force to be rolled along down to the Sea of Oblivion.

Again thanking Fate for the information and advice given, the River commenced making a diligent search from its fountain head, turning up every patch of sand, and compelling each pebble to shift its place. News of the diligent search soon spread, and the

Sands of Inaction hearing the report became much disturbed. During the disturbance that followed the hearing of the report, the Pebbles of Discontent becoming loosened were carried away one by one, by the revived force of the current, disclosing to view the unsightly black Boulder of Sloth. Not at all approving of the disturbance and commotion going on around it, and yet not liking to take any trouble, the great Boulder of Sloth determined on offering all the resistance it was capable of, viz., its own dead weight.

Coming up to the Boulder, the renewed spirit of the River commanded it to move on, as it must no longer be a bar to progress. Meeting with no reply, the spirit of the River was incensed at its contemptuous silence, and at once began to use rough measures, increasing in force by degrees, until, making one grand effort, the Boulder of Sloth began to give way, and at last toppled over completely. Pleased with its victory, the spirit of the River would not give the Boulder of Sloth one moment's rest, but kept on rolling it over and over, until it disappeared in the Sea of Oblivion.

While the great battle was going on between the renewed spirit of the River and the great Boulder of Sloth, and its other enemies, fishes and other water animals, hearing of the great change, came swarming up the stream in shoals. Aquatic birds also, hearing that the River was once more peopled, soon re-appeared on its bosom. The plants and trees feeling the benefit of the change, sent up new shoots, or young ones sprang up with a vigorous growth. Birds and land animals also smelling the fresh pure water, once more frequented its banks, and slaked their thirst in its now limpid stream.

When the spirit of the River returned victorious, it could hardly recognise itself, or its own clean scoured channel, and when it was greeted with joyous acclamations on all sides, it gratefully thanked Fate for the lessons of wisdom received, and firmly resolved thenceforth to continue its renewed course of life.

Having finished his story, the president said that as they would have to get up early the next day they had better go to bed, and accordingly all retired. At daybreak the next morning the khansamah awoke them with the announcement that chota hazreh was ready, which made them all jump up and dress quickly. When the camp equipage had left, the president explained that he had ordered the Sulkhun shikari to be ready with men, and he proposed that they should ride to Putwut, and about half way to Sulkhun, dismount there and strike into the jungle to the left, where forming an extended line and wheeling to the right, they should shoot their way into camp, when by the time they arrived breakfast would be ready.

This proposal being agreed to, they all mounted and crossed the Soane, in the middle of which, while letting their horses drink, they took a parting draught of its healthful waters.

At rather less than half way to Sulkhun, they found the shikari waiting with several men to act as beaters, where having dismounted and given the syces (grooms) orders to go on to camp, they spread themselves in a line and struck off into the jungle to the left, gradually wheeling to the right. They had not gone far when a deer was seen bounding over some low bushes, but having been perceived a moment before by Brown, the animal was brought down in splendid style by a ball while on the leap.

This shot roused other animals, and another deer, a pig, a hare and a peacock fell right and left in about a minute. Having shot enough venison and pork, it was determined on to shoot only small game for the remainder of the walk, so taking the smooth bores from the attendants, they soon made up a load for two men, bagging three hares, three brace of grey and two brace of black partridges, five brace of quails, and two young pea-fowl. While the men were beating the bushes, one of the party (Jones) saw a nice young porker scampering off, and remembering a former barbecue, his career was soon brought to a close.

CHAPTER XLVII.

THE STOREKEEPER'S ACCOUNT AT FAULT.

THE shikari conducted them so well, that they emerged from the jungle right on the road, about one hundred and fifty yards from the village of Sulkhun. On reaching the tents they found that breakfast was waiting, and as they were ready it was ordered to be brought at once. Refreshing themselves with a good wash, they all sat down with ravenous appetites, which the abundance on the table hardly satisfied.

Breakfast being over, and the beaters paid, they found the shikari in attendance, and went with him to inspect the menagerie, kept in a hut engaged for the purpose in the village. After settling accounts with the shikari, the president instructed him to tie up the victim that night, and make the other necessary preparations for a hankwa the next day.

These matters being arranged they returned to the tents, and the various heads of departments took the opportunity to make a general overhaul and inspection of everything in their several departments. The storekeeper soon found that he could not make his beer and brandy account tally. On inquiring into the matter of the discrepancy, the servants only implicated each other, without any one making a distinct charge ; so a general council being immediately held, it was resolved that as the liquids could only have disappeared with the connivance of all the servants, a rateable proportion should be deducted from their several wages to pay for the abstracted liquor.

When the servants were assembled it was announced to them, that as they did not choose to confess who had taken the liquids, the whole cost would be deducted from their wages rateably.

This decision caused great consternation, but as they knew that there was no help for it, they retired not over pleased, and shortly after a great row was heard and seen among them, when they were all collected together to discuss the justice of their employers' decision. But as the matter could not apparently be settled by word of mouth, two or three couples soon got by the ears, scratching and pulling each other by the hair. Some of the more peaceable interfered to separate the combatants, but were themselves drawn into the fray.

The row gradually increasing, and the preparations for dinner being entirely suspended meanwhile, the caterer and one or two more of the party, thought it was high time to take a more active part in the disturbance than being mere spectators of the comic scene.

Going quickly to the scene of the disturbance, a sound cuff right and left, and a Saxon grip, soon brought the angry ones to their senses, and a threat of a further fine if the dinner were delayed or spoiled, sent the cook and others off at once to their duties.

When the caterer and others returned and had seated themselves, the president informed them that when a similar row takes place amongst native servants, the masters are sure for some time after to be extra well served, and prophesied that they would have a splendid dinner that evening, which came true to the letter.

As it was too late to go out again that day, hot water, which had been ordered beforehand was brought, and each one occupied himself with thoroughly cleaning his guns, so as to prevent the possibility of any mischance at the hankwa the next day. By the time that the guns were cleaned, oiled and carefully loaded, it had got dusk, and shortly after the shikari came to report having tied up the victim, and made the other preparations.

He also reported that there were certain signs of two tigers at least being at the Jherria, so that there was every prospect that the hankwa would not be a blank. Dismissing the man with instructions to have the beaters ready by daybreak, the president ordered dinner to be brought while they all cleaned themselves.

The dinner, as prophesied by the president, was found to be excellent; the barbecue especially, the only fault that the caterer could find with one preparation arose from the scarcity of eggs, which were not procurable that day, otherwise the pillau would have been perfect.

After feasting gloriously, they found a capital fire blazing a bright welcome, and while seated around it, when other subjects began to flag, the president was called upon for a story, but demurring to being so frequently called upon, he said that it would be only fair to call first upon each one of the party in turn for either a story or a song, and all having complied with the request, the last one called in his turn upon the president, who, instead of story or song, recited the following—

MONODY OF THE DESERTED DOVE.

Upon a leafless tree on high
A mournful turtle lonely sat,
Filling the ears of passers-by
With doleful wailing for her mate.

"Ah, faithless! whither hast thou flown,
Deserting me to cruel fate;
The livelong day me finds alone
Asking in vain thy cause of hate?

Ah me! didst e'er thou think to grieve,
And sorrow's pangs not rend my breast?
What luckless day could I thee leave,
And hope to find a moment's rest?

My moans thou absent canst not hear?
Now life's sweet joys are o'er, alas!
My bosom pants with unknown fear,
Nor know I how the days I pass.

> Death now would be a sweet release
> From pains I can no longer bear;
> My absent mate his love doth cease,
> And others' notes I could not hear."
>
> Filling the wood with mournful cry,
> Death heard her pass the heavy day;
> Swift as the light swoop'd down from high
> A hungry hawk on hapless prey.

The president having finished the recital, then said it was time for all to go to bed, as they would have to be up by daylight at latest, and accordingly all retired.

Most of the party slept so soundly that, when they were awaked with some difficulty the next morning, it seemed as if they had hardly slept an hour. As one or two were inclined for a little more sleep, the president told them plainly that he and all who were ready would start in exactly ten minutes, so that if they chose they might still be able to go, otherwise by lingering they would surely be left behind.

Knowing that the president would be as good as his word, and not wishing to lose the chance of shooting the tigers, or at least of witnessing the exciting scene, the drowsy ones jumped up without further delay, and were speedily ready, claiming however five minutes' grace to get a bite and a cup of hot coffee, which was barely consented to.

All being ready at last, they found the shikari and the rokhs or stoppers waiting, and mounting their horses they rode in silence as far into the jungle as was prudent; then dismounting and sending the horses back into camp, they proceeded with as little noise as possible to their several machauns.

When they were all seated, with their artillery handily arranged, and the rokhs well placed, the shikari departed to give the signal for the commencement of the hankwa, or drive. After waiting what in their impatience seemed an age, the signal was telegraphed down and back, and then was heard the first beat of the centre drum, instantly followed by that of the other drums, and the simultaneous shouts of the large semicircle of beaters.

Presently, out popped a boar, which stood a moment, as if considering what the row was about; but, his ears giving him warning that other animals were afoot, and which he was not inclined to meet, he made a sudden rush, and was soon out of sight.

Scarcely had the pig vanished, when a large bear came shambling along, looking behind him now and then, evidently not at all approving of being disturbed in his meditated repose after the labours of the night. He, too, thought it best to clear out soon from such a neighbourhood, and was succeeded by a pot-bellied hyena, giving proofs that his nocturnal ramblings had not been unsuccessful, but who managed to shuffle out of the row with creditable dispatch.

These were succeeded by a few smaller animals, and then, after waiting on the tiptoe of expectation, a huge tiger was seen coming along majestically, as if it scorned to flee. Allowing it to come full into view, two rifles spoke, and on the instant another tiger, or rather tigress, bounded in front.

Then followed a general discharge, some firing at the tiger, and others at the tigress. Owing to their over-excitement, not one ball was fatal; the tiger, however, was lying with his spine broken, and roaring awfully, but the tigress nearly escaped, when a fortunate shot broke her back also.

As all the guns had been emptied, every one was busy in reloading, when the beaters were seen approaching. Shouting to them to keep off, they divided their fire, but, owing to the movements of the animals, and their own unusual over-excitement, neither of the tigers could be killed. After re-loading once more, a steadier aim was taken, and the tiger's roarings were finally silenced.

The tigress, however, had managed to drag herself into a clump of high grass, and could not be seen, and, as it was dangerous for any one to go near while there was the possibility of life in her, they were obliged to be content with each one firing carefully according to his judgment. The last one of the party having fired, they again loaded, and, as the tigress made no noise or sign, the shikari was ordered to reconnoitre with two or three men.

Proceeding very cautiously to the clump of grass, on searching it they at first found only a large snake dead, but almost immediately one of the men made a sudden start backwards, which caused the others to retreat rapidly as the tigress was heard and seen, dragging herself along to seize one of them. The men having got out of the way, three of the party, taking deliberate aim, soon put the tigress out of her misery.

When she too was still in death, the beaters sent up a triumphant shout that made the welkin ring again. While the party were descending from their several machauns, the shikari and beaters were busy in cutting poles, &c., for carrying off the tigers.

On examination, the tiger was found to have received no less than eleven balls and the tigress nine; and such of the balls as struck on the head or fore-legs, or rather fore shoulder, were found to be completely flattened.

On one and another expressing themselves ashamed at such apparent butchery, the president said he could not concur in such an opinion. The tigers were the largest he had seen for some years, and, were it not that their spines had been broken early in the fight, they would have carried off the other balls and have escaped into the jungle, where they would no doubt have died. Their own excitement after the first shot each, together with the roarings and contortions of the animals, made it impossible (for him at least) to take a steady aim. It was unfortunate that they took so many balls to kill them, but it was well that such monsters *were* killed.

CHAPTER XLVIII.

THE LARGEST TIGERS SHOT FOR SOME YEARS.

AFTER examining the tigers, they went to look at the snake, and found it to be one of the non-venomous species, which attains to ten feet or so when full grown, the one shot being at least nine feet long, and about two inches thick. This kind of snake (dhamin) is very destructive where poultry are kept, being extremely fond of eggs, young chickens, or ducklings, which it will abstract from under the sitting or brooding hen or duck without disturbing her.

Being satisfied with their inspection, they ordered the snake to be taken to camp with the tigers; and then taking two or three men with them, they started for the camp, leaving the shikari to bring on the tigers in the usual way.

On the road back to camp they managed each to have a shot; bagging three brace of partridges and two peacocks. The morning air and exercise, together, had so sharpened their appetites, that breakfast was ordered immediately on their return, and was served while they were paying the necessary attention to their toilettes.

During breakfast the beaters came in, bringing the tigers and snake in triumphant procession, and with more than the usual noisy accompaniment. When their hunger was at last satisfied, the paymaster was requested to settle accounts with the beaters, &c., during which process the shikari suggested a little extra present, in honour of the largest tigers shot for some years, which was accordingly agreed to.

The party then amused themselves watching the operation of

skinning the tigers, until, finding the sun too hot, they retired to the tent, and, after commenting on their morning's work for some time, one and another called upon the president for a story, who, after considering awhile, proceeded to relate the following native story (which he said might possibly amuse them) of—

A JACKAL AND AN ALLIGATOR.

A jackal going every day to a certain river to drink, regularly saw an alligator which frequented that part of the river. Seeing each other daily, in course of time an intimacy sprang up between them, which however did not last long, owing to the evil disposition of the alligator.

On a certain day, the alligator, taking offence at the jackal for not doing him some service on which he had depended, determined on his destruction. Knowing that the jackal came regularly at a certain hour to drink, after troubling the water and so making it muddy, the better to conceal himself, the alligator waited patiently the coming of the jackal, and, on his arrival, making a spring, he seized him by the leg.

The wily jackal guessed the whole matter at once, and instantly conceived a plan of delivering himself from his pretended but treacherous friend. Seeing the muddy state of the water, he cried out, "How fortunate it was, as the water is so muddy, that I thought of bringing my walking-stick, to try the depth before stepping in myself."

The alligator, thinking that the jackal spoke the truth, thereupon quietly let go his leg, when the latter, finding himself at liberty, quickly placed a safe distance between them, and, turning round, said to the alligator, "You fool! does a jackal ever use a walking-stick?" and then ran off to another part of the river to drink.

The alligator finding himself deceived, and stung by the taunts of the jackal, determined on revenging himself for the trick

THE ALLIGATOR TURNS UP HIS TOES. 303

played on him. During his rambles on land one day, he chanced to come to the jackal's house, and, not finding him at home, went and hid himself behind the entrance, intending on his return to snap him up.

Soon after that the jackal, having had a good dinner, was coming home to have a nap, when he smelt a strong fishy odour. Divining the scheme instantly, the jackal stopped and called out, " House, why don't you wish me good evening, as usual. I suppose some enemy must be inside."

The alligator, thinking to deceive, tried to disguise his voice, and desired the jackal to come into his own house without fear.

The jackal, having thus cleverly unmasked his pretended friend, cried out, " You fool! does a house ever speak?" and, wagging his tail, went off to find other quarters.

Foiled in this scheme also, the alligator thought of a capital plan to catch the jackal. Remembering a certain field where dead bodies were thrown by the villagers, and knowing that his enemy always went there for his dinner, the alligator went and laid himself down amongst the bones near a carcase, and waited patiently for several hours the arrival of his enemy.

At last the jackal came, and, seeing the alligator, instantly understanding the snare, he cried out, "This cheat is only shamming; dead alligators always turn on their backs and shake their toes."

The alligator hearing that, thought he might as well turn over, as by so doing he would then get his enemy into his power.

No sooner had he given proofs, as he thought, of being really defunct, than the jackal called out, "You fool! does a dead animal ever move?" and laughing heartily ran off, wagging his tail harder than ever.

The alligator was greatly nettled at being once more baffled, and cogitated a long time over various plans, till, as he conceived, he had hit upon a scheme that was certain of success.

Knowing that the jackal used to meet his lady-love regularly in a field covered with long grass, near the river, the alligator went the next day and laid himself down near the trysting-place, where, after waiting patiently for several hours, sleep insensibly overcame him.

The jackal coming along soon after, finding his enemy fast asleep, ran off and stole a brand from a hut, with which he set fire to the grass all round.

The alligator awaking with the heat, and finding himself surrounded with fire, from which there was no escape, died, grinding his teeth with rage at the superior cunning of his enemy.

The jackal, finding his enemy this time really dead, after the fire had exhausted itself, gave vent to several loud hoo-ahs! which soon brought a pack of his kindred around him, and they all had a hearty feast on baked alligator, in the course of which the jackal, relating all the circumstances, caused his friends a good deal of merriment.

The moral of the tale is, that schemers in laying traps for others are often entrapped themselves.

On finishing the story, the president said that he related it to show not only the estimation in which the jackal was held by the natives of India for wit and cunning, but their own storytelling abilities, and their sense of humour.

Just as the president had finished his story, the khansamah came to report that the larder needed replenishing, and as their sederunt had lasted long enough, the information was rather agreeable than otherwise.

While a man went to call the shikari and some beaters, the whole party looked to their guns, &c., and all being ready they set out for an afternoon's walk to the west of the camp, arranging to return through the jungle to the south.

When they had gone about a mile, or less, from the tents, they saw some curlews flying rather wildly about some trees, and marching up close they succeeded between them in bagging five of them.

As they were trying to discover the cause of the commotion, the skikari pointed out to them a large wild cat, crouched high up in the fork of one of the trees, when Jones, who had long been anxious to obtain the skull and whole skin of the genus, took careful aim with his rifle, and fired.

To the surprise of all who were looking on, the cat seemed to be unhurt, and they declared that the ball had missed the mark altogether, but Jones said that he had aimed too carefully for that to be the case, and that if a man were sent up the tree it would be found that the ball had cut its throat.

Presently, the cat was seen to rise gradually, arching its back, and glaring down on them fiercely, as if it were going to spring down on them, but, while they were all watching it, the cat's head suddenly dropped, and at the same moment the sharp eyes of one of the natives detected bloodmarks on the lower branches.

As the beast was dead, or nearly so, one of the beaters was directed to climb up, and when he had reached the cat he said that without a strong knife or an axe he could not throw the carcase down, as the claws were dug deep into the branch.

Another of the beaters having taken up a hunting-knife to the first man, the wood was cut away and the cat thrown down, and then it was seen that its throat had been very cleverly cut by the ball, so that Jones, the marksman, obtained a perfect specimen.

Continuing their walk along the edge of the jungle, they bagged several brace of grey and black partridges and quails, two old peacocks with splendid tails, and a brace of young pea-fowl. Pushing then into the jungle, they shot first a sambhur, then a spotted deer, and a sounder of wild pigs being disturbed by the reports, a general volley was fired at them as they were scampering off helter-skelter, bringing down a boar, a sow, and three fine porkers.

Having now more game than they could well carry, Wilcox, with one of the beaters, was left on guard while the rest hastened into camp with as much as they could all carry, and on arrival sent back the men with others to bring in the remainder.

When all had been brought in, it made a goodly show—one sambhur, one spotted deer, two large peacocks, two small ditto, one large boar pig, one sow, three fine porkers, five brace of grey and three brace of black partridges, four brace of quails, and five curlews.

With such abundance it was difficult to decide on what to keep for the tent, and what to give away. At last it was determined on that all the sambhur meat should be smoke-dried, the saddle of the spotted deer, two of the porkers, and the smaller birds (partridges, quails, and curlews) were to be reserved for themselves, and all the rest was to be divided among the servants.

Having returned early from their very successful walk, the caterer was soon busy with the khansamah, who was ordered to have one porker barbecued, while another was to be converted into chops and curry; the curlews and partridges to be stewed as one dish, and the quails to be roasted, which, with sambhur soup and sundry other accompaniments, the caterer thought, perhaps, would be enough, as well as giving satisfaction.

CHAPTER XLIX.

TIGERS AT THE GHAGUR.

TO prevent the game from getting bad, the services of the beaters and of all the spare servants not engaged in the culinary department were pressed into skinning, plucking feathers, or jerking the sambhur meat, for which latter purpose large fires were lighted, and kept burning all night, so that the camp presented a scene of great activity that night.

Having set these several operations going, while amusing themselves further with the various members of the menagerie, the time rapidly slipped away, so that evening came on before they were aware of it.

While preparing for dinner, the shikari came to report that there were two tigers at the Ghagur, near Murkoondee, that had killed a buffalo the evening previous, and a bullock that afternoon; that on receiving the above information he had at once sent off men to give notice for a hankwa the next morning, thinking that the gentlemen would not be angry at his not waiting for their orders first, adding that, had he done so, it would have been too late to make the necessary preparations that day, and if the day were lost a victim would have to be tied up.

All the party being pleased at the prospect of some more tiger shooting, the president assured the shikari that he had done quite right in not waiting for orders, and was thereupon directed to have everything in readiness by the morning.

Dinner being announced at that moment, the shikari was dismissed, and all sat down with ravenous appetites, having taken no lunch that day. Whether it were owing to the dinner being admirably cooked and served, or that each one had brought a large stock of nature's best sauce, hunger, the various dishes were highly appreciated, and a full measure of justice done to each, due praise being accorded to the caterer and all concerned in their preparation.

Having adjourned to the fire, the president announced that it was time to think of ascending the Kowie Ghât, on to the Kymore plateau, as the various supplies were running short, and put it to the vote to leave Sulkhun the next day, after the tiger-hunt.

The time at Sulkhun having been passed so agreeably, all were loth to leave it so soon, and an amendment was put by Robinson to stay at least three more clear days there before starting on the return.

The president, however, showed in black and white the number of days that it would take to reach Chunar, allowing a day or two at various places for sport, adding that if they left as he suggested, their supplies would exactly run out with the last day's march, providing no accidents happened.

This kind of argument being conclusive, it was at last settled that the time of starting should depend upon the result of the next day's hankwa, that is, if they bagged the tigers; if not, they would then stay another day.

The time of their return having drawn so near, and the prospect of their pleasant trip and party being speedily broken up and ended, cast a damper on all, seeing which, the president called on one of them for a song to dissipate the gloom.

The call having been responded to by each in turn, the president as the last was called upon, but he said that it was time to go to bed, as they would have to be up very early next day, and suited action to the word, the others not being slow in following suit.

The next morning early, some time before daybreak, the president aroused the others, making the drowsy ones get up by cleverly pulling off all the bed coverings at one sweep.

When they had washed and were dressed, they found the chota hazreh ready, the shikari and rokhs (stoppers) waiting, and the horses saddled, at the tent door.

After discussing the light breakfast, each one looked to his guns and ammunition (Brown not forgetting his pistols, which did such service on a former occasion, but which fortunately were not required this time), and all being ready, they mounted their horses and proceeded at a canter to the edge of the jungle at Murkoondee.

While they were having breakfast, the shikari and the rokhs had been sent on ahead, and on their arrival they found them at the edge of the jungle, where dismounting, they sent their horses into the village, and silently proceeded to the machauns.

After they were seated and the rokhs suitably stationed, the shikari departed to give the signal, and in a short time the first beat of the drum was heard, followed by the simultaneous shouts of the numerous beaters, making row enough to disgust any number of animals crouched within a mile of the horrible din.

A number of inferior animals having been allowed to pass unchallenged, after awhile a tigress was now and then seen creeping along behind some bushes, as if she were aware of something " uncanny" in front of her, but which she was obliged to meet, by the horrid din behind her drawing nearer every moment.

At last she came into full view as she was turning the corner of some bushes, and within shot of the nearest machaun, when Smith, by a well-aimed shot right in her heart, dropped her without a struggle.

While all were on the *qui vive* for the appearance of the tiger, suddenly they heard a great outcry amongst the beaters, which they subsequently ascertained was caused by the tiger breaking through the line and escaping, fortunately without doing any further harm than slightly scratching the arm of one of the men while springing past him.

The beaters having then come close up, when they had all

descended from their machauns the president inquired into the matter, and it was the opinion of all that the tiger was a cowardly ungallant brute.

It appeared from the statements of the beaters nearest to the scene, that the tiger allowed the tigress to assume the post of honour and danger in preceding him, he following in her wake and closely imitating her actions, in stealthily creeping along close under the bushes.

When the tiger heard the shot, instead of exhibiting any signs of anger he was thoroughly and unmistakably scared, and making a sudden start on one side, he turned round, and dashing through the line of beaters, made off as fast as he could, slightly wounding one of the men as he was passing.

If the ignoble brute could only have heard and understood the indignant remarks of the sportsmen and beaters, and the abusive epithets liberally showered upon him by the latter, it would cause him to hide his head for ever, and never more presume to show himself in the society of any of his own genus for very shame.

The hankwa being over so soon, and the jungle of the neighbourhood not having been much disturbed, it was proposed by some of the party to have two or three hours' shooting before returning to camp.

The president, however, overruled this proposal by saying that he thought it would be better to return to camp, have breakfast over quickly, and set out for the next halting-place, adding that he had received information of another party being on their way to the Valley, and it would be only fair to leave them something to shoot.

This last consideration deciding the matter, they returned to the village of Murkoondee, where mounting their horses, they were soon back to Sulkhun, and to the bewilderment of some of them, they found only one, the breakfast tent, remaining, the others, with most of the camels, having disappeared.

The president, in explanation, said that as he felt sure that they would agree with what he had said in the jungle at Murkoondee, he had quietly given orders the previous evening for everything not wanted to be packed up, and the moment that they started for the hankwa, the sleeping tents, &c., were to be packed and the camels started, adding that the servants had done uncommonly well, for if they turned round (which they did) they might at that moment see some of their baggage animals just at the top of Kowie Ghât.

After laughing heartily at the president's so cleverly stealing a march upon them, they sat down to breakfast with excellent appetites, one and another expressing themselves as delighted with the trip, and only sorry that it was so nearly at an end.

Brown, Jones, and Robinson were more than half inclined to be offended at all the beer having been sent off, as they thought that the president well deserved a bumper vote of thanks for the many pleasant days that they had enjoyed, especially in the lovely Valley of the Soane.

The president in accepting the implied vote of thanks, said that he thought the beer would do them more good if taken after arrival at Adulgunge, their next station, instead of before starting from Sulkhun, as they would have to march eight to ten miles in the sun.

With reference to tiger shooting, the president said further, that he feared they had had their last hankwa, as far as tigers were concerned; but he was glad of such a good finale, the tigress of that morning having been killed instantly by one ball.

Breakfast being over, they found the shikari and beaters waiting, when, after the paymaster had settled with them (giving the wounded man a small extra gratuity), lighting their cheroots or pipes, they went to the village to inspect the menagerie, where the president settled accounts and arranged with the shikari for the transport of all their pets to Chunar, and where they would arrive about the same time as themselves.

This matter being settled, they returned to what had been their camp, and finding the breakfast tent and the rest of the baggage packed up and gone, they mounted their horses and set out for Adulgunge, stopping at the top of Kowie Ghát for a few minutes to have a last look round at the lovely scenery.

As they were drawing near to Adulgunge, remembering an intimation from the khansamah as to the state of the larder, the president, spying a small herd of antelopes on the plain to the right, about a quarter of a mile off, proposed to the rest to ring them.

The others never having engaged in the process, the president explained that two of them should make a considerable detour to the right and two to the left, their horses going at a walking pace so as not to alarm the antelopes. When they had got about half-way round, one from each side would go ahead, dividing the further half circle about equally, the two remaining here doing the same by the nearer,

CHAPTER L.

RINGING THE ANTELOPES.

IF the antelopes got alarmed before the circle was completed, and made off, those nearest were to ride up and try to head them back. Should the herd not be alarmed, they would gradually contract the circle, getting nearer to the herd and to each other, and when the herd broke and scattered, they were to fire at the bucks if they had a chance, the two black ones especially, letting the does escape.

Having understood the plan, Jones and Wilcox went to the right, Brown and Smith to the left, while the president and Robinson remained stationary awhile.

When the others had got round the herd, the president detached Robinson to the right, while he went to the left; and seeing the herd shaking their little tails, a sure sign that they were about to bolt, he gave the signal for closing up.

Everything went admirably, for as the antelopes broke into a trot, the nearest horseman rode hard and turned them back, the others doing the same in their direction, until they got within shot, when the herd, thoroughly scared, broke away singly and escaped, leaving behind the two black bucks and a doe.

Then, dismounting, they blooded the deer, and having placed them across three of the horses, they proceeded on foot the rest of the way to the camp, which was less than a mile off, where, on arrival, a glass of beer proved acceptable, and was heartily enjoyed.

After they had washed and rested themselves for an hour or so, a servant came in, saying that there was a herd of deer not far off the encampment. This news made them all jump up, and on going outside the tent they saw a herd of about twenty antelopes to the west, and about half a mile off.

When the president had viewed them for awhile, he said that, in the position that the herd was, in an open plain, without any bush, or even an ant-hill, near, it would be extremely difficult to stalk them so as to get near enough for a shot.

The only plan that he could think of was to ring them on foot, which, as he knew the ground, would be very fatiguing; but if the best walkers would not object to taking the opposite side of the intended circle, he would at once make arrangements.

Brown and Robinson having volunteered for the opposite side, the president summoned a dozen of the unoccupied camel-men and servants, and, allotting two to each, sent four of the party to the right and left, leaving it to each one to instruct his men where to go and what to do, and arranging with all of them to close in upon seeing him hoist his handkerchief on the end of his gun.

Accordingly, half an hour after the others had started (the president meanwhile having distributed the men that were left with him, and seeing the herd surrounded at all points), he gave the signal for closing up.

As the circle was necessarily a large one, it took some considerable time for the several members to close up, but when they did come sufficiently near to alarm the antelopes, one and another of the bucks began shaking his tail, when suddenly they broke, bounding and leaping in regular succession, as if they were playing at "follow-my-leader," and "leap-frog" combined, until they came within shot, when they were turned.

Breaking away in another direction, they were once more turned by a shot, but the second shot, and the noise and eagerness that the servants made and displayed, so scared them that they broke away singly and escaped, having given the opportunity of bagging only two.

By the time that they got back to the camp, they were forced to admit the truth of the president's remark as to its being fatiguing, for what with walking, and running over tussocks of grass, small ant-hills, fox and rat holes, after the deer, they were pretty well blown.

A good wash, and a bottle of soda-water with a dash of brandy in it, otherwise called a "peg" in those parts, having set them up somewhat, they went to inspect the deer, when the caterer gave orders for the meat off one of them to be cut into thin strips, well rubbed with salt and ground chillies, dried, and so preserved, and after reserving sufficient for themselves for present purposes, he directed the other deer, together with what remained of those shot earlier in the day, to be divided amongst the servants.

As dinner would not be ready for some time longer, while they were enjoying themselves in the cool dusk of the evening, the president proposed sending a man to a certain village that evening, to inquire if there was a chance of finding any wild pigs in the sugar-cane field, which he had noted while coming along, and whether they could have any beaters from the village to drive the pigs out the next morning.

The proposal being readily agreed to, a man was sent off at once, and during dinner he returned, saying that numbers of pigs were there usually, and that twenty men and boys would be ready by sunrise.

Meanwhile, the president amused them with various anecdotes anent antelope hunting and shooting, one or two of which were to the following effect :—

You remember, he said, the story I told you about poor little Jacky having been suckled by one of the sluts of a friend of mine? Well, that slut was a cross between a retriever and a thorough pariah, and she herself was crossed by a thorough pariah; consequently, the pups that she then threw were three parts pariah.

My friend being a bit of a humorist, when young Jacky came into the family circle, a day or two before my own arrival, the two pups that were selected to be saved, owing to their being most like the mother, were both black sluts, and were named by him severally, Tobacco, and Pipes.

When these two pups grew up to man's, or I should say woman's, that is, full-grown slut's, estate, it was something singular how hunting, particularly deer hunting, propensities developed in both of them, but more especially in Baccy, as she was generally called.

When we put on our hats and coats of an afternoon, and took our walkingsticks or guns, as the case might be, Baccy knew as well as we did that we were going for a walk, and used to exhibit her delight by jumping up to one or other of us, barking all the time for joy, until we were fairly out of the premises.

On such occasions, Baccy used generally to be the first to nose a pig in a bush, nor could she be got away from it until Master Piggy had been unroosted, and then it was amusing to see her manœuvres in trying to seize the pig, while at the same time escaping from its attempts to rip her up with its tusks, and in such encounters she never met with a scratch.

Nothing, however, seemed to give Baccy greater delight than being put on the scent of a deer. Take her up to a spot of deer's blood, and however languid and listless she might have appeared a minute previous, she would fire up with excitement, and then it was beautiful to see how she would quarter the ground, discover the next trace, and follow it up until she came upon the wounded deer, which would not then go much farther before she pulled it down by the ear, and held on to it until we came up.

One day a most amusing circumstance occurred. We had gone out one afternoon for our usual walk, at a time of the year when the grass on the plain was high enough to hide a million of deer lying down, when one or other of us shot an antelope, wounding it grievously; and, after watching its course for some time, we marked where it couched.

But when we went up to the supposed place, we were utterly at fault—no deer could be found anywhere. Taking the bearings afresh, we quartered the ground ourselves, until we came upon a spot of blood, when, calling the dogs about us, we put Baccy's nose to the spot.

Just at that moment, Master Jacky, who had till then indulged in a little horsemanship on the back of one of the dogs, chose to change his steed, and, before we could prevent it mounted Baccy (one of his foster-sisters), at a time when her blood was up, and away he went at a good speed, the slut following unerringly all the windings of the deer until she came upon it.

Having put the deer up, Baccy started in pursuit at increased speed, and it was laughable to see Jacky holding on to Baccy as she went tearing after the deer, the monkey's instinct telling it that if it attempted to get off while going at that rate it might get seriously hurt.

We had the chase in view all the time, and when Baccy came up with the deer, she sprang at its head, and, seizing it by the ear, brought it down and held it until we came up, Jacky maintaining his post admirably all the time, proving himself to be a first-rate jockey. Nevertheless, he seemed very glad when we came up, jumping off Baccy's back, climbing up the nearest of us, and nestling in his bosom, all of a tremble.

On another occasion, for some reason we had left all the dogs and the monkey at home, and on our return, when about half-way between Romph and Adulgunge, my friend took a running long-shot at a doe antelope, which took effect, as we soon saw that one of its forelegs was broken.

Watching it for some time, we suddenly missed it, and knew it had couched; then, taking the bearings, we made, as we thought, a straight course for it, but we were again all of us at fault, utterly unable to find the deer.

We then sent the servant that was with us on to the house, less than a mile off, with orders to bring only Baccy, as we wished to see how she would act by herself, we meanwhile searching in all directions for traces of blood.

When the man returned with the slut, we put her nose to the first spot of blood we had found, and led her on to the next, giving her as it turned out the right direction; and then it was beautiful to see how she followed up the trace, until she came upon the deer, proving herself to be a born deerhound.

After Baccy had roused the deer, the chase became very exciting, and to us not a little fatiguing, running over such ground, while trying to keep the hunt in sight.

The deer made two or three useless attempts to throw the dog off the scent, by doubling back in the high grass, but it would not do with such a born hunter after her, and at last the deer was forced to leave the grass, and take to the jungle to the north of Romph-hill, where Baccy pulled her down, not far from the Customs' Station at Chupka.

The president then recited the following verses on

THE STRICKEN DEER.

As through the woods I roam'd one day,
  I came upon a wounded doe,
That, looking at me, seem'd to say,
  " See what your heartless race can do.

",'Mid peaceful herd I rov'd about;
  No cause had I my fears t' alarm,
Nor ever once had enter'd thought
  Of aught that could befall of harm.

"One while we listless fed at ease,
  And now we coursed o'er the plain;
Choosing the blade that did most please,
  We sought the cool repose again.

" This hapless day our choice was gram;
  While nibbling full the tender leaves,
A savage hunter treach'rous came,
  And hid himself behind some trees.

THE STRICKEN DEER.

"Fearless, at length we went too close,
　Dreaming of naught to mar our joys;
Marking the herd, poor me he chose,
　And sudden made a fearful noise.

"I instant felt a dreadful pain—
　His cruel ball had op'd my side;
Madly I bounded o'er the plain—
　In thicket's shade methought to hide.

"My joys, alas! I feel are past—
　No more can I in freedom roam.
Life's ebbing stream leaves me too fast,
　And helpless now I wait my doom."

Briefly it clos'd its painful life,
　By hunter's hand thought little worth.
Without the aid of ruthless knife,
　In heaving throes its soul gush'd forth.

Poor doe! my thoughts I sad express'd,
　Thou hadst no sharp retort of mine,
But hadst thou not thus heedless press'd
　On death, thy life had still been thine.

CHAPTER LI.

DIFFERENCE IN VENISON.

DINNER being then announced, they adjourned to the tent, nothing loth, where they had the opportunity of tasting antelope-venison cooked in various ways, and of comparing it with the venison of other deer, of which they had partaken so much lately, the general opinion being that, although by no means to be despised, yet it wanted flavour and juiciness, which might be attributed to difference in feeding.

The president remarked that feeding made all the difference; sambhur, spotted, and other kinds of deer browsing on the tender succulent leaves of various bushes and the soft-jungle grass, while the antelope, being a very timid, wary animal, found only on large open plains, is confined chiefly to the coarse grass on it for its sustenance, although they may occasionally be found in young growing corn, or other grain fields, where the field borders on the plain, and is sufficiently open to allow of a wide range of vision.

The antelope, as a rule, is never found in the jungle, only taking to it to throw off its pursuer when hard pressed by a leopard or other animal.

The president added that that dinner gave no just criterion of antelope-venison, the deer having been killed too recently; that, when the meat is kept for a day or two, as they would find hereafter, it acquires a more gamey flavour.

After dinner, while assembled round the fire, the president informed them that there was a man in a certain village, not far from where they were then, who used to have a pack of four black thorough pariahs, that, like Baccy, were naturally born hunters, and that he had sent a servant that evening to request the man to give them the services of himself and his dogs tomorrow afternoon.

Having been much pleased with their sport that day, one and another of the party proposed staying in that neighbourhood for three or four days, but the president said that " their various supplies running short would not admit of a lengthened stay.

"He could keep them there for a fortnight, and give them antelope hunting and shooting until they were all thoroughly satiated, did time allow of it, but, according to arrangement, they were to stay only one clear day at Adulgunge.

" However, as he wished to show them one or two more plans for circumventing even such a wary animal as the antelope, and one day's stay there not being enough for the purpose, he thought that they might stay two clear days more at Adulgunge, but they must make up for it by not stopping anywhere else on the road ;" and this being agreed to, as they were all pretty well tired, they turned into bed.

The next morning, about sunrise, they went on the road to Romph, to a sugar-cane field, which was for their purpose of a very convenient shape, being a nearly perfect parallelogram, where they found a number of men waiting ; and, after enjoining on all the party not to miss any shot, but kill every pig they could get a chance of shooting at, as, by so doing, they would be doing the cultivators real service, the president commenced operations.

Posting two of the party at equal distances apart on each of the longer sides, ten to fifteen yards from the canes, and one each at the shorter, the president ordered the beaters to enter the field at one of the shorter sides, where he himself was stationed, thus giving the others the best chances for a shot, giving the beaters directions to return to his end, and so drive out those pigs that might double back.

In a very short time several shots from the three sides were heard, when an old boar and three smaller pigs, that had managed to double back, not liking the great disturbance, tried to escape by suddenly bolting out at the president's end of the field, but, a quick shot flooring him, caused the smaller ones to rush back into the canes, only to be again routed out.

After the canes had been beaten through twice, from end to end, the villagers reporting that there were no more pigs in the field, the president ordered all the dead to be brought to him, and when the party had all assembled, they found the result to be two boars, one sow, and five porkers, which the president thought was very creditable, although about as many more had managed to get clear off.

As so much pig-meat would be a great deal more than they or the servants could consume, the villagers being told that they might take as much as they chose for the village, they at once selected the two boars and the sow, showing plainly that they thought more of quantity than quality.

Directing some of the villagers to take their share of the pigs to the village, and ordering the rest to come to the camp, bringing the porkers with them, they returned to the tents, where they found a capital breakfast waiting, and to which they sat down with excellent appetites.

After breakfast, the beaters were paid, and went away apparently highly pleased with their morning's work and its results; and then, as the servants had pitched the camp where there was little or no shade (receiving a good rating for so doing from the president), the party were confined to the tents, amusing themselves with chess or in other ways, until a servant came to announce lunch being ready.

Just as they had finished lunch, a servant reported a man having come by order, as he said, with two black village dogs (Bruno, Brown's dog, had meanwhile given tongue to the same effect), so, rising hastily to prevent hostilities, they went out to see the man and his natural hunters.

After a little conversation with the man, he said that two of the best dogs were dead, one being killed by a leopard, and the other in a fight with dogs of another village, but that the two he had brought were very good game dogs, and had brought him and his family many a meal.

One and another of the party having expressed decidedly unfavourable opinions, Brown said that he would reserve his opinion until he had seen them tried, but, nevertheless, he could not just then believe that such veritable looking curs had any hunting "go" in them.

Directing the man to wait half an hour or so, the president ordered some broken meat to be brought for the dogs, but the owner, interfering, said, "that would spoil them, for if they had anything *then* to eat, they would not hunt. After you have seen their performance, and they have earned their dinner, give them what you please."

As the man had the dogs in a rude leash, he was directed to make himself at home with the servants, while they returned to the tent for a quiet smoke, and also to wait until the sun went down a little more.

Between two and three o'clock, taking a servant with each one, and the villager with his dogs, they started for the large plain to the east of Adulgunge, where was a herd of antelopes a considerable distance off; and, separating about a hundred yards apart, they gradually got within about sixty yards, when the two who were nearest fired, bringing down a buck and wounding another, which at first fell, but, quickly rising, was making off when the president shouted to the man to put his dogs on.

When the dogs came up to the place where the antelope had fallen on being shot, and obtained the scent, the hair on their bodies seemed to stand up on end, and the villager not being able to hold them in any longer, slipped the leash, and away they went, nosing the ground beautifully, following the deer in all its windings until they came up with it, when they gallantly attacked and pulled it down.

The chase was a very exciting one, leading them over more than a mile of very rough ground for running, and as they were coming up they found that the two dogs (being young) were not powerful enough to permanently hold the deer down, it being a full grown fawn-coloured buck.

When they had come up they soon relieved the dogs of their difficulty, and the villager having secured his dogs, they blooded the deer, and asked him if they should give the dogs the entrails, but he said, " No ;" adding that, " they might let the dogs lap the blood if they wished, but that would make them only the more savage, and the next deer they would most likely tear." Wishing then to see how the dogs would act, they let them lap up the blood.

Before leaving the tents the president left directions with the servants that, when they heard any shots, other men were to come out to relieve those sent in with the deer, and when they had sent off the two antelopes and were ready to start again, fresh men had joined them.

After a good hour's walk they came upon another herd, more numerous than the first, and succeeded in bringing down two black bucks and wounding another fawn-coloured one.

When the dogs had been brought up and put on the trail, their excitement was something to see; and when they were let loose they tore along as if their previous exercise had only made their limbs supple.

When the dogs came up with the deer, as the man said, they were savage, and no mistake about it, as they flew at the deer's throat, had it down in a moment, and if the villager and some of the party had not come up as quickly as they did, they would soon have had its heart out. To look at them they were quite a picture of savagery, their eyes bloodshot, their hair on end, and their whole frames quivering with excitement.

After the dogs had been secured with some trouble, the deer

was blooded, and as the sun was getting low, and a long hour's walk was before them, it was time to return to camp.

While on their return Brown expressed his great surprise and pleasure at the performances of the dogs, and was anxious to strike a bargain with the owner for them.

But the president interfered, saying that Bruno and the pariahs would never agree. Moreover, he said that if Brown did buy them it would be money thrown away, for the dogs would surely make their escape, in a few hours probably, and return to their own village.

He said further that if Brown did succeed in getting them home (which he much doubted), the dogs would be of little or no use to him, as they would only pine for their freedom, and on the first occasion of being taken out to hunt, on being loosed he would see no more of them.

He thought that they would be better off if left with their present owner, which was reluctantly consented to.

CHAPTER LII.

HOW TO PREPARE VENISON.

ON their return to the tents the deer were skinned, disembowelled, and as much as was intended for their own use broken up, the entrails being given to the dogs, with which they gorged themselves, while the villager was presented and dismissed with half of one of the deer and one rupee (two shillings), with which he was greatly pleased, the rest of the antelopes being divided amongst the various servants.

Having paid the much-needed attention to their toilettes, dinner being shortly after announced, they all sat down to it with excellent appetites, greatly conduced by the running exercise they had been engaged in that afternoon.

The wild porker barbecued was highly relished, the sugar-cane diet having apparently made it more tender than any of those previously tasted. But the saddle and a haunch of antelope venison gave such unqualified satisfaction, that they were eager to know where the meat came from.

The president and caterer in explanation said that he had ordered the saddle and haunches of one of the antelopes shot in the morning of the previous day to be well washed, wiped dry, enveloped separately in clean cloths, and buried two or more feet deep in the ground for twenty-four hours, which had the effect of rendering the meat mellow and juicy, as well as bringing out the game flavour.

After dinner Robinson would insist on proposing a bumper to the president, adding that they did not appear to have come yet to the end of his resources, and wondered for himself what the next surprise would be.

The president, in returning thanks, said that after living a few years in and on the border of the jungle, if a man did not learn a thing or two he deserved to live on rice or pulse. With regard to surprises, he could only speak oracularly, "they would see what they would see;" and then, as they were all tired, he proposed their going to bed, to which no objection was made.

The next morning, when they were all ready for a walk about sunrise, seeing a mob of servants and some villagers with three bullocks in tether, one and another exclaimed, "Here's another surprise!" and wondered what on earth they could be for; when Smith, wag as he was, suggested, "Of course, two were to mount each animal, and so go a-hunting."

Brown, with a merry twinkle in his eye, said, "Well, that *is* a queer start. Going a-hunting antelopes on bullock back! But, live and learn, so here goes"—and had just managed to put his right leg across one of the animals, when the bullock, giving a sudden hoist up behind, sent him all of a heap on to the villager who was holding the rope, knocking him down and causing him to let go of the rope, which the bullock took advantage of, capering about, kicking up his heels generally, and making a straight course for his village, with a posse of servants after him.

After the hearty roars of laughter had somewhat subsided, Brown, on picking himself up, with a comically rueful countenance said, "Here's a pretty go! My steed has bolted, leaving me to sing, 'My lodging is on the cold ground;' however" (feeling himself all over), "it is well it is no worse, no bones or gun broken," adding, "Thank you, I will not try any more bullock riding to-day."

When Brown's steed had been recaptured and brought back, the president explained that antelopes being accustomed to see bullocks feeding on the plain, and also to parties of men driving one or two bullocks, loaded with produce, across the plain from one village to another, bullocks are occasionally used for stalking purposes.

The plan to be adopted that day was this,—the bullocks would have a sack or two thrown across each, with some of the camel or elephant furniture, to give them the appearance of being loaded. Two of the party, with one servant besides the driver, would then start on the plain in different directions with each bullock, and when they sighted a herd of antelopes (or even a single one, although single ones were more difficult to approach near, through soon taking alarm), the driver would go in their direction, each party keeping in the rear, or on the off-side of the bullock, so as to have the bullock between them and the antelopes, and when within shot the driver would be ordered to stand still while they fired.

Having understood the plan of procedure, the three parties started in different directions, Brown and Jones with one bullock, Robinson and Wilcox with another, and Smith and the president with the third.

In about an hour after starting, the president and Smith returned with a doe and a fawn buck. Smith was so pleased with the ruse that he tried hard to induce the president to go out again; but the latter objected, owing to the probability of the others bringing some in.

Smith, however, was not to be restrained—so, taking a fresh servant, he went out by himself with the bullock, and brought in another buck before either of the other parties had returned.

Shortly after Smith's second return, Wilcox and Robinson came in with one doe, another being wounded, which had couched in some long grass, and could not be found, notwithstanding a diligent search for a long time.

In about an hour after that Brown and Jones came in with a black buck and a doe, which they had to bring in themselves, as the wicked bullock, which had played him such a trick in the morning, positively refused the load, throwing them off as often as they tried to load him. Were it not for this bother they might have been in more than an hour ago.

A good wash and a much-needed change of clothes gave time for breakfast to be served, and to which ample justice was done.

After breakfast the bullock-drivers were dismissed with a liberal present, besides one of the antelopes, and when they had enjoyed a rest of an hour or so, the president (taking a glance round the plain with a telescope, and seeing numbers of antelopes in different directions) communicated his own excitement to the others on asking if they were inclined for any more exercise that day.

All eagerly assenting, he made a signal to the servants, and half-a-dozen men were soon seen coming along, each with a good-sized, leafy bough—in fact, a portable bush—which the president, unknown to the others, had ordered to be got ready.

All eyes being turned towards the president, he said that "that was only another jungle ruse. When they were all ready they would each take a separate course on the plain, the bush-bearer carrying it as was most convenient until they came in sight of any antelopes, when he would gently elevate it and go slowly towards them, holding the bush upright in front of him, the sportsman also keeping well behind it until they got within shot.

"Sometimes a sportsman will carry his own bush, but that is fatiguing work if he has to go far after the deer. If, however, when once out on the plain, he will stick his bush in a rat-hole, and sit down by the side of it patiently, any antelopes that may be in sight are almost sure to fall into the snare, their curiosity exciting them to examine it closer."

When they were all ready they set out each in a different direction, and were successful beyond expectation in being able to return with an antelope each in about two hours.

The president having purposely taken the windward side, and having soon come upon some antelopes, and circumvented them, he fired and brought down a fawn buck.

His shot started the herd (about twenty), which went galloping close by Wilcox, who dropped another, and this shot caused them to change their course, and join another small herd.

Smith, who had been making for the second herd, was able to bring one down while they were moving about confusedly, and this shot broke up the combined herd, some starting off singly, others in small parties going to join other small groups.

Brown, after his morning's exertions, determining to do the easy, after he had got well out on the plain, ordered his man to stick the bush in a hole, which, being done, Brown said afterwards, "he must have had the best chance of all; for, after the third shot, a considerable number of antelopes, from different directions, began galloping towards him, until not less than forty stood and were huddled so close together, about twenty-five yards off, that, had he fired into their midst, he must have brought down two or three at a shot. Waiting until he got a chance at a separate one, he shot it and came home."

This shot gave Robinson a chance, and as the herd broke away towards him he was able to stop one.

Jones adopted the same plan as Brown, but, in regard to numbers, "he thought that there must have been two or three hundred antelopes racing about all round him, so that for some time he could not make up his mind which to fire at. A good-sized fawn buck at length coming almost within biscuit throw, he fired, and brought it along."

CHAPTER LIII.

ANTELOPES MIGRATE.

ON their way back to the camp all of them could not but remark the number of antelopes all round them, and on subsequently relating their several experiences as above, the president said that they were remarkably fortunate in coming there at the period of the migration of the antelopes.

From the experience of others, but more especially his own—having lived in the district for some years, he had traversed those plains round about in all directions, and could certify that it has happened that for weeks together not an antelope was to be seen anywhere, while at other times the plains would swarm with them singly, or in small or large herds; proving conclusively, in his opinion, that at certain periods, most probably when the grass had been cropped too short for their sustenance, antelopes migrated from one part of the district to another, where there was a greater supply of grass uncropped on the plains, and *vice versâ*.

In order to show how suddenly the antelopes appear and disappear thereabouts, the president said further, that when going out on official duty he always took his double-barrel with him, and usually a brace of pistols in his pocket, both gun and pistols being for use against *feræ naturæ* of whatever kind might be met with.

On one occasion, while about leaving his house to mount his horse, his servant asked, as usual, if he should bring the gun, but he said "No, as deer and other animals seemed to have deserted the neighbourhood completely," and left the house without either gun or pistols. The provoking result was, that he had not gone a mile from the house when, at the turn of the road, he came upon a herd of about fifteen antelopes within close pistol shot, and they were huddled so close together that, had he his gun to use, he could not have failed in bringing down two or three at one shot. That he was wild at the mischance you may be very sure.

While they were examining the deer, one and another could not keep from looking out on the plain round them, and, seeing the numbers of antelopes, they were very desirous of going out again after them.

The president, however, objected strongly to the proposal, saying that "he did not think it right to slaughter wild animals merely because they were numerous, unless they were prolific and destructive to agriculture in general, such as wild pigs, rabbits, hares, &c.

"The wild pigs breeding about four times a year, and bringing forth eight to twelve at each farrow, living moreover chiefly at the cultivator's expense, their slaughter in any number was justifiable. This cannot be said of antelopes, which, breeding at most twice a year, and bringing forth one or two fawns at a birth, live principally on the coarse grass of wide, open plains, and by cropping it confer a general benefit on the district.

"If this coarse grass were not cropped as it is by antelopes, but allowed to grow to its natural height, during the hot weather it would become so dry that the least spark would set it on fire, and the consequence would be a general conflagration extending for miles, as on the American prairies.

"As it was they had a good deal more meat in the camp than all hands together could possibly consume; but it would not be wasted, as the surrounding villagers would be only too glad of the meat."

Having reserved an ample supply for themselves, the servants were told to take as much as they chose for all hands in the camp, and four antelopes still remaining, a servant was sent to the

DISTRIBUTION OF THE TROPHIES. 333

villages nearest, with the intimation that each might have an antelope on sending for it, and in a very short time no surplus remained.

At dinner that evening they had antelope venison to perfection, cooked in various forms, all of which gave eminent satisfaction, and on adjourning to the open air around the fire, after a little general conversation the president said, in answer to a remark, that he thought that there must have been one or two thousand antelopes on the plains around them that day, increasing in numbers towards the evening, all going in a westerly direction apparently.

The president then further said that, having to start very early the next day, with the object of avoiding a hot march in the sun, which would otherwise be before them, besides being pretty well tired, they should retire early, which was forthwith agreed to.

On the third day after leaving Adulgunge, they returned to Chunar, all with more or less reluctance, considerable, however, in each one; whence, after two days' stay, they dispersed to their several avocations in different directions.

On the day after their return to Chunar, the shikari arrived with the miscellaneous members of the menagerie (all in good order and well-conditioned, as stated in ships' manifests), and with whom accounts were finally settled.

The remainder of the day was passed in apportioning the various pets amongst the members of the party, and in distributing by lot the several trophies of the tour—such as tigers', leopards', bears' skins, skulls, claws, &c.; porcupines' quills, peacocks' feathers, and other collections, those wanting particular articles making exchanges amongst themselves subsequently, while the remainder of the sambhur and other jerked or dried venison was equally divided amongst the several members of the party.

The following day was taken up by the paymaster in taking stock and settling the accounts of the tour, which having been done, the balance of expenditure over and above what each one had subscribed at the commencement of the tour, was divided amongst the party, and promptly settled.

On the evening before separating, the president gave them one more and last very agreeable surprise, in a dinner composed principally of Guzeerati beef (prepared in various ways, and all excellent), the like of which none of the others had ever previously tasted.

The delicate flavour and extreme tenderness of the hump (salted and boiled), and round (boiled), called for the especial commendations of all, and the surprise was general at none of them having met with the like before.

In answer to various remarks and inquiries, the president said that he thought that Guzeerati were the smallest of all known cattle, as certainly they made the most delicate eating beef in the whole world.

The Guzeerati cattle generally (at least those that he had seen, for he had never been to the province of Guzeerat, and so could not speak from any extensive knowledge of them) were so small that an English butcher's porter could easily carry a full-grown live ox on his knot.

He supposed it must be owing only to entire ignorance in the matter, otherwise he could not help thinking that Guzeerati cattle, if introduced into England, would be found a profitable speculation, as the small animals would cost very little for their keep, soon becoming as round as a barrel, and much the shape of it, while the beef would command the highest price.

Once introduced, there would soon be an extensive competition amongst breeders for stock, and Epicurean palates could not fail of appreciating the beef. Any attempt, however, to increase the size of the animal, by crossing with larger species, with the view of *improving the breed*, would, he thought, only result in making the texture of the beef coarse and tough, and so destroy all the delicate flavour and tenderness.

In bringing this rambling account to an end, it must not be supposed that, because (for the convenience of having no break in the story) Sunday has not been mentioned, therefore it has been entirely ignored, as such an inference would not be correct.

Enlightened persons in India, as elsewhere, whether in cities or the country, travelling on business or on a sporting tour, find the *rest* of the Sabbath indispensable; and those who do not observe it, soon have reason to come to the conclusion that *they were not wise*.

When travelling in the interior of India, although such persons must necessarily be from five to fifty, or a hundred, miles away from the sound of the nearest "church-going bell," yet the Day of Rest (if only as an example to the heathen around them) should be observed by them in as decorous a manner as circumstances will admit of.

In the hope that his readers have been reasonably interested and amused, before finally taking his leave, the writer would offer a little advice to intending Indian sporting tourists.

Although a sporting tour of a month or two in the jungle of India, at the proper time of the year (the cold weather) may be, and is, very health-conducing and thoroughly enjoyable, yet, in going after the larger or fiercer denizens of the forest, prudence, caution, and presence of mind are no less indispensable than courage and the *best apparatus*, or arms of precision, as the pedantic phrase is nowadays.

A man that is, so to speak, afraid of a mouse, and has no confidence in his nerves, or is armed only with Brown Bess, unless he is tired of life, has no business in the jungles; he had much better stay at home, and be a carpet knight.

Too many persons in India, principally young men, on whom all lessons of experience are lost, persist in going after tigers on foot, but such a procedure can only be characterized as *foolhardiness*.

When a tiger's strength is so great that it can kill and easily drag off a large buffalo, and when its agility is equal to its strength, or, at any rate, far superior to that of a man, the chances of an encounter on foot are ten thousand to one against the man; consequently, when a man goes into heavy jungle after a tiger *on foot*, it is no mark of wisdom; he simply enough puts himself thereby on a level with the brute, and, in so doing, vacates his position as one of the *lords* of creation.

A man going after a tiger on foot in scrubby or thick jungle, or high grass, although armed with the best-invented double barrel, yet, in order to be more than a match for the brute, he requires to be possessed of equal strength, agility, lightness of tread, acuteness of vision and ear, and sense of smelling, otherwise the contest, in the writer's opinion, is unequal, the chances being greatly against him.

Of course, in stalking sambhur or other animals, the sportsman is liable at any moment to rouse or come upon a tiger, but in such cases it is simply a misadventure, and, as in other circumstances, must be made the best of, but which can hardly be put on a par with deliberately going on foot to attack such an active, lithe, and ferocious brute.

Advocates for tiger-shooting on foot say that a man, armed with a good double barrel, is more than a match for a tiger. The writer is of a different opinion, and (although he freely admits that many tigers have been shot by parties on foot) points to the number of accidents and valuable lives lost through the practice as proofs of the many chances there are against a man in such an unequal encounter.

Given the qualifications of a tiger as above mentioned, add to them the *possibility* of missing, or only slightly wounding and not killing the tiger or effectually disabling him, the gun hanging fire, bad caps, a stumble or other mischance, and then let the young sportsman in India calculate whether the trophy of a tiger's skull, skin, and claws is worth running such a great risk to obtain; for, unless the tiger be killed by the first shot, or effectually disabled from doing any injury, the sportsman's life in about two seconds would not be worth a rotten carrot, as, once seized by a tiger, a man is on a par with a mouse seized by a cat, there being about as much chance of saving his life in the one case as in the other.

When any one in India asks you to go out with him after a tiger, *on foot*, take my advice, young man—don't go.

With this last remark the writer makes his salaam.

THE END.

www.ingramcontent.com/pod-product-compliance
Lightning Source LLC
Chambersburg PA
CBHW031852220426
43663CB00006B/595